TExES

Science 7-12 (236)

SECRETS

Study Guide

Your Key to Exam Success

TExES Test Review for the
Texas Examinations
of Educator Standards

Dear Future Exam Success Story:

First of all, **THANK YOU** for purchasing Mometrix study materials!

Second, congratulations! You are one of the few determined test-takers who are committed to doing whatever it takes to excel on your exam. **You have come to the right place.** We developed these study materials with one goal in mind: to deliver you the information you need in a format that's concise and easy to use.

In addition to optimizing your guide for the content of the test, we've outlined our recommended steps for breaking down the preparation process into small, attainable goals so you can make sure you stay on track.

We've also analyzed the entire test-taking process, identifying the most common pitfalls and showing how you can overcome them and be ready for any curveball the test throws you.

Standardized testing is one of the biggest obstacles on your road to success, which only increases the importance of doing well in the high-pressure, high-stakes environment of test day. Your results on this test could have a significant impact on your future, and this guide provides the information and practical advice to help you achieve your full potential on test day.

Your success is our success

We would love to hear from you! If you would like to share the story of your exam success or if you have any questions or comments in regard to our products, please contact us at **800-673-8175** or **support@mometrix.com**.

Thanks again for your business and we wish you continued success!

Sincerely,
The Mometrix Test Preparation Team

Need more help? Check out our flashcards at: http://MometrixFlashcards.com/TExES

Written and edited by the Mometrix Exam Secrets Test Prep Team
Printed in the United States of America

TABLE OF CONTENTS

INTRODUCTION 5

SECRET KEY #1 – PLAN BIG, STUDY SMALL 6
- Information Organization 6
- Time Management 6
- Study Environment 6

SECRET KEY #2 – MAKE YOUR STUDYING COUNT 7
- Retention 7
- Modality 7

SECRET KEY #3 – PRACTICE THE RIGHT WAY 8
- Practice Test Strategy 9

SECRET KEY #4 – PACE YOURSELF 10

SECRET KEY #5 – HAVE A PLAN FOR GUESSING 11
- When to Start the Guessing Process 11
- How to Narrow Down the Choices 12
- Which Answer to Choose 13

TEST-TAKING STRATEGIES 14
- Question Strategies 14
- Answer Choice Strategies 15
- General Strategies 16
- Final Notes 17

SCIENTIFIC INQUIRY AND PROCESSES 18

PHYSICS 33

CHEMISTRY 54

CELL STRUCTURE AND PROCESSES 79

HEREDITY AND EVOLUTION OF LIFE 95

DIVERSITY OF LIFE 108

INTERDEPENDENCE OF LIFE AND ENVIRONMENTAL SYSTEMS 122

EARTH'S HISTORY AND THE STRUCTURE AND FUNCTION OF EARTH SYSTEMS 126

COMPONENTS AND PROPERTIES OF THE SOLAR SYSTEM AND THE UNIVERSE 148

TEXES PRACTICE TEST 157

ANSWERS AND EXPLANATIONS 177

THANK YOU 189

ADDITIONAL BONUS MATERIAL 190

Introduction

Thank you for purchasing this resource! You have made the choice to prepare yourself for a test that could have a huge impact on your future, and this guide is designed to help you be fully ready for test day. Obviously, it's important to have a solid understanding of the test material, but you also need to be prepared for the unique environment and stressors of the test, so that you can perform to the best of your abilities.

For this purpose, the first section that appears in this guide is the **Secret Keys**. We've devoted countless hours to meticulously researching what works and what doesn't, and we've boiled down our findings to the five most impactful steps you can take to improve your performance on the test. We start at the beginning with study planning and move through the preparation process, all the way to the testing strategies that will help you get the most out of what you know when you're finally sitting in front of the test.

We recommend that you start preparing for your test as far in advance as possible. However, if you've bought this guide as a last-minute study resource and only have a few days before your test, we recommend that you skip over the first two Secret Keys since they address a long-term study plan.

If you struggle with **test anxiety**, we strongly encourage you to check out our recommendations for how you can overcome it. Test anxiety is a formidable foe, but it can be beaten, and we want to make sure you have the tools you need to defeat it.

Secret Key #1 – Plan Big, Study Small

There's a lot riding on your performance. If you want to ace this test, you're going to need to keep your skills sharp and the material fresh in your mind. You need a plan that lets you review everything you need to know while still fitting in your schedule. We'll break this strategy down into three categories.

Information Organization

Start with the information you already have: the official test outline. From this, you can make a complete list of all the concepts you need to cover before the test. Organize these concepts into groups that can be studied together, and create a list of any related vocabulary you need to learn so you can brush up on any difficult terms. You'll want to keep this vocabulary list handy once you actually start studying since you may need to add to it along the way.

Time Management

Once you have your set of study concepts, decide how to spread them out over the time you have left before the test. Break your study plan into small, clear goals so you have a manageable task for each day and know exactly what you're doing. Then just focus on one small step at a time. When you manage your time this way, you don't need to spend hours at a time studying. Studying a small block of content for a short period each day helps you retain information better and avoid stressing over how much you have left to do. You can relax knowing that you have a plan to cover everything in time. In order for this strategy to be effective though, you have to start studying early and stick to your schedule. Avoid the exhaustion and futility that comes from last-minute cramming!

Study Environment

The environment you study in has a big impact on your learning. Studying in a coffee shop, while probably more enjoyable, is not likely to be as fruitful as studying in a quiet room. It's important to keep distractions to a minimum. You're only planning to study for a short block of time, so make the most of it. Don't pause to check your phone or get up to find a snack. It's also important to **avoid multitasking**. Research has consistently shown that multitasking will make your studying dramatically less effective. Your study area should also be comfortable and well-lit so you don't have the distraction of straining your eyes or sitting on an uncomfortable chair.

The time of day you study is also important. You want to be rested and alert. Don't wait until just before bedtime. Study when you'll be most likely to comprehend and remember. Even better, if you know what time of day your test will be, set that time aside for study. That way your brain will be used to working on that subject at that specific time and you'll have a better chance of recalling information.

Finally, it can be helpful to team up with others who are studying for the same test. Your actual studying should be done in as isolated an environment as possible, but the work of organizing the information and setting up the study plan can be divided up. In between study sessions, you can discuss with your teammates the concepts that you're all studying and quiz each other on the details. Just be sure that your teammates are as serious about the test as you are. If you find that your study time is being replaced with social time, you might need to find a new team.

Secret Key #2 – Make Your Studying Count

You're devoting a lot of time and effort to preparing for this test, so you want to be absolutely certain it will pay off. This means doing more than just reading the content and hoping you can remember it on test day. It's important to make every minute of study count. There are two main areas you can focus on to make your studying count:

Retention

It doesn't matter how much time you study if you can't remember the material. You need to make sure you are retaining the concepts. To check your retention of the information you're learning, try recalling it at later times with minimal prompting. Try carrying around flashcards and glance at one or two from time to time or ask a friend who's also studying for the test to quiz you.

To enhance your retention, look for ways to put the information into practice so that you can apply it rather than simply recalling it. If you're using the information in practical ways, it will be much easier to remember. Similarly, it helps to solidify a concept in your mind if you're not only reading it to yourself but also explaining it to someone else. Ask a friend to let you teach them about a concept you're a little shaky on (or speak aloud to an imaginary audience if necessary). As you try to summarize, define, give examples, and answer your friend's questions, you'll understand the concepts better and they will stay with you longer. Finally, step back for a big picture view and ask yourself how each piece of information fits with the whole subject. When you link the different concepts together and see them working together as a whole, it's easier to remember the individual components.

Finally, practice showing your work on any multi-step problems, even if you're just studying. Writing out each step you take to solve a problem will help solidify the process in your mind, and you'll be more likely to remember it during the test.

Modality

Modality simply refers to the means or method by which you study. Choosing a study modality that fits your own individual learning style is crucial. No two people learn best in exactly the same way, so it's important to know your strengths and use them to your advantage.

For example, if you learn best by visualization, focus on visualizing a concept in your mind and draw an image or a diagram. Try color-coding your notes, illustrating them, or creating symbols that will trigger your mind to recall a learned concept. If you learn best by hearing or discussing information, find a study partner who learns the same way or read aloud to yourself. Think about how to put the information in your own words. Imagine that you are giving a lecture on the topic and record yourself so you can listen to it later.

For any learning style, flashcards can be helpful. Organize the information so you can take advantage of spare moments to review. Underline key words or phrases. Use different colors for different categories. Mnemonic devices (such as creating a short list in which every item starts with the same letter) can also help with retention. Find what works best for you and use it to store the information in your mind most effectively and easily.

Secret Key #3 – Practice the Right Way

Your success on test day depends not only on how many hours you put into preparing, but also on whether you prepared the right way. It's good to check along the way to see if your studying is paying off. One of the most effective ways to do this is by taking practice tests to evaluate your progress. Practice tests are useful because they show exactly where you need to improve. Every time you take a practice test, pay special attention to these three groups of questions:

- The questions you got wrong
- The questions you had to guess on, even if you guessed right
- The questions you found difficult or slow to work through

This will show you exactly what your weak areas are, and where you need to devote more study time. Ask yourself why each of these questions gave you trouble. Was it because you didn't understand the material? Was it because you didn't remember the vocabulary? Do you need more repetitions on this type of question to build speed and confidence? Dig into those questions and figure out how you can strengthen your weak areas as you go back to review the material.

Additionally, many practice tests have a section explaining the answer choices. It can be tempting to read the explanation and think that you now have a good understanding of the concept. However, an explanation likely only covers part of the question's broader context. Even if the explanation makes sense, **go back and investigate** every concept related to the question until you're positive you have a thorough understanding.

As you go along, keep in mind that the practice test is just that: practice. Memorizing these questions and answers will not be very helpful on the actual test because it is unlikely to have any of the same exact questions. If you only know the right answers to the sample questions, you won't be prepared for the real thing. **Study the concepts** until you understand them fully, and then you'll be able to answer any question that shows up on the test.

It's important to wait on the practice tests until you're ready. If you take a test on your first day of study, you may be overwhelmed by the amount of material covered and how much you need to learn. Work up to it gradually.

On test day, you'll need to be prepared for answering questions, managing your time, and using the test-taking strategies you've learned. It's a lot to balance, like a mental marathon that will have a big impact on your future. Like training for a marathon, you'll need to start slowly and work your way up. When test day arrives, you'll be ready.

Start with the strategies you've read in the first two Secret Keys—plan your course and study in the way that works best for you. If you have time, consider using multiple study resources to get different approaches to the same concepts. It can be helpful to see difficult concepts from more than one angle. Then find a good source for practice tests. Many times, the test website will suggest potential study resources or provide sample tests.

Practice Test Strategy

If you're able to find at least three practice tests, we recommend this strategy:

Untimed and Open-Book Practice

Take the first test with no time constraints and with your notes and study guide handy. Take your time and focus on applying the strategies you've learned.

Timed and Open-Book Practice

Take the second practice test open-book as well, but set a timer and practice pacing yourself to finish in time.

Timed and Closed-Book Practice

Take any other practice tests as if it were test day. Set a timer and put away your study materials. Sit at a table or desk in a quiet room, imagine yourself at the testing center, and answer questions as quickly and accurately as possible.

Keep repeating timed and closed-book tests on a regular basis until you run out of practice tests or it's time for the actual test. Your mind will be ready for the schedule and stress of test day, and you'll be able to focus on recalling the material you've learned.

Secret Key #4 – Pace Yourself

Once you're fully prepared for the material on the test, your biggest challenge on test day will be managing your time. Just knowing that the clock is ticking can make you panic even if you have plenty of time left. Work on pacing yourself so you can build confidence against the time constraints of the exam. Pacing is a difficult skill to master, especially in a high-pressure environment, so **practice is vital**.

Set time expectations for your pace based on how much time is available. For example, if a section has 60 questions and the time limit is 30 minutes, you know you have to average 30 seconds or less per question in order to answer them all. Although 30 seconds is the hard limit, set 25 seconds per question as your goal, so you reserve extra time to spend on harder questions. When you budget extra time for the harder questions, you no longer have any reason to stress when those questions take longer to answer.

Don't let this time expectation distract you from working through the test at a calm, steady pace, but keep it in mind so you don't spend too much time on any one question. Recognize that taking extra time on one question you don't understand may keep you from answering two that you do understand later in the test. If your time limit for a question is up and you're still not sure of the answer, mark it and move on, and come back to it later if the time and the test format allow. If the testing format doesn't allow you to return to earlier questions, just make an educated guess; then put it out of your mind and move on.

On the easier questions, be careful not to rush. It may seem wise to hurry through them so you have more time for the challenging ones, but it's not worth missing one if you know the concept and just didn't take the time to read the question fully. Work efficiently but make sure you understand the question and have looked at all of the answer choices, since more than one may seem right at first.

Even if you're paying attention to the time, you may find yourself a little behind at some point. You should speed up to get back on track, but do so wisely. Don't panic; just take a few seconds less on each question until you're caught up. Don't guess without thinking, but do look through the answer choices and eliminate any you know are wrong. If you can get down to two choices, it is often worthwhile to guess from those. Once you've chosen an answer, move on and don't dwell on any that you skipped or had to hurry through. If a question was taking too long, chances are it was one of the harder ones, so you weren't as likely to get it right anyway.

On the other hand, if you find yourself getting ahead of schedule, it may be beneficial to slow down a little. The more quickly you work, the more likely you are to make a careless mistake that will affect your score. You've budgeted time for each question, so don't be afraid to spend that time. Practice an efficient but careful pace to get the most out of the time you have.

Secret Key #5 – Have a Plan for Guessing

When you're taking the test, you may find yourself stuck on a question. Some of the answer choices seem better than others, but you don't see the one answer choice that is obviously correct. What do you do?

The scenario described above is very common, yet most test takers have not effectively prepared for it. Developing and practicing a plan for guessing may be one of the single most effective uses of your time as you get ready for the exam.

In developing your plan for guessing, there are three questions to address:

- When should you start the guessing process?
- How should you narrow down the choices?
- Which answer should you choose?

When to Start the Guessing Process

Unless your plan for guessing is to select C every time (which, despite its merits, is not what we recommend), you need to leave yourself enough time to apply your answer elimination strategies. Since you have a limited amount of time for each question, that means that if you're going to give yourself the best shot at guessing correctly, you have to decide quickly whether or not you will guess.

Of course, the best-case scenario is that you don't have to guess at all, so first, see if you can answer the question based on your knowledge of the subject and basic reasoning skills. Focus on the key words in the question and try to jog your memory of related topics. Give yourself a chance to bring the knowledge to mind, but once you realize that you don't have (or you can't access) the knowledge you need to answer the question, it's time to start the guessing process.

It's almost always better to start the guessing process too early than too late. It only takes a few seconds to remember something and answer the question from knowledge. Carefully eliminating wrong answer choices takes longer. Plus, going through the process of eliminating answer choices can actually help jog your memory.

Summary: Start the guessing process as soon as you decide that you can't answer the question based on your knowledge.

How to Narrow Down the Choices

The next chapter in this book (**Test-Taking Strategies**) includes a wide range of strategies for how to approach questions and how to look for answer choices to eliminate. You will definitely want to read those carefully, practice them, and figure out which ones work best for you. Here though, we're going to address a mindset rather than a particular strategy.

Your chances of guessing an answer correctly depend on how many options you are choosing from.

How many choices you have	How likely you are to guess correctly
5	20%
4	25%
3	33%
2	50%
1	100%

You can see from this chart just how valuable it is to be able to eliminate incorrect answers and make an educated guess, but there are two things that many test takers do that cause them to miss out on the benefits of guessing:

- Accidentally eliminating the correct answer
- Selecting an answer based on an impression

We'll look at the first one here, and the second one in the next section.

To avoid accidentally eliminating the correct answer, we recommend a thought exercise called **the $5 challenge**. In this challenge, you only eliminate an answer choice from contention if you are willing to bet $5 on it being wrong. Why $5? Five dollars is a small but not insignificant amount of money. It's an amount you could afford to lose but wouldn't want to throw away. And while losing $5 once might not hurt too much, doing it twenty times will set you back $100. In the same way, each small decision you make—eliminating a choice here, guessing on a question there—won't by itself impact your score very much, but when you put them all together, they can make a big difference. By holding each answer choice elimination decision to a higher standard, you can reduce the risk of accidentally eliminating the correct answer.

The $5 challenge can also be applied in a positive sense: If you are willing to bet $5 that an answer choice *is* correct, go ahead and mark it as correct.

Summary: Only eliminate an answer choice if you are willing to bet $5 that it is wrong.

Which Answer to Choose

You're taking the test. You've run into a hard question and decided you'll have to guess. You've eliminated all the answer choices you're willing to bet $5 on. Now you have to pick an answer. Why do we even need to talk about this? Why can't you just pick whichever one you feel like when the time comes?

The answer to these questions is that if you don't come into the test with a plan, you'll rely on your impression to select an answer choice, and if you do that, you risk falling into a trap. The test writers know that everyone who takes their test will be guessing on some of the questions, so they intentionally write wrong answer choices to seem plausible. You still have to pick an answer though, and if the wrong answer choices are designed to look right, how can you ever be sure that you're not falling for their trap? The best solution we've found to this dilemma is to take the decision out of your hands entirely. Here is the process we recommend:

Once you've eliminated any choices that you are confident (willing to bet $5) are wrong, select the first remaining choice as your answer.

Whether you choose to select the first remaining choice, the second, or the last, the important thing is that you use some preselected standard. Using this approach guarantees that you will not be enticed into selecting an answer choice that looks right, because you are not basing your decision on how the answer choices look.

This is not meant to make you question your knowledge. Instead, it is to help you recognize the difference between your knowledge and your impressions. There's a huge difference between thinking an answer is right because of what you know, and thinking an answer is right because it looks or sounds like it should be right.

Summary: To ensure that your selection is appropriately random, make a predetermined selection from among all answer choices you have not eliminated.

Test-Taking Strategies

This section contains a list of test-taking strategies that you may find helpful as you work through the test. By taking what you know and applying logical thought, you can maximize your chances of answering any question correctly!

It is very important to realize that every question is different and every person is different: no single strategy will work on every question, and no single strategy will work for every person. That's why we've included all of them here, so you can try them out and determine which ones work best for different types of questions and which ones work best for you.

Question Strategies

Read Carefully

Read the question and answer choices carefully. Don't miss the question because you misread the terms. You have plenty of time to read each question thoroughly and make sure you understand what is being asked. Yet a happy medium must be attained, so don't waste too much time. You must read carefully, but efficiently.

Contextual Clues

Look for contextual clues. If the question includes a word you are not familiar with, look at the immediate context for some indication of what the word might mean. Contextual clues can often give you all the information you need to decipher the meaning of an unfamiliar word. Even if you can't determine the meaning, you may be able to narrow down the possibilities enough to make a solid guess at the answer to the question.

Prefixes

If you're having trouble with a word in the question or answer choices, try dissecting it. Take advantage of every clue that the word might include. Prefixes and suffixes can be a huge help. Usually they allow you to determine a basic meaning. Pre- means before, post- means after, pro - is positive, de- is negative. From prefixes and suffixes, you can get an idea of the general meaning of the word and try to put it into context.

Hedge Words

Watch out for critical hedge words, such as *likely*, *may*, *can*, *sometimes*, *often*, *almost*, *mostly*, *usually*, *generally*, *rarely*, and *sometimes*. Question writers insert these hedge phrases to cover every possibility. Often an answer choice will be wrong simply because it leaves no room for exception. Be on guard for answer choices that have definitive words such as *exactly* and *always*.

Switchback Words

Stay alert for *switchbacks*. These are the words and phrases frequently used to alert you to shifts in thought. The most common switchback words are *but*, *although*, and *however*. Others include *nevertheless*, *on the other hand*, *even though*, *while*, *in spite of*, *despite*, *regardless of*. Switchback words are important to catch because they can change the direction of the question or an answer choice.

Face Value

When in doubt, use common sense. Accept the situation in the problem at face value. Don't read too much into it. These problems will not require you to make wild assumptions. If you have to go beyond creativity and warp time or space in order to have an answer choice fit the question, then you should move on and consider the other answer choices. These are normal problems rooted in reality. The applicable relationship or explanation may not be readily apparent, but it is there for you to figure out. Use your common sense to interpret anything that isn't clear.

Answer Choice Strategies

Answer Selection

The most thorough way to pick an answer choice is to identify and eliminate wrong answers until only one is left, then confirm it is the correct answer. Sometimes an answer choice may immediately seem right, but be careful. The test writers will usually put more than one reasonable answer choice on each question, so take a second to read all of them and make sure that the other choices are not equally obvious. As long as you have time left, it is better to read every answer choice than to pick the first one that looks right without checking the others.

Answer Choice Families

An answer choice family consists of two (in rare cases, three) answer choices that are very similar in construction and cannot all be true at the same time. If you see two answer choices that are direct opposites or parallels, one of them is usually the correct answer. For instance, if one answer choice says that quantity *x* increases and another either says that quantity *x* decreases (opposite) or says that quantity *y* increases (parallel), then those answer choices would fall into the same family. An answer choice that doesn't match the construction of the answer choice family is more likely to be incorrect. Most questions will not have answer choice families, but when they do appear, you should be prepared to recognize them.

Eliminate Answers

Eliminate answer choices as soon as you realize they are wrong, but make sure you consider all possibilities. If you are eliminating answer choices and realize that the last one you are left with is also wrong, don't panic. Start over and consider each choice again. There may be something you missed the first time that you will realize on the second pass.

Avoid Fact Traps

Don't be distracted by an answer choice that is factually true but doesn't answer the question. You are looking for the choice that answers the question. Stay focused on what the question is asking for so you don't accidentally pick an answer that is true but incorrect. Always go back to the question and make sure the answer choice you've selected actually answers the question and is not merely a true statement.

Extreme Statements

In general, you should avoid answers that put forth extreme actions as standard practice or proclaim controversial ideas as established fact. An answer choice that states the "process should be used in certain situations, if..." is much more likely to be correct than one that states the "process should be discontinued completely." The first is a calm rational statement and doesn't even make a definitive, uncompromising stance, using a hedge word *if* to provide wiggle room, whereas the second choice is a radical idea and far more extreme.

Benchmark

As you read through the answer choices and you come across one that seems to answer the question well, mentally select that answer choice. This is not your final answer, but it's the one that will help you evaluate the other answer choices. The one that you selected is your benchmark or standard for judging each of the other answer choices. Every other answer choice must be compared to your benchmark. That choice is correct until proven otherwise by another answer choice beating it. If you find a better answer, then that one becomes your new benchmark. Once you've decided that no other choice answers the question as well as your benchmark, you have your final answer.

Predict the Answer

Before you even start looking at the answer choices, it is often best to try to predict the answer. When you come up with the answer on your own, it is easier to avoid distractions and traps because you will know exactly what to look for. The right answer choice is unlikely to be word-for-word what you came up with, but it should be a close match. Even if you are confident that you have the right answer, you should still take the time to read each option before moving on.

General Strategies

Tough Questions

If you are stumped on a problem or it appears too hard or too difficult, don't waste time. Move on! Remember though, if you can quickly check for obviously incorrect answer choices, your chances of guessing correctly are greatly improved. Before you completely give up, at least try to knock out a couple of possible answers. Eliminate what you can and then guess at the remaining answer choices before moving on.

Check Your Work

Since you will probably not know every term listed and the answer to every question, it is important that you get credit for the ones that you do know. Don't miss any questions through careless mistakes. If at all possible, try to take a second to look back over your answer selection and make sure you've selected the correct answer choice and haven't made a costly careless mistake (such as marking an answer choice that you didn't mean to mark). This quick double check should more than pay for itself in caught mistakes for the time it costs.

Pace Yourself

It's easy to be overwhelmed when you're looking at a page full of questions; your mind is confused and full of random thoughts, and the clock is ticking down faster than you would like. Calm down and maintain the pace that you have set for yourself. Especially as you get down to the last few minutes of the test, don't let the small numbers on the clock make you panic. As long as you are on track by monitoring your pace, you are guaranteed to have time for each question.

Don't Rush

It is very easy to make errors when you are in a hurry. Maintaining a fast pace in answering questions is pointless if it makes you miss questions that you would have gotten right otherwise. Test writers like to include distracting information and wrong answers that seem right. Taking a little extra time to avoid careless mistakes can make all the difference in your test score. Find a pace that allows you to be confident in the answers that you select.

Keep Moving

Panicking will not help you pass the test, so do your best to stay calm and keep moving. Taking deep breaths and going through the answer elimination steps you practiced can help to break through a stress barrier and keep your pace.

Final Notes

The combination of a solid foundation of content knowledge and the confidence that comes from practicing your plan for applying that knowledge is the key to maximizing your performance on test day. As your foundation of content knowledge is built up and strengthened, you'll find that the strategies included in this chapter become more and more effective in helping you quickly sift through the distractions and traps of the test to isolate the correct answer.

Now it's time to move on to the test content chapters of this book, but be sure to keep your goal in mind. As you read, think about how you will be able to apply this information on the test. If you've already seen sample questions for the test and you have an idea of the question format and style, try to come up with questions of your own that you can answer based on what you're reading. This will give you valuable practice applying your knowledge in the same ways you can expect to on test day.

Good luck and good studying!

Scientific Inquiry and Processes

Laboratory Accidents

Any spills or accidents should be **reported** to the teacher so that the teacher can determine the safest clean-up method. The student should start to wash off a **chemical** spilled on the skin while reporting the incident. Some spills may require removal of contaminated clothing and use of the **safety shower**. Broken glass should be disposed of in a designated container. If someone's clothing catches fire they should walk to the safety shower and use it to extinguish the flames. A fire blanket may be used to smother a **lab fire**. A fire extinguisher, phone, spill neutralizers, and a first aid box are other types of **safety equipment** found in the lab. Students should be familiar with **routes** out of the room and the building in case of fire. Students should use the **eye wash station** if a chemical gets in the eyes.

Safety Procedures

Students should wear a **lab apron** and **safety goggles**. Loose or dangling clothing and jewelry, necklaces, and earrings should not be worn. Those with long hair should tie it back. Care should always be taken not to splash chemicals. Open-toed shoes such as sandals and flip-flops should not be worn, nor should wrist watches. Glasses are preferable to contact lenses since the latter carries a risk of chemicals getting caught between the lens and the eye. Students should always be supervised. The area where the experiment is taking place and the surrounding floor should be free of clutter. Only the lab book and the items necessary for the experiment should be present. Smoking, eating, and chewing gum are not permitted in the lab. Cords should not be allowed to dangle from work stations. There should be no rough-housing in the lab. Hands should be washed after the lab is complete.

Fume Hoods

Because of the potential safety hazards associated with chemistry lab experiments, such as fire from vapors and the inhalation of toxic fumes, a **fume hood** should be used in many instances. A fume hood carries away vapors from reagents or reactions. Equipment or reactions are placed as far back in the hood as practical to help enhance the collection of the fumes. The **glass safety shield** automatically closes to the appropriate height, and should be low enough to protect the face and body. The safety shield should only be raised to move equipment in and out of the hood. One should not climb inside a hood or stick one's head inside. All spills should be wiped up immediately and the glass should be cleaned if a splash occurs.

Common Safety Hazards

Some specific safety hazards possible in a chemistry lab include:

- **Fire**: Fire can be caused by volatile solvents such as ether, acetone, and benzene being kept in an open beaker or Erlenmeyer flask. Vapors can creep along the table and ignite if they reach a flame or spark. Solvents should be heated in a hood with a steam bath, not on a hot plate.
- **Explosion**: Heating or creating a reaction in a closed system can cause an explosion, resulting in flying glass and chemical splashes. The system should be vented to prevent this.
- **Chemical and thermal burns**: Many chemicals are corrosive to the skin and eyes.
- **Inhalation of toxic fumes**: Some compounds severely irritate membranes in the eyes, nose, throat, and lungs.

- **Absorption** of toxic chemicals such as dimethyl sulfoxide (DMSO) and nitrobenzene through the skin.
- **Ingestion** of toxic chemicals.

Safety Gloves

There are many types of **gloves** available to help protect the skin from cuts, burns, and chemical splashes. There are many considerations to take into account when choosing a glove. For example, gloves that are highly protective may limit dexterity. Some gloves may not offer appropriate protection against a specific chemical. Other considerations include degradation rating, which indicates how effective a glove is when exposed to chemicals; breakthrough time, which indicates how quickly a chemical can break through the surface of the glove; and permeation rate, which indicates how quickly chemicals seep through after the initial breakthrough. Disposable latex, vinyl, or nitrile gloves are usually appropriate for most circumstances, and offer protection from incidental splashes and contact. Other types of gloves include butyl, neoprene, PVC, PVA, viton, silver shield, and natural rubber. Each offers its own type of protection, but may have drawbacks as well. **Double-gloving** can improve resistance or dexterity in some instances.

Proper Handling and Storage of Chemicals

Students should take care when **carrying chemicals** from one place to another. Chemicals should never be taken from the room, tasted, or touched with bare hands. **Safety gloves** should be worn when appropriate and glove/chemical interactions and glove deterioration should be considered. Hands should always be **washed** thoroughly after a lab. Potentially hazardous materials intended for use in chemistry, biology, or other science labs should be secured in a safe area where relevant **Safety Data Sheets (SDS)** can be accessed. Chemicals and solutions should be used as directed and labels should be read before handling solutions and chemicals. Extra chemicals should not be returned to their original containers, but should be disposed of as directed by the school district's rules or local ordinances. Local municipalities often have hazardous waste disposal programs. Acids should be stored separately from other chemicals. Flammable liquids should be stored away from acids, bases, and oxidizers.

Bunsen Burners

When using a **Bunsen burner**, loose clothing should be tucked in, long hair should be tied back, and safety goggles and aprons should be worn. Students should know what to do in case of a fire or accident. When lighting the burner, strikers should always be used instead of matches. Do not touch the hot barrel. Tongs (never fingers) should be used to hold the material in the flame. To heat liquid, a flask may be set upon wire gauze on a tripod and secured with an iron ring or clamp on a stand. The flame is extinguished by turning off the gas at the source.

Safety Procedures Related to Animals

Animals to be used for **dissections** should be obtained from a company that provides animals for this purpose. Road kill or decaying animals that a student brings in should not be used. It is possible that such an animal may have a pathogen or a virus, such as rabies, which can be transmitted via the saliva of even a dead animal. Students should use gloves and should not participate if they have open sores or moral objections to dissections. It is generally accepted that biological experiments may be performed on lower-order life forms and invertebrates, but not on mammalian vertebrates and birds. No animals should be harmed physiologically. Experimental animals should be kept, cared for, and handled in a safe manner and with compassion. Pathogenic (anything able to cause a disease) substances should not be used in lab experiments.

Lab Notebooks

A **lab notebook** is a record of all pre-lab work and lab work. It differs from a lab report, which is prepared after lab work is completed. A lab notebook is a formal record of lab preparations and what was done. **Observational recordings** should not be altered, erased, or whited-out to make corrections. Drawing a single line through an entry is sufficient to make changes. Pages should be numbered and should not be torn out. Entries should be made neatly, but don't necessarily have to be complete sentences. **Entries** should provide detailed information and be recorded in such a way that another person could use them to replicate the experiment. **Quantitative data** may be recorded in tabular form, and may include calculations made during an experiment. Lab book entries can also include references and research performed before the experiment. Entries may also consist of information about a lab experiment, including the objective or purpose, the procedures, data collected, and the results.

Lab Reports

A **lab report** is an item developed after an experiment that is intended to present the results of a lab experiment. Generally, it should be prepared using a word processor, not hand-written or recorded in a notebook. A lab report should be formally presented. It is intended to persuade others to accept or reject a hypothesis. It should include a brief but descriptive **title** and an **abstract**. The abstract is a summary of the report. It should include a purpose that states the problem that was explored or the question that was answered. It should also include a **hypothesis** that describes the anticipated results of the experiment. The experiment should include a **control** and one **variable** to ensure that the results can be interpreted correctly. Observations and results can be presented using written narratives, tables, graphs, and illustrations. The report should also include a **summation** or **conclusion** explaining whether the results supported the hypothesis.

Types of Laboratory Glassware

Two types of flasks are Erlenmeyer flasks and volumetric flasks. **Volumetric flasks** are used to accurately prepare a specific volume and concentration of solution. **Erlenmeyer flasks** can be used for mixing, transporting, and reacting, but are not appropriate for accurate measurements.

A **pipette** can be used to accurately measure small amounts of liquid. Liquid is drawn into the pipette through a bulb. The liquid measurement is read at the **meniscus**. There are also plastic disposable pipettes. A **repipette** is a hand-operated pump that dispenses solutions.

Beakers can be used to measure mass or dissolve a solvent into a solute. They do not measure volume as accurately as a volumetric flask, pipette, graduated cylinder, or burette.

Graduated cylinders are used for precise measurements and are considered more accurate than Erlenmeyer flasks or beakers. To read a graduated cylinder, it should be placed on a flat surface and read at eye level. The surface of a liquid in a graduated cylinder forms a lens-shaped curve. The measurement should be taken from the bottom of the curve. A ring may be placed at the top of tall, narrow cylinders to help avoid breakage if they are tipped over.

A **burette**, or buret, is a piece of lab glassware used to accurately dispense liquid. It looks similar to a narrow graduated cylinder, but includes a stopcock and tip. It may be filled with a funnel or pipette.

Microscopes

There are different kinds of microscopes, but **optical** or **light microscopes** are the most commonly used in lab settings. Light and lenses are used to magnify and view samples. A specimen or sample is placed on a slide and the slide is placed on a stage with a hole in it. Light passes through the hole and illuminates the sample. The sample is magnified by lenses and viewed through the eyepiece. A simple microscope has one lens, while a typical compound microscope has three lenses. The light source can be room light redirected by a mirror or the microscope can have its own independent light source that passes through a condenser. In this case, there are diaphragms and filters to allow light intensity to be controlled. Optical microscopes also have coarse and fine adjustment knobs.

Other types of microscopes include **digital microscopes**, which use a camera and a monitor to allow viewing of the sample. **Scanning electron microscopes (SEMs)** provide greater detail of a sample in terms of the surface topography and can produce magnifications much greater than those possible with optical microscopes. The technology of an SEM is quite different from an optical microscope in that it does not rely on lenses to magnify objects, but uses samples placed in a chamber. In one type of SEM, a beam of electrons from an electron gun scans and actually interacts with the sample to produce an image.

Wet mount slides designed for use with a light microscope typically require a thin portion of the specimen to be placed on a standard glass slide. A drop of water is added and a cover slip or cover glass is placed on top. Air bubbles and fingerprints can make viewing difficult. Placing the cover slip at a 45-degree angle and allowing it to drop into place can help avoid the problem of air bubbles. A **cover slip** should always be used when viewing wet mount slides. The viewer should start with the objective in its lowest position and then fine focus. The microscope should be carried with two hands and stored with the low-power objective in the down position. **Lenses** should be cleaned with lens paper only. A **graticule slide** is marked with a grid line, and is useful for counting or estimating a quantity.

Balances

Balances such as triple-beam balances, spring balances, and electronic balances measure mass and force. An **electronic balance** is the most accurate, followed by a **triple-beam balance** and then a **spring balance**. One part of a **triple-beam balance** is the plate, which is where the item to be weighed is placed. There are also three beams that have hatch marks indicating amounts and hold the weights that rest in the notches. The front beam measures weights between 0 and 10 grams, the middle beam measures weights in 100 gram increments, and the far beam measures weights in 10 gram increments. The sum of the weight of each beam is the total weight of the object. A triple beam balance also includes a set screw to calibrate the equipment and a mark indicating the object and counterweights are in balance.

Chromatography

Chromatography refers to a set of laboratory techniques used to separate or analyze **mixtures**. Mixtures are dissolved in their mobile phases. In the stationary or bonded phase, the desired component is separated from other molecules in the mixture. In chromatography, the analyte is the substance to be separated. **Preparative chromatography** refers to the type of chromatography that involves purifying a substance for further use rather than further analysis. **Analytical chromatography** involves analyzing the isolated substance. Other types of chromatography include column, planar, paper, thin layer, displacement, supercritical fluid, affinity, ion exchange, and size exclusion chromatography. Reversed phase, two-dimensional, simulated moving bed, pyrolysis, fast protein, counter current, and chiral are also types of chromatography. **Gas chromatography** refers to the separation technique in which the mobile phase of a substance is in gas form.

Review Video: Paper Chromatography
Visit mometrix.com/academy and enter code: 543963

Reagents and Reactants

A **reagent** or **reactant** is a chemical agent for use in chemical reactions. When preparing for a lab, it should be confirmed that glassware and other equipment has been cleaned and/or sterilized. There should be enough materials, reagents, or other solutions needed for the lab for every group of students completing the experiment. Distilled water should be used instead of tap water when performing lab experiments because distilled water has most of its impurities removed. Other needed apparatus such as funnels, filter paper, balances, Bunsen burners, ring stands, and/or microscopes should also be set up. After the lab, it should be confirmed that sinks, workstations, and any equipment used have been cleaned. If chemicals or specimens need to be kept at a certain temperature by refrigerating them or using another storage method, the temperature should be checked periodically to ensure the sample does not spoil.

Diluting Acids

When preparing a solution of **dilute acid**, always add the concentrated acid solution to water, not water to concentrated acid. Start by adding ~2/3 of the total volume of water to the graduated cylinder or volumetric flask. Next, add the concentrated acid to the water. Add additional water to the diluted acid to bring the solution to the final desired volume.

Cleaning After Acid Spills

In the event of an **acid spill**, any clothes that have come into contact with the acid should be removed and any skin contacted with acid must be rinsed with clean water. To the extent a window can be opened or a fume hood can be turned on, do so. Do not try force circulation, such as by adding a fan, as acid fumes can be harmful if spread.

Next, pour one of the following over the spill area: sodium bicarbonate, baking soda, soda ash, or cat litter. Start from the outside of the spill and then move towards the center, in order to prevent splashing. When the clumps have thoroughly dried, sweep up the clumps and dispose of them as chemical waste.

Centrifuges

A **centrifuge** is used to separate the components of a heterogeneous mixture (consisting of two or more compounds) by spinning it. The solid precipitate settles in the bottom of the container and the liquid component of the solution, called the **centrifugate**, is at the top. A well-known application of this process is using a centrifuge to separate blood cells and plasma. The heavier cells settle on the bottom of the test tube and the lighter plasma stays on top. Another example is using a salad spinner to help dry lettuce.

Spectrophotometry

Spectrophotometry involves measuring the amount of visible light absorbed by a colored solution. There are **analog** and **digital spectrometers** that measure percent absorbency and percent transmittance. A **single beam spectrometer** measures relative light intensity. A **double beam spectrometer** compares light intensity between a reference sample and a test sample. Spectrometers measure the wavelength of light. Spectrometry not only involves working with visible light, but also near-ultraviolet and near-infrared light. A **spectrophotometer** includes an illumination source. An output wavelength is selected and beamed at the sample, the sample absorbs light, and the detector responds to the light and outputs an analog electronic current in a usable form. A spectrophotometer may require calibration. Some types can be used to identify unknown chemicals.

Electrophoresis, Calorimetry, and Titration

- **Electrophoresis** is the separation of molecules based on electrical charge. This is possible because particles disbursed in a fluid usually carry electric charges on their surfaces. Molecules are pulled through the fluid toward the positive end if the molecules have a negative charge and are pulled through the fluid toward the negative end if the molecules have a positive charge.
- **Calorimetry** is used to determine the heat released or absorbed in a chemical reaction.
- **Titration** helps determine the precise endpoint of a reaction. With this information, the precise quantity of reactant in the titration flask can be determined. A burette is used to deliver the second reactant to the flask and an indicator or pH meter is used to detect the endpoint of the reaction.

Review Video: Titration
Visit mometrix.com/academy and enter code: 550131

Field Studies and Research Projects

Field studies may facilitate scientific inquiry in a manner similar to indoor lab experiments. Field studies can be interdisciplinary in nature and can help students learn and apply scientific concepts and processes. **Research projects** can be conducted in any number of locations, including school campuses, local parks, national parks, beaches, or mountains. Students can practice the general techniques of observation, data collection, collaborative planning, and analysis of experiments. Field studies give students the chance to learn through hands-on applications of scientific processes, such as map making in geography, observation of stratification in geology, observation of life cycles of plants and animals, and analysis of water quality.

Students should watch out for obvious outdoor **hazards**. These include poisonous flora and fauna such as poison ivy, poison oak, and sumac. Depending on the region of the United States in which the field study is being conducted, hazards may also include rattlesnakes and black widow or brown recluse spiders. Students should also be made aware of potentially hazardous situations specific to **geographic locales** and the possibility of coming into contact with **pathogens**.

Field studies allow for great flexibility in the use of traditional and technological methods for **making observations** and **collecting data**. For example, a nature study could consist of a simple survey of bird species within a given area. Information could be recorded using still photography or a video camera. This type of activity gives students the chance to use technologies other than computers. Computers could still be used to create a slide show of transferred images or a digital lab report. If a quantitative study of birds was being performed, the simple technique of using a pencil and paper to tabulate the number of birds counted in the field could also be used. Other techniques used during field studies could include collecting specimens for lab study, observing coastal ecosystems and tides, and collecting weather data such as temperature, precipitation amounts, and air pressure in a particular locale.

Metric and International System of Units

The **metric system** is the accepted standard of measurement in the scientific community. The **International System of Units (SI)** is a set of measurements (including the metric system) that is almost globally accepted. The United States, Liberia, and Myanmar have not accepted this system. **Standardization** is important because it allows the results of experiments to be compared and reproduced without the need to laboriously convert measurements. The SI is based partially on the **meter-kilogram-second (MKS) system** rather than the **centimeter-gram-second (CGS) system**. The MKS system considers meters, kilograms, and seconds to be the basic units of measurement, while the

CGS system considers centimeters, grams, and seconds to be the basic units of measurement. Under the MKS system, the length of an object would be expressed as 1 meter instead of 100 centimeters, which is how it would be described under the CGS system.

Basic Units of Measurement

Using the **metric system** is generally accepted as the preferred method for taking measurements. Having a **universal standard** allows individuals to interpret measurements more easily, regardless of where they are located. The basic units of measurement are: the **meter**, which measures length; the **liter**, which measures volume; and the **gram**, which measures mass. The metric system starts with a base unit and increases or decreases in units of 10. The prefix and the base unit combined are used to indicate an amount. For example, deka- is 10 times the base unit. A dekameter is 10 meters; a dekaliter is 10 liters; and a dekagram is 10 grams. The prefix hecto- refers to 100 times the base amount; kilo- is 1,000 times the base amount. The prefixes that indicate a fraction of the base unit are deci-, which is 1/10 of the base unit; centi-, which is 1/100 of the base unit; and milli-, which is 1/1000 of the base unit.

Common Prefixes

The prefixes for multiples are as follows: **deka** (da), 10^1 (deka is the American spelling, but deca is also used); **hecto** (h), 10^2; **kilo** (k), 10^3; **mega** (M), 10^6; **giga** (G), 10^9; **tera** (T), 10^{12}; **peta** (P), 10^{15}; **exa** (E), 10^{18}; **zetta** (Z), 10^{21}; and **yotta** (Y), 10^{24}. The prefixes for subdivisions are as follows: **deci** (d), 10^{-1}; **centi** (c), 10^{-2}; **milli** (m), 10^{-3}; **micro** (μ), 10^{-6}; **nano** (n), 10^{-9}; **pico** (p), 10^{-12}; **femto** (f), 10^{-15}; **atto** (a), 10^{-18}; **zepto** (z), 10^{-21}; and **yocto** (y), 10^{-24}. The rule of thumb is that prefixes greater than 10^3 are capitalized. These abbreviations do not need a period after them. A decimeter is a tenth of a meter, a deciliter is a tenth of a liter, and a decigram is a tenth of a gram. Pluralization is understood. For example, when referring to 5 mL of water, no "s" needs to be added to the abbreviation.

Basic SI Units of Measurement

SI uses **second(s)** to measure time. Fractions of seconds are usually measured in metric terms using prefixes such as millisecond (1/1,000 of a second) or nanosecond (1/1,000,000,000 of a second). Increments of time larger than a second are measured in **minutes** and **hours**, which are multiples of 60 and 24. An example of this is a swimmer's time in the 800-meter freestyle being described as 7:32.67, meaning 7 minutes, 32 seconds, and 67 one-hundredths of a second. One second is equal to 1/60 of a minute, 1/3,600 of an hour, and 1/86,400 of a day. Other SI base units are the **ampere** (A) (used to measure electric current), the **kelvin** (K) (used to measure thermodynamic temperature), the **candela** (cd) (used to measure luminous intensity), and the **mole** (mol) (used to measure the amount of a substance at a molecular level). **Meter** (m) is used to measure length and **kilogram** (kg) is used to measure mass.

Significant Figures

The mathematical concept of **significant figures** or **significant digits** is often used to determine the accuracy of measurements or the level of confidence one has in a specific measurement. The significant figures of a measurement include all the digits known with certainty plus one estimated or uncertain digit. There are a number of rules for determining which digits are considered "important" or "interesting." They are: all non-zero digits are *significant*, zeros between digits are *significant*, and leading and trailing zeros are *not significant* unless they appear to the right of the non-zero digits in a decimal. For example, in 0.01230 the significant digits are 1230, and this number would be said to be accurate to the hundred-thousandths place. The zero indicates that the amount has actually been measured as 0. Other zeros are considered place holders, and are not important. A decimal point may be placed after zeros to indicate their importance (in 100. for example). **Estimating**, on the other hand, involves approximating a value rather than calculating the exact number. This may be used to quickly determine a value that is close to the actual number when complete accuracy does not matter or is not possible. In science, estimation may be used when it is impossible to measure or calculate an exact amount, or to quickly approximate an answer when true calculations would be time consuming.

Graphs and Charts

Graphs and charts are effective ways to present scientific data such as observations, statistical analyses, and comparisons between dependent variables and independent variables. On a line chart, the **independent variable** (the one that is being manipulated for the experiment) is represented on the horizontal axis (the x-axis). Any **dependent variables** (the ones that may change as the independent variable changes) are represented on the y-axis. An **XY** or **scatter plot** is often used to plot many points. A "best fit" line is drawn, which allows outliers to be identified more easily. Charts and their axes should have titles. The x and y interval units should be evenly spaced and labeled. Other types of charts are **bar charts** and **histograms**, which can be used to compare differences between the data collected for two variables. A **pie chart** can graphically show the relation of parts to a whole.

Data Presentation

Data collected during a science lab can be organized and **presented** in any number of ways. While **straight narrative** is a suitable method for presenting some lab results, it is not a suitable way to present numbers and quantitative measurements. These types of observations can often be better presented with **tables** and **graphs**. Data that is presented in tables and organized in rows and columns may also be used to make graphs quite easily. Other methods of presenting data include illustrations, photographs, video, and even audio formats. In a **formal report**, tables and figures are labeled and referred to by their labels. For example, a picture of a bubbly solution might be labeled Figure 1, Bubbly Solution. It would be referred to in the text in the following way: "The reaction created bubbles 10 mm in size, as shown in Figure 1, Bubbly Solution." Graphs are also labeled as figures. Tables are labeled in a different way. Examples include: Table 1, Results of Statistical Analysis, or Table 2, Data from Lab 2.

Statistical Precision and Errors

Errors that occur during an experiment can be classified into two categories: random errors and systematic errors. **Random errors** can result in collected data that is wildly different from the rest of the data, or they may result in data that is indistinguishable from the rest. Random errors are not consistent across the data set. In large data sets, random errors may contribute to the variability of data, but they will not affect the average. Random errors are sometimes referred to as noise. They may be caused by a student's inability to take the same measurement in exactly the same way or by outside factors that are not considered variables, but influence the data. A **systematic error** will show up consistently across a sample or data set, and may be the result of a flaw in the experimental design. This type of error affects the average, and is also known as bias.

Scientific Notation

Scientific notation is used because values in science can be very large or very small, which makes them unwieldy. A number in **decimal notation** is 93,000,000. In **scientific notation**, it is 9.3×10^7. The first number, 9.3, is the **coefficient**. It is always greater than or equal to 1 and less than 10. This number is followed by a multiplication sign. The base is always 10 in scientific notation. If the number is greater than ten, the exponent is positive. If the number is between zero and one, the exponent is negative. The first digit of the number is followed by a decimal point and then the rest of the number. In this case, the number is 9.3. To get that number, the decimal point was moved seven places from the end of the number, 93,000,000. The number of places, seven, is the exponent.

Statistical Terminology

Mean - The average, found by taking the sum of a set of numbers and dividing by the number of numbers in the set.

Median - The middle number in a set of numbers sorted from least to greatest. If the set has an even number of entries, the median is the average of the two in the middle.

Mode - The value that appears most frequently in a data set. There may be more than one mode. If no value appears more than once, there is no mode.

Range - The difference between the highest and lowest numbers in a data set.

Standard deviation - Measures the dispersion of a data set or how far from the mean a single data point is likely to be.

Regression analysis - A method of analyzing sets of data and sets of variables that involves studying how the typical value of the dependent variable changes when any one of the independent variables is varied and the other independent variables remain fixed.

Scientific Inquiry

Teaching with the concept of **scientific inquiry** in mind encourages students to think like scientists rather than merely practice the rote memorization of facts and history. This belief in scientific inquiry puts the burden of learning on students, which is a much different approach than expecting them to simply accept and memorize what they are taught. The standards for science as inquiry are intended to be comprehensive, encompassing a student's K-12 education. More are addressed as students gain knowledge. The **National Science Education Standards** state that engaging students in inquiry helps them develop the following five skills:

- Understand scientific concepts.
- Appreciate "how we know" what we know in science.
- Understand the nature of science.
- Develop the skills necessary to become independent inquirers about the natural world.
- Develop the skills necessary to use the skills, abilities, and attitudes associated with science.

Scientific Knowledge

The National Science Education Standards suggest that **science** as a whole and its unifying concepts and processes are a way of thought that is taught throughout a student's K-12 education. There are eight areas of content, and all the concepts, procedures, and underlying principles contained within make up the body of **scientific knowledge**. The areas of content are: unifying concepts and processes in science, science as inquiry, physical science, life science, earth and space science, science and technology, science in personal and social perspectives, and history and nature of science. Specific unifying concepts and processes included in the standards and repeated throughout the content areas are: systems, order, and organization; evidence, models, and explanation; change, constancy, and measurement; evolution and equilibrium; and form and function.

History of Scientific Knowledge

When one examines the history of **scientific knowledge**, it is clear that it is constantly **evolving**. The body of facts, models, theories, and laws grows and changes over time. In other words, one scientific discovery leads to the next. Some advances in science and technology have important and long-lasting effects on science and society. Some discoveries were so alien to the accepted beliefs of the time that not only were they rejected as wrong, but were also considered outright blasphemy. Today, however, many beliefs once considered incorrect have become an ingrained part of scientific knowledge, and have also been the basis of new advances. Examples of advances include: Copernicus's heliocentric view of the universe, Newton's laws of motion and planetary orbits, relativity, geologic time scale, plate tectonics, atomic theory, nuclear physics, biological evolution, germ theory, industrial revolution, molecular biology, information and communication, quantum theory, galactic universe, and medical and health technology.

Important Terminology

- A **scientific fact** is considered an objective and verifiable observation.
- A **scientific theory** is a greater body of accepted knowledge, principles, or relationships that might explain why something happens.
- A **hypothesis** is an educated guess that is not yet proven. It is used to predict the outcome of an experiment in an attempt to solve a problem or answer a question.
- A **law** is an explanation of events that always leads to the same outcome. It is a fact that an object falls. The law of gravity explains why an object falls. The theory of relativity, although generally accepted, has been neither proven nor disproved.
- A **model** is used to explain something on a smaller scale or in simpler terms to provide an example. It is a representation of an idea that can be used to explain events or applied to new situations to predict outcomes or determine results.

Scientific Inquiry and Scientific Method

Scientists use a number of generally accepted techniques collectively known as the **scientific method**. The scientific method generally involves carrying out the following steps:

- Identifying a problem or posing a question
- Formulating a hypothesis or an educated guess
- Conducting experiments or tests that will provide a basis to solve the problem or answer the question
- Observing the results of the test
- Drawing conclusions

An important part of the scientific method is using acceptable experimental techniques. Objectivity is also important if valid results are to be obtained. Another important part of the scientific method is peer review. It is essential that experiments be performed and data be recorded in such a way that experiments can be reproduced to verify results.

Scientific Inquiry Skills for Elementary Students

The six abilities that **grades K-4 students** should acquire are as follows:

- They should be able to ask questions about objects, organisms, and events in the environment.
- They should be able to devise a simple investigation to answer a question.
- They should be able to use tools such as magnifying glasses, rulers, and balances to gather data and make observations.
- They should be able to use the gathered data and observations to provide an explanation.

- They should be able to talk about, draw pictures, or use another method to communicate the results of an investigation and what they learned.
- With respect to the nature of scientific inquiry and scientists, students should understand that investigations involve formulating questions and answers, using different methods of discovering and disclosing answers, using basic tools, observing, sharing answers, and looking at and understanding others' work.

Scientific Inquiry Skills for Middle Grade Students

The five abilities that **grades 5-8 students** should acquire are as follows:

- They should be able to reformulate and clarify questions until they can be answered through scientific investigation.
- They should be able to create and carry out a scientific investigation, interpret the data to provide explanations, and use further data to revise explanations.
- They should be able to identify the tools necessary to gather and analyze data. They should be able to use computer hardware and software to store, organize, and gather data.
- They should be able to provide descriptions and explanations, create models, and make predictions based on the body of knowledge they possess.
- They should be able to explain cause and effect relationships using explanations and data from experiments.

Scientific Inquiry Skills for Older Students

The six abilities that **grades 9-12 students** should acquire are as follows:

- They should be able to identify questions and concepts that guide scientific investigation. In other words, they should be able to create a hypothesis and an appropriate experiment to test that hypothesis.
- They should be able to design and conduct a scientific investigation from start to finish. This includes being able to guide the inquiry by choosing the proper technologies and methods, determining variables, selecting an appropriate method for presenting data, and conducting peer review.
- They should be able to use technology and mathematics in investigations.
- They should be able to formulate and revise scientific explanations and models.
- They should be able to recognize and analyze alternative explanations. In other words, they should be able to devise other possibilities based on the current body of knowledge.
- They should be able to communicate and defend a scientific argument in both written and oral form.

Greenhouse Effect

The **greenhouse effect** refers to a naturally occurring and necessary process. **Greenhouse gases**, which are ozone, carbon dioxide, water vapor, and methane, trap infrared radiation that is reflected toward the atmosphere. Without the greenhouse effect, it is estimated that the temperature on Earth would be 30 degrees less on average. The problem occurs because human activity generates more greenhouse gases than necessary. Practices that increase the amount of greenhouse gases include the burning of natural gas and oil, farming practices that result in the release of methane and nitrous oxide, factory operations that produce gases, and deforestation practices that decrease the amount of oxygen available to offset greenhouse gases. Population growth also increases the volume of gases released. Excess greenhouse gases cause more infrared radiation to become trapped, which increases the temperature at the Earth's surface.

Ozone Depletion

Ultraviolet light breaks O_2 into two very reactive oxygen atoms with unpaired electrons, which are known as **free radicals**. A free radical of oxygen pairs with another oxygen molecule to form **ozone** (O_3). Ultraviolet light also breaks ozone (O_3) into O_2 and a free radical of oxygen. This process usually acts as an ultraviolet light filter for the planet. Other free radical catalysts are produced by natural phenomena such as volcanic eruptions and by human activities. When these enter the atmosphere, they disrupt the normal cycle by breaking down ozone so it cannot absorb more ultraviolet radiation. One such catalyst is the chlorine in chlorofluorocarbons (CFCs). CFCs were used as aerosols and refrigerants. When a CFC like CF_2Cl_2 is broken down in the atmosphere, chlorine free radicals are produced. These act as catalysts to break down ozone. Whether a chlorine free radical reacts with an ozone or oxygen molecule, it is able to react again.

Human Impacts on Ecosystems

Human impacts on **ecosystems** take many forms and have many causes. They include widespread disruptions and specific niche disturbances. Humans practice many forms of **environmental manipulation** that affect plants and animals in many biomes and ecosystems. Many human practices involve the consumption of natural resources for food and energy production, the changing of the environment to produce food and energy, and the intrusion on ecosystems to provide shelter. These general behaviors include a multitude of specific behaviors, including the use and overuse of pesticides, the encroachment upon habitat, over hunting and over fishing, the introduction of plant and animal species into non-native ecosystems, and the introduction of hazardous wastes and chemical byproducts into the environment. These behaviors have led to a number of consequences, such as acid rain, ozone depletion, deforestation, urbanization, accelerated species loss, genetic abnormalities, endocrine disruption in populations, and harm to individual animals.

Global Warming

Global warming may cause the permanent loss of glaciers and permafrost. There might also be increases in air pollution and acid rain. Rising temperatures may lead to an increase in sea levels as polar ice melts, lower amounts of available fresh water as coastal areas flood, species extinction because of changes in habitat, increases in certain diseases, and a decreased standard of living for humans. Less fresh water and losses of habitat for humans and other species can also lead to decreased agricultural production and food supply shortages. Increased desertification leads to habitat loss for humans and other species. There may be more moisture in the atmosphere due to evaporation.

Acid Rain and Eutrophication

Acid rain is made up water droplets for which the pH has been lowered due atmospheric pollution. The common sources of this pollution are **sulfur** and **nitrogen** that have been released through the burning of fossil fuels. This can lead to a lowering of the pH of lakes and ponds, thereby destroying aquatic life, or damaging the leaves and bark of trees. It can also destroy buildings, monuments, and statues made of rock.

Eutrophication is the depletion of oxygen in a body of water. It may be caused by an increase in the amount of nutrients, particularly **phosphates**, which leads to an increase in plant and algae life that use up the oxygen. The result is a decrease in water quality and death of aquatic life. Sources of excess phosphates may be detergents, industrial run-off, or fertilizers that are washed into lakes or streams.

Waste Disposal Methods

- Landfills – **Methane** (CH_4) is a greenhouse gas emitted from landfills. Some is used to generate electricity and some gets into the atmosphere. **CO_2** is also emitted, and landfill gas can contain nitrogen, oxygen, water vapor, sulfur, mercury, and radioactive contaminants such as tritium. **Landfill leachate** contains acids from car batteries, solvents, heavy metals, pesticides, motor oil, paint, household cleaning supplies, plastics, and many other potentially harmful substances. Some of these are dangerous when they get into the ecosystem.
- Incinerators – These contribute to air pollution in that they can release nitric and sulfuric oxides, which cause **acid rain**.
- Sewage – When dumped in raw form into oceans, sewage can introduce **fecal contaminants** and **pathogenic organisms**, which can harm ocean life and cause disease in humans.

Effects of Consumerism

Economic growth and quality of living are associated with a wasteful cycle of production. Goods are produced as cheaply as possible with little or no regard for the **ecological effects**. The ultimate goal is profitability. The production process is wasteful, and often introduces **hazardous byproducts** into the environment. Furthermore, byproducts may be dumped into a landfill instead of recycled. When consumer products get dumped in landfills, they can leach **contamination** into groundwater. Landfills can also leach gases. These are or have been dumping grounds for illegal substances, business and government waste, construction industry waste, and medical waste. These items also get dumped at illegal dump sites in urban and remote areas.

Ethical and Moral Concerns

Ethical and moral concerns related to genetic engineering arise in the scientific community and in smaller communities within society. Religious and moral beliefs can conflict with the economic interests of businesses, and with research methods used by the scientific community. For example, the United States government allows genes to be patented. A company has patented the gene for breast and ovarian cancer and will only make it available to researchers for a fee. This leads to a decrease in research, a decrease in medical solutions, and possibly an increase in the occurrence of breast and ovarian cancers. The possibility of lateral or incidental discoveries as a result of research is also limited. For example, a researcher working on a genetic solution to treat breast cancer might accidentally discover a cure for prostate cancer. This, however, would not occur if the researcher could not use the patented gene in the first place.

Energy Production

- Coal-fired power plants: These generate electricity fairly cheaply, but are the largest source of **greenhouse gases**.
- Gasoline: Gasoline is cheap, generates less CO_2 than coal, and requires less water than coal. But it nevertheless releases a substantial amount of **CO_2** in the aggregate and is a limited resource. The burning of gas and other fossil fuels releases carbon dioxide (a greenhouse gas) into the atmosphere.

- Nuclear power plants: A small nuclear power plant can cheaply produce a large amount of electricity. But the waste is potentially harmful and a substantial amount of **water** is required to generate electricity. The cost of storing and transporting the **radioactive waste** is also very large.
- Hydropower: Hydropower is sustainable and environmentally benign once established. A disadvantage is that the building of a dam and the re-routing of a river can be very **environmentally disruptive**.
- Wind power: Wind power is sustainable, non-polluting, and requires little to no cooling water. But it will not produce power in the absence of **wind** and requires a large area over which the turbines can be laid out.
- Solar power: Solar power is sustainable, can be used for a single house or building, and generates peak energy during times of peak usage. But production is limited to when the sun is shining, the panels themselves are expensive to make, and making the panels generates harmful **toxins**.
- Geothermal power: Geothermal power is sustainable, relatively cheap, and non-polluting. Disadvantages are that it can only be utilized in areas with specific **volcanic activity**.

Remote Sensing

Remote sensing refers to the gathering of data about an object or phenomenon without physical or intimate contact with the object being studied. The data can be viewed or recorded and stored in many forms (visually with a camera, audibly, or in the form of data). Gathering weather data from a ship, satellite, or buoy might be thought of as remote sensing. The monitoring of a fetus through the use of ultrasound technology provides a remote image. Listening to the heartbeat of a fetus is another example of remote sensing. Methods for remote sensing can be grouped as radiometric, geodetic, or acoustic. Examples of **radiometric remote sensing** include radar, laser altimeters, light detection and ranging (LIDAR) used to determine the concentration of chemicals in the air, and radiometers used to detect various frequencies of radiation. **Geodetic remote sensing** involves measuring the small fluctuations in Earth's gravitational field. Examples of **acoustic remote sensing** include underwater sonar and seismographs.

Cell Phones and GPS

A **cell phone** uses **radio waves** to communicate information. When speaking into a cell phone, the user's voice is converted into an electrical signal which is transmitted via radio waves to a cell tower, then to a satellite, then to a cell tower near the recipient, and then to the recipient's cell phone. The recipient's cell phone converts the digital signal back into an electrical signal.

A similar process occurs when data is transmitted over the **Internet** via a wireless network. The cell phone will convert any outgoing communication into a radio wave that will be sent to a wireless router. The router is "wireless" in the sense that the router is not wired to the phone. But the router is connected to the Internet via a cable. The router converts the radio signal into digital form and sends the communication through the Internet. The same basic process also occurs when a cell phone receives information from the Internet.

Wireless networks use radio frequencies of 2.4 GHz or 5 GHz.

Global Positioning System (GPS) is a system of **satellites** that orbit the Earth and communicate with mobile devices to pinpoint the mobile device's **position**. This is accomplished by determining the distance between the mobile device and at least three satellites. A mobile device might calculate a distance of 400 miles between it and the first satellite. The possible locations that are 400 miles from the first satellite and the mobile device will fall along a circle. The possible locations on Earth relative to the other two satellites will fall somewhere along different circles. The point on Earth at which these three circles intersect is the location of the mobile device. The process of determining position based on distance measurements from three satellites is called **trilateration**.

Physics

Energy Transformation

Energy is constantly changing forms and being transferred back and forth. A pendulum swinging is an example of both a kinetic to potential and a potential to kinetic **energy transformation**. When a pendulum is moved from its center point (the point at which it is closest to the ground) to the highest point before it returns, it is an example of a kinetic to potential transformation. When it swings from its highest point toward the center, it is considered a potential to kinetic transformation. The sum of the potential and kinetic energy is known as the **total mechanical energy**. Stretching a rubber band gives it potential energy. That potential energy becomes kinetic energy when the rubber band is released.

Review Video: Energy
Visit mometrix.com/academy and enter code: 677735

Mechanics

Mechanics is the study of matter and motion, and the topics related to matter and motion, such as force, energy, and work. Discussions of mechanics will often include the concepts of vectors and scalars. **Vectors** are quantities with both magnitude and direction, while **scalars** have only magnitude. **Scalar quantities** include length, area, volume, mass, density, energy, work, and power. **Vector quantities** include displacement, velocity, acceleration, momentum, and force.

Velocity and Accelerations

There are two types of velocity to consider: average velocity and instantaneous velocity. Unless an object has a constant velocity or we are explicitly given an equation for the velocity, finding the **instantaneous velocity** of an object requires the use of calculus. If we want to calculate the **average velocity** of an object, we need to know two things: the displacement, or the distance it has covered, and the time it took to cover this distance. The formula for average velocity is simply the distance traveled divided by the time required. In other words, the average velocity is equal to the change in position divided by the change in time. Average velocity is a vector and will always point in the same direction as the displacement vector (since time is a scalar and always positive).

Acceleration is the change in the velocity of an object. Typically, the acceleration will be a constant value. Like position and velocity, acceleration is a vector quantity and will therefore have both magnitude and direction.

Review Video: Speed and Velocity
Visit mometrix.com/academy and enter code: 645590

Review Video: Velocity and Acceleration
Visit mometrix.com/academy and enter code: 671849

Newton's First Law of Motion

Newton's First Law of Motion

An object at rest or in motion will remain at rest or in motion unless acted upon by an external force.

This phenomenon is commonly referred to as **inertia**, the tendency of a body to remain in its present state of motion. In order for the body's state of motion to change, it must be acted on by an unbalanced force.

Newton's Second Law of Motion

Newton's Second Law of Motion

An object's **acceleration** is directly proportional to the **net force** acting on the object, and inversely proportional to the object's **mass**.

It is generally written in equation form $F = ma$, where F is the net force acting on a body, m is the mass of the body, and a is its acceleration. Note that since the mass is always a positive quantity, the acceleration is always in the same direction as the force.

Newton's Third Law of Motion

Newton's Third Law of Motion

For every force, there is an equal and opposite force.

When a hammer strikes a nail, the nail hits the hammer just as hard. If we consider two objects, *A* and *B*, then we may express any contact between these two bodies with the equation $F_{AB} = -F_{BA}$, where the order of the subscripts denotes which body is exerting the force. At first glance, this law might seem to forbid any movement at all since every force is being countered with an equal opposite force, but these equal opposite forces are acting on different bodies with different masses, so they will not cancel each other out.

Review Video: Newton's First Law of Motion
Visit mometrix.com/academy and enter code: 590367

Review Video: Newton's Second Law of Motion
Visit mometrix.com/academy and enter code: 737975

Review Video: Newton's Third Law of Motion
Visit mometrix.com/academy and enter code: 838401

Kinetic and Potential Energy

The two types of energy most important in mechanics are potential and kinetic energy. **Potential energy** is the amount of energy an object has stored within itself because of its position or orientation. There are many types of potential energy, but the most common is **gravitational potential energy**. It is the energy that an object has because of its height (h) above the ground. It can be calculated as $PE = mgh$, where m is the object's mass and g is the acceleration of gravity. **Kinetic energy** is the energy of an object in motion, and is calculated as $KE = mv^2/2$, where v is the magnitude of its velocity. When an object is dropped, its potential energy is converted into kinetic energy as it falls. These two equations can be used to calculate the velocity of an object at any point in its fall.

Review Video: Potential and Kinetic Energy
Visit mometrix.com/academy and enter code: 491502

Weight, Mass, and Acceleration

The **weight** of an object is the force of gravity on the object, and may be defined as the mass times the acceleration of gravity: $w = mg$. **Mass** is the amount of matter an object contains. When an object falls, it will **accelerate** at the same speed regardless of its mass, provided that gravity is the only force working on the object. Where mass can come into play is when there is significant **air resistance**. The force due to air resistance is a function of the object's size, shape, and velocity, but not mass. Thus, the air resistance force on two identically sized and shaped objects of different masses will be the same, but the heavier object will not be as affected, since it requires a greater force to overcome its momentum.

Work

Work can be thought of as the amount of energy expended in accomplishing some goal. The simplest equation for **mechanical work** (W) is $W = Fd$, where F is the force exerted and d is the displacement of the object on which the force is exerted. This equation requires that the force be applied in the same direction as the displacement. If this is not the case, then the work may be calculated as $W = Fd\cos(\theta)$, where θ is the angle between the force and displacement vectors. If force and displacement have the same direction, then work is positive; if they are in opposite directions, then work is negative; and if they are perpendicular, the work done by the force is zero.

If a man pushes a block horizontally across a surface with a constant force of 10 N for a distance of 20 m, the work done by the man is 200 N-m or 200 J. If instead the block is sliding and the man tries to slow its progress by pushing against it, his work done is -200 J, since he is pushing in the direction opposite the motion. If the man pushes vertically downward on the block while it slides, his work done is zero, since his force vector is perpendicular to the displacement vector of the block.

Review Video: Work
Visit mometrix.com/academy and enter code: 681834

Acceleration

When an object is thrown upward the acceleration throughout its flight is 9.8 meters per second squared (m/s^2) downward. This is Earth's **gravity** (g) close to its surface. It is the acceleration of all objects when there is no resistance, such as that of air.

If an object is held **stationary**, there is no work performed. This is because the formula for work performed is equal to the force times distance, or **displacement** ($W = F \times d[\cos\theta]$). Displacement is a vector measurement, and there must be displacement for work to be done. If an object is being held up, forces are at work, but are canceling each other out. No work is being done.

Density

A key property determining whether an object will float or sink in water is its **density**. The general rule is that if an object is less dense than water, it floats; if it is denser than water, it sinks. The density of an object is equal to its mass divided by its volume ($d = m/v$). It is important to note the difference between an **object's** density and a **material's** density. Water has a density of one gram per cubic centimeter, while steel has a density approximately eight times that. Despite having a much higher material density, an object made of steel may still float. A hollow steel sphere, for instance, will float easily because the density of the object includes the air contained within the sphere. An object may also float only in certain orientations. An ocean liner that is placed in the water upside down, for instance, may not remain afloat. An object will float only if it can displace a mass of water equal to its own mass.

Review Video: Mass, Weight, Volume, Density, and Specific Gravity
Visit mometrix.com/academy and enter code: 920570

Archimedes's Principle

Archimedes's principle states that a buoyant (upward) force on a submerged object is equal to the weight of the liquid displaced by the object. Water has a density of one gram per cubic centimeter. Anything that floats in water has a lower effective density, and anything that sinks has a higher effective density. This principle of buoyancy can also be used to calculate the volume of an irregularly shaped object. The mass of the object (m) minus its apparent mass in the water (m_a) divided by the density of water (ρ_w), gives the object's volume: $V = (m - m_a)/\rho_w$.

Projectile, Circular, and Periodic Motion

- **Projectile motion**: occurs where an object thrown into the air near the earth's surface moves along an arched path under the effect of gravity alone
- **Circular motion**: movement of an object in a rotating circular path
- **Periodic motion**: motion that is repeated at recurring intervals, such as the swinging of a pendulum

Collision and Conservation of Momentum

- **Elastic collision**: collision in which the total kinetic energy between two bodies before the collision equals the total kinetic energy after the collision. An example would be a collision between two gas molecules, in which the two molecules only change direction after a collision, but not kinetic energy.
- **Inelastic collision**: collision in which the total kinetic energy between two bodies increases or decreases after a collision. An example would be a collision in which a moving car strikes a parked car, resulting in a single body with a different kinetic energy than either of the original two bodies. In this case, kinetic energy could be lost because of friction between the tires and the road or changes in the car bodies because of the collision.
- **Law of conservation of momentum**: for a collision between two bodies with no external forces, the vector sum of the momentums is not affected by the interaction and remains constant.

Types of Energy Transformation

Other examples of energy transformations include:

- Electric to mechanical: Ceiling fan
- Chemical to heat: burning coal
- **Chemical to light**: Phosphorescence and luminescence (which allow objects to glow in the dark) occur because energy is absorbed by a substance (charged) and light is re-emitted comparatively slowly
- **Heat to electricity**: Examples include thermoelectric, geothermal, and ocean thermal.
- Heat to mechanical: steam engine
- **Nuclear to heat**: Examples include nuclear reactors and power plants.
- **Mechanical to sound**: Playing a violin or almost any instrument
- Sound to electric: Microphone
- Light to electric: Solar panels
- Electric to light: Light bulbs

Motion and Displacement

Motion is a change in the location of an object, and is the result of an unbalanced net force acting on the object. Understanding motion requires the understanding of three basic quantities: displacement, velocity, and acceleration.

When something moves from one place to another, it has undergone **displacement**. Displacement along a straight line is a very simple example of a vector quantity. If an object travels from position $x = -5$ cm to $x = 5$ cm, it has undergone a displacement of 10 cm. If it traverses the same path in the opposite direction, its displacement is -10 cm. A vector that spans the object's displacement in the direction of travel is known as a **displacement vector**.

Review Video: Displacement
Visit mometrix.com/academy and enter code: 236197

Gravitational Force and Friction

Gravitational force is a universal force that causes every object to exert a force on every other object. The gravitational force between two objects can be described by the formula, $F = Gm_1m_2/r^2$, where m_1 and m_2 are the masses of two objects, r is the distance between them, and G is the gravitational constant, $G = 6.672 \times 10^{-11}$ N-m²/kg². In order for this force to have a noticeable effect, one or both of the objects must be extremely large, so the equation is generally only used in problems involving planetary bodies. For problems involving objects on the earth being affected by earth's gravitational pull, the force of gravity is simply calculated as $F = mg$, where g is 9.8 m/s² toward the ground.

Friction is a force that arises as a resistance to motion where two surfaces are in contact. The maximum magnitude of the **frictional force** (f)can be calculated as $f = F_c\mu$, where F_c is the contact force between the two objects and μ is a **coefficient of friction** based on the surfaces' material composition. Two types of friction are static and kinetic. To illustrate these concepts, imagine a book resting on a table. The force of its weight (W) is equal and opposite to the force of the table on the book, or the normal force (N). If we exert a small force (F) on the book, attempting to push it to one side, a frictional force (f) would arise, equal and opposite to our force. At this point, it is a **static frictional force** because the book is not moving. If we increase our force on the book, we will eventually cause it to move. At this point, the frictional force opposing us will be a **kinetic frictional force**. Generally, the kinetic frictional force is lower than static frictional force (because the frictional coefficient for static friction is larger), which means that the amount of force needed to maintain the movement of the book will be less than what was needed to start it moving.

Review Video: Friction
Visit mometrix.com/academy and enter code: 716782

Simple Machines

Simple machines include the inclined plane, lever, wheel and axle, and pulley. These simple machines have no internal source of energy. More complex or compound machines can be formed from them. Simple machines provide a force known as a mechanical advantage and make it easier to accomplish a task. The inclined plane enables a force less than the object's weight to be used to push an object to a greater height. A lever enables a multiplication of force. The wheel and axle allows for movement with less resistance. Single or double pulleys allow for easier direction of force. The wedge and screw are forms of the inclined plane. A wedge turns a smaller force working over a greater distance into a larger force. The screw is similar to an incline that is wrapped around a shaft.

Review Video: Simple Machines
Visit mometrix.com/academy and enter code: 950789

Mechanical Advantage

A certain amount of **work** is required to move an object. The amount cannot be reduced, but by changing the way the work is performed a **mechanical advantage** can be gained. A certain amount of work is required to raise an object to a given vertical height. By getting to a given height at an angle, the effort required is reduced, but the distance that must be traveled to reach a given height is increased. An example of this is walking up a hill. One may take a direct, shorter, but steeper route, or one may take a more meandering, longer route that requires less effort. Examples of wedges include doorstops, axes, plows, zippers, and can openers.

Review Video: Mechanical Advantage
Visit mometrix.com/academy and enter code: 482323

Levers

A **lever** consists of a bar or plank and a pivot point or fulcrum. Work is performed by the bar, which swings at the pivot point to redirect the force. There are three types of levers: first, second, and third class. Examples of a **first-class lever** include balances, see-saws, nail extractors, and scissors (which also use wedges). In a **second-class lever** the fulcrum is placed at one end of the bar and the work is performed at the other end. The weight or load to be moved is in between. The closer to the fulcrum the weight is, the easier it is to move. Force is increased, but the distance it is moved is decreased. Examples include pry bars, bottle openers, nutcrackers, and wheelbarrows. In a **third-class lever** the fulcrum is at one end and the positions of the weight and the location where the work is performed are reversed. Examples include fishing rods, hammers, and tweezers.

Review Video: Levers
Visit mometrix.com/academy and enter code: 103910

Wheel and Axle

The center of a **wheel and axle** can be likened to a fulcrum on a rotating lever. As it turns, the wheel moves a greater distance than the axle, but with less force. Obvious examples of the wheel and axle are the wheels of a car, but this type of simple machine can also be used to exert a greater force. For instance, a person can turn the handles of a winch to exert a greater force at the turning axle to move an object. Other examples include steering wheels, wrenches, faucets, waterwheels, windmills, gears, and belts. **Gears** work together to change a force. The four basic types of gears are spur, rack and pinion, bevel, and worm gears. The larger gear turns slower than the smaller, but exerts a greater force. Gears at angles can be used to change the direction of forces.

Review Video: Simple Machines - Wheel and Axle
Visit mometrix.com/academy and enter code: 574045

Pulleys

A **single pulley** consists of a rope or line that is run around a wheel. This allows force to be directed in a downward motion to lift an object. This does not decrease the force required, just changes its direction. The load is moved the same distance as the rope pulling it. When a **combination pulley** is used, such as a double pulley, the weight is moved half the distance of the rope pulling it. In this way, the work effort is doubled. Pulleys are never 100% efficient because of friction. Examples of pulleys include cranes, chain hoists, block and tackles, and elevators.

Review Video: Pulley
Visit mometrix.com/academy and enter code: 495865

Conductors and Insulators

- **Conductor**: This is a material that provides little resistance to heat transfer between its particles.
- **Insulator**: This is a material that provides resistance to heat transfer between its particles.

Valence Electrons and Conduction

When studying atoms at a microscopic level, it can be seen that some materials such as metals have properties that allow electrons to flow easily. Metals are good **conductors** of electricity because their valence electrons are loosely held in a network of atoms. This is because the valence shells of metal atoms have weak attractions to their nuclei. This results in a "sea of electrons," and electrons can flow between atoms with little resistance. In **insulating** materials such as glass, they hardly flow at all. In between materials can be called **semiconducting materials**, and have intermediate conducting behavior. At low temperatures, some materials become superconductors and offer no resistance to the flow of electrons. **Thermal conductivity** refers to a material's capacity to conduct heat.

Review Video: Resistance of Electric Currents
Visit mometrix.com/academy and enter code: 668423

Electric Motors

An **electric motor** converts electric energy into **mechanical energy**. Energy can be provided by an AC or DC source. The power provided has many practical applications. The basic premise of a motor is that the electric current passing through a wire or coil creates a magnetic field that opposes the poles of a permanent magnet. The repelling forces between one pole of the electromagnet and the opposing pole of the fixed magnet cause the coil to move about ½ a turn. As it approaches the pole of like attraction, the coil would normally stop moving. In a motor, however, the current is reversed at this time, which reverses the poles and again forces rotation. In a **DC motor**, a switch or commuter can be used to reverse the charge. In an **AC motor**, the charge alternates on its own. The coil is attached to a shaft that is rotated, which provides the mechanical energy necessary to do work.

Electrical Generators and Electric Potential

An **electrical generator** is the opposite of a motor in that it transforms magnetic force into electrical energy. Like a motor, however, it uses an electromagnetic field and a permanent magnet to achieve electromagnetic induction. Generators do not create electricity, but rather convert mechanical energy into electric energy. Smaller gas generators are used as backup or primary power sources of electricity for equipment, homes, and other small-scale applications. Larger generators may use mechanical energy from many different sources, including water, steam, wind, compressed air, or even a hand crank.

The current does not flow through the bird because it and the wire have the same **electric potential**. Therefore, there is no reason for current to move from the wire to the bird. If the bird touched something else in addition to the wire and became grounded, the electrons would flow through the bird and electrocute it.

Static Electricity

Static electricity occurs when the net electric charge is non-zero, motionless, and produces an electrostatic discharge in two objects brought together. The objects' charges are changed to achieve a balance. **Polarization** is when there is a zero net charge that is unevenly distributed, which leads to a bound charge. The motion of charged particles in a given direction is known as **electric current**. It does not produce a net loss or gain of charge.

Review Video: Static Electricity
Visit mometrix.com/academy and enter code: 113722

Friction

A glass rod and a plastic rod can illustrate the concept of static electricity due to **friction**. Both start with no charge. A glass rod rubbed with silk produces a positive charge, while a plastic rod rubbed with fur produces a negative charge. The **electron affinity** of a material is a property that helps determine how easily it can be charged by friction. Materials can be sorted by their affinity for electrons into a **triboelectric series**. Materials with greater affinities include celluloid, sulfur, and rubber. Materials with lower affinities include glass, rabbit fur, and asbestos. In the example of a glass rod and a plastic one, the glass rod rubbed with silk acquires a positive charge because glass has a lower affinity for electrons than silk. The electrons flow to the silk, leaving the rod with fewer electrons and a positive charge. When a plastic rod is rubbed with fur, electrons flow to the rod and result in a negative charge.

Power, Watt, and Transformer

- **Power**: Measured in watts, electric power refers to the rate at which electrical energy is transferred by an electric circuit. It can be calculated using **Joule's law**: $P = VI$, where P is power, V is the potential difference (in volts) and I is current (in amps). Power can be generated, transmitted, and converted into various forms of light.
- **Watt**: A watt is the unit used to measure power. One watt is equal to one joule of energy per second.
- **Transformer**: A transformer is a device that uses induction to transfer current from one circuit to another. Two wound coils act as a pair of **inductors**. Voltage can be modified to be transferred to another circuit (as in transmission lines) or to a load, such as an electrical device plugged into a socket.

Models Explaining Electric Current

Models that can be used to explain the flow of **electric current**, potential, and circuits include water, gravity, and roller coasters. For example, just as gravity is a force and a mass can have a potential for energy based on its location, so can a charge within an electrical field. Just as a force is required to move an object uphill, a force is also required to move a charge from a low to high potential. Another example is water. Water does not flow when it is level. If it is lifted to a point and then placed on a downward path, it will flow. A roller coaster car requires work to be performed to transport it to a point where it has potential energy (the top of a hill). Once there, gravity provides the force for it to flow (move) downward. If either path is broken, the flow or movement stops or is not completed.

Electric Charge and Atomic Structure

The attractive force between the electrons and the nucleus is called the **electric force**. A positive (+) charge or a negative (-) charge creates a field of sorts in the empty space around it, which is known as an **electric field**. The direction of a positive charge is away from it and the direction of a negative charge is towards it. An electron within the force of the field is pulled towards a positive charge because an electron has a negative charge. A particle with a positive charge is pushed away, or repelled, by another positive charge. Like charges repel each other and opposite charges attract. **Lines of force** show the paths of charges. The **magnitude** of the force is directly proportional to the magnitude of the charges (q) and inversely proportional to the square of the distance (r) between the two objects: $F = kq_1q_2/r^2$, where $k = 9 \times 10^9$ N-m^2/C^2. This relationship is known as **Coulomb's Law**. Electric charge is measured with the unit Coulomb (C). It is the amount of charge moved in one second by a steady current of one ampere (1C = 1A × 1s).

Review Video: Electric Charge
Visit mometrix.com/academy and enter code: 323587

Review Video: Electric Force
Visit mometrix.com/academy and enter code: 717639

Induction and Insulators

Insulators are materials that prevent the movement of electrical charges, while conductors are materials that allow the movement of electrical charges. This is because conductive materials have free electrons that can move through the entire volume of the conductor. This allows an external charge to change the charge distribution in the material. In **induction**, a neutral conductive material, such as a sphere, can become charged by a positively or negatively charged object, such as a rod. The charged object is placed close to the material without touching it. This produces a force on the free electrons, which will either be attracted to or repelled by the rod, polarizing (or separating) the charge. The sphere's electrons will flow into or out of it when touched by a ground. The sphere is now charged. The charge will be opposite that of the charging rod.

Conduction and Law of Conservation of Charge

Charging by **conduction** is similar to charging by induction, except that the material transferring the charge actually touches the material receiving the charge. A negatively or positively charged object is touched to an object with a neutral charge. Electrons will either flow into or out of the neutral object and it will become charged. Insulators cannot be used to conduct charges. Charging by conduction can also be called charging by **contact**. The **law of conservation of charge** states that the total number of units before and after a charging process remains the same. No electrons have been created. They have just been moved around. The removal of a charge on an object by conduction is called grounding.

Dielectric, Electroscope, and Van de Graaff Generator

- **Dielectric**: This refers to a nonconducting substance of electric current that can usually sustain an electric field or maintain polarization. It differs from an insulator, which is typically defined as a material used to prevent the flow of current.

- **Electroscope**: This refers to an instrument used to detect a charge on another object. One somewhat low-tech type is the gold foil electroscope. It includes a conducting part connected to thin leaves of gold or aluminum foil which separate when a charged object is touched with the conducting part. The reason for this separation is that like charges repel each other. Electroscopes require high levels of voltage and are used with high voltage sources, such as static electricity and electrostatic machines. An electroscope cannot be used to determine whether a charge is positive or negative.
- **Van de Graaff generator**: This device, typically composed of a hollow metal ball and belt, is used to produce static electricity or high-voltage electricity with a low current.

Electric Potential

Electric potential, or electrostatic potential or voltage, is an expression of potential energy per unit of charge. It is measured in volts (V) as a scalar quantity. The formula used is $V = E/Q$, where V is voltage, E is electrical potential energy, and Q is the charge. **Voltage** is typically discussed in the context of electric potential difference between two points in a circuit. Voltage can also be thought of as a measure of the rate at which energy is drawn from a source in order to produce a flow of electric charge.

Circuits and Current

A **circuit** is a closed path along which electrons can travel with minimal resistance except at particular locations. **Electric current** is the sustained flow of electrons that are part of an electric charge moving along a path in a circuit. This differs from a **static electric charge**, which is a constant non-moving charge rather than a continuous flow. The rate of flow of electric charge is expressed using the ampere (amp or A) and can be measured using an ammeter. A current of 1 ampere means that 1 coulomb of charge passes through a given area every second. Electric charges typically only move from areas of high electric potential to areas of low electric potential.

Ohm's Law

Electric currents experience **resistance** as they travel through a circuit. Resistance is the hindrance to the flow of an electric charge. Different objects have different levels of resistance. The **ohm** (Ω) is the measurement unit of electric resistance. The symbol is the Greek letter omega. **Ohm's Law**, which is expressed as $I = V/R$, states that current flow (I, measured in amps) through an object is equal to the potential difference from one side to the other (V, measured in volts) divided by resistance (R, measured in ohms). An object with a higher resistance will have a lower current flow through it given the same potential difference.

Simple Circuits

Movement of electric charge along a path between areas of high electric potential and low electric potential, with a resistor or load device between them, is the definition of a **simple circuit**. It is a closed conducting path between the high and low potential points, such as the positive and negative terminals on a battery. One example of a circuit is the flow from one terminal of a car battery to the other. The electrolyte solution of water and sulfuric acid provides work in chemical form to start the flow. A frequently used classroom example of circuits involves using a D cell (1.5 V) battery, a small light bulb, and a piece of copper wire to create a circuit to light the bulb.

Series Circuits

Series circuits are circuits in which there is only one path through which electrons can flow. An example of a series circuit is a string of old-fashioned Christmas tree lights. If a load in this type of circuit is removed, disabled, or switched off, the circuit is open and electricity does not flow. In the series circuit below, three resistors are in series, and their equivalent resistance is:

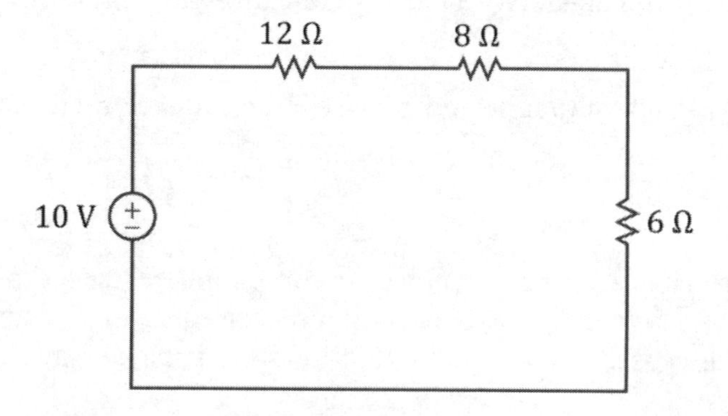

$$R_{eq} = R_1 + R_2 + \cdots + R_n = 12 + 8 + 6 = 26\Omega$$

Parallel Circuit

A **parallel circuit** is one in which there is more than one path through which electrons can travel. In a parallel circuit, the same voltage exists across all parallel paths, though the current may be vastly different among them. For the parallel circuit below, the equivalent resistance is:

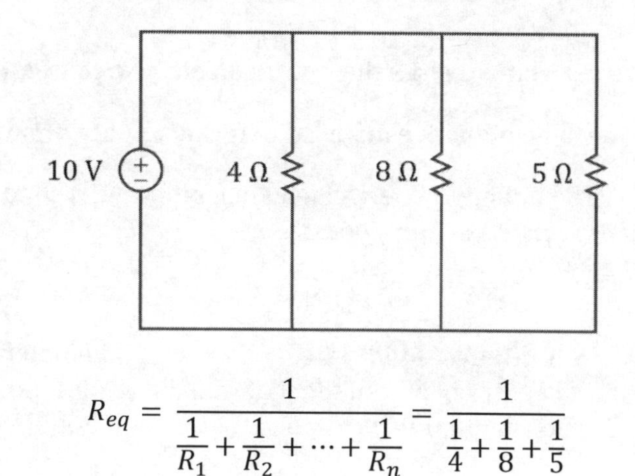

$$R_{eq} = \frac{1}{\frac{1}{R_1} + \frac{1}{R_2} + \cdots + \frac{1}{R_n}} = \frac{1}{\frac{1}{4} + \frac{1}{8} + \frac{1}{5}}$$

Short Circuit, Breakers, and Fuses

Short circuit: This refers to a low-resistance connection between two nodes of an electrical circuit, which results in an excessive electric current, or overcurrent. For example, a D cell battery with no load (such as a light bulb within the circuit) would result in a high rate of charge flow between terminals. This could cause unwanted or unintended high temperatures or rapid energy loss. Other short circuit circumstances could lead to circuit damage, fire, or explosion.

Because of the risks, circuit **breakers** are used as safety features to prevent overcurrent. Once a fault is detected, the circuit breaker acts like a switch to interrupt flow. It can be reset once the condition is corrected.

A **fuse** has a component that melts, which interrupts the flow of charges. Fuses differ from breakers in that fuses are one-time interrupters that must be replaced before the circuit can be restored.

Direct and Alternating Current

Direct current (DC) is the flow of an electric charge in one direction. Batteries and solar cells typically use direct current.

Alternating current (AC) is current that periodically reverses direction. AC is typically used in houses and other buildings.

Diodes and Inverters

A **diode** is an electronic device used to conduct electric current in one direction. The process of conduction in one direction is known as **rectification**. A rectifier is used to convert alternating current to direct current. Diodes are also used to remove modulation from radio signals.

An **inverter** is the opposite of a rectifier in that it converts direct current to alternating current. **Electromotive force (emf)** is what causes electrons to move when there is potential difference between two points (voltage). Devices that can provide emf include batteries, voltaic cells, thermoelectric devices, solar cells, electrical generators, transformers, and Van de Graaff generators.

Circuit Terminology

Circuit breaker: stops the flow of an electric charge through a circuit by creating a break in the path. A fuse also creates a break.

Resistor: a device used in a circuit that opposes the flow of an electric charge.

Transistor: a device made of a semiconductive material that can amplify or switch an electric charge.

Semiconductor: a material with conductivity between an insulator and a conductor. These materials replaced earlier electric devices such as vacuum tubes.

Solid State Devices

Solid state device: Used in modern circuits, solid state devices are solid materials in which the charge carriers, or electrons, are contained entirely within the material. Examples include transistors, microprocessors, integrated circuits, light-emitting diodes (LEDs), and liquid-crystal displays (LCDs).

Magnets and Magnetism

A **magnet** is a piece of metal, such as iron, steel, or magnetite (lodestone) that can affect another substance within its field of force that has like characteristics. Magnets can either attract or repel other substances. Magnets have two **poles**: north and south. Like poles repel and opposite poles (pairs of north and south) attract. The magnetic field is a set of invisible lines representing the paths of attraction and repulsion.

Magnetism can occur naturally, or ferromagnetic materials can be magnetized. Certain matter that is magnetized can retain its magnetic properties indefinitely and become a permanent magnet. Other matter can lose its magnetic properties. For example, an iron nail can be temporarily magnetized by stroking it repeatedly in the same direction using one pole of another magnet. Once magnetized, it can attract or repel other magnetically inclined materials, such as paper clips. Dropping the nail repeatedly will cause it to lose its magnetic properties.

Magnetic Fields and Atomic Structure

The motions of subatomic structures (nuclei and electrons) produce a **magnetic field**. It is the direction of the spin and orbit that indicate the direction of the field. The strength of a magnetic field is known as the magnetic moment. As electrons spin and orbit a nucleus, they produce a magnetic field.

Pairs of electrons that spin and orbit in opposite directions cancel each other out, creating a **net magnetic field** of zero. Materials that have an unpaired electron are magnetic. Those with a weak attractive force are referred to as **paramagnetic materials**, while **ferromagnetic materials** have a strong attractive force. A **diamagnetic material** has electrons that are paired, and therefore does not typically have a magnetic moment. There are, however, some diamagnetic materials that have a weak magnetic field.

A magnetic field can be formed not only by a magnetic material, but also by electric current flowing through a wire. When a coiled wire is attached to the two ends of a battery, for example, an **electromagnet** can be formed by inserting a ferromagnetic material such as an iron bar within the coil. When electric current flows through the wire, the bar becomes a magnet. If there is no current, the magnetism is lost. A **magnetic domain** occurs when the magnetic fields of atoms are grouped and aligned. These groups form what can be thought of as miniature magnets within a material. This is what happens when an object like an iron nail is temporarily magnetized. Prior to magnetization, the organization of atoms and their various polarities are somewhat random with respect to where the north and south poles are pointing. After magnetization, a significant percentage of the poles are lined up in one direction, which is what causes the magnetic force exerted by the material.

Review Video: Magnetic Field Part I
Visit mometrix.com/academy and enter code: 953150

Review Video: Magnetic Field Part II
Visit mometrix.com/academy and enter code: 710249

Wave Types

Waves are divided into types based on the direction of particle motion in a medium and the direction of wave propagation.

- **Longitudinal waves**: These are waves that travel in the same direction as the particle movement. They are sometimes called pressure, compression, or density waves. Longitudinal sound waves are the easiest to produce and have the highest speed. A longitudinal wave consists of compressions and rarefactions, such as those seen by extending and collapsing a Slinky toy.
- **Shear or transverse waves**: These types of waves move perpendicular to the direction of the particle movement. For example, if the particles in a medium move up and down, a transverse wave will move forward. Transverse waves are possible only in solids and are slower than longitudinal waves.
- **Surface (circular) waves**: These waves travel at the surface of a material and move in elliptical orbits. They are a little slower than shear waves.
- **Plate waves**: These waves move in elliptical orbits and only occur in very thin pieces of material.

Wave Interactions

Waves can be in phase or out of phase, which is similar to the concept of being in sync or out of sync. For example, if two separate waves originate from the same point and the peaks (crests) and valleys (troughs) are exactly aligned, they are said to be **in phase**. If the peak of a wave aligns with the valley of another wave, they are **out of phase**. When waves are in phase their displacement is doubled. If they are out of phase they cancel each other out. If they are somewhere in between being completely in phase and completely out of phase, the wave interaction is a wave that is the sum of the **amplitudes** of all points along the wave. If waves originate from different points, the amplitude of particle displacement is the combined sum of the particle displacement amplitude of each individual wave.

Waveforms

Waveforms refer to the shapes and forms of waves as they are depicted on graphs. Forms include sinusoidal, square, triangle, and sawtooth. **Sinusoidal** refers to a waveform in which the amplitude (displacement from the rest position) is proportional to the sine (side opposite of angle/hypotenuse) of a variable such as time. Square, triangle, and sawtooth waveforms are **non-sinusoidal**, and are usually based on formulas. **Square waves** are used to depict digital information. **Pulse waves**, also known as rectangular waves, are a non-sinusoidal form similar to square waves, and are found in synthesizer programming. **Triangle waves**, like square waves, only have odd harmonics. The harmonic of a wave is the integer multiple of a base frequency. **Sawtooth waves** have both even and odd harmonics, and produce a sound particularly suited for synthesizing bowed string instruments.

Wave Interference

When waves traveling in the same medium interact, it is known as **wave interference**. While a single wave generally remains the same in terms of waveform, frequency, amplitude, and wavelength, several waves traveling through particles in a medium take on a more complicated appearance after they interact. The final properties of a wave are dependent on many factors, such as the points of origin of waves and whether they are in phase, out of phase, or somewhere in between. **Constructive interference** refers to what happens when two crests or two troughs of a wave meet. The resulting amplitude of the crest or trough is doubled. **Destructive interference** is what happens when the crest of one wave and the trough of another that are the same shape meet. When this occurs, the two waves cancel each other out.

Transfer of Energy in Waves

Waves have **energy** and can transfer energy when they interact with matter. Although waves transfer energy, they do not transport **matter**. They are a disturbance of matter that transfers energy from one particle to an adjacent particle. There are many types of waves, including sound, seismic, water, light, micro, and radio waves. The two basic categories of waves are mechanical and electromagnetic. **Mechanical waves** are those that transmit energy through matter. **Electromagnetic waves** can transmit energy through a vacuum. A **transverse wave** provides a good illustration of the features of a wave, which include crests, troughs, amplitude, and wavelength.

Wave Terminology

- **Frequency** is a measure of how often particles in a medium vibrate when a wave passes through the medium with respect to a certain point or node. Usually measured in Hertz (Hz), frequency might refer to cycles per second, vibrations per second, or waves per second. One Hz is equal to one cycle per second.
- **Period** is a measure of how long it takes to complete a cycle. It is the inverse of frequency; where frequency is measure in cycles per second, period can be thought of as seconds per cycle, though it is measured in units of time only.
- **Speed** refers to how fast or slow a wave travels. It is measured in terms of distance divided by time. While frequency is measured in terms of cycles per second, speed might be measured in terms of meters per second.

- **Amplitude** is the maximum amount of displacement of a particle in a medium from its rest position, and corresponds to the amount of energy carried by the wave. High-energy waves have greater amplitudes; low energy waves have lesser amplitudes. Amplitude is a measure of a wave's strength.
- **Rest position**, also called equilibrium, is the point at which there is neither positive nor negative displacement.
- **Crest**, also called the peak, is the point at which a wave's positive or upward displacement from the rest position is at its maximum.
- **Trough**, also called a valley, is the point at which a wave's negative or downward displacement from the rest position is at its maximum.
- A **wavelength** is one complete wave cycle. It could be measured from crest to crest, trough to trough, rest position to rest position, or any point of a wave to the corresponding point on the next wave.

Phenomenon of Sound

Sound is a pressure disturbance that moves through a medium in the form of mechanical waves. Sound requires a medium to travel through, such as air, water, or other matter since it is the vibrations that transfer energy to adjacent particles, not the actual movement of particles over a great distance. Sound is transferred through the movement of atomic particles, which can be atoms or molecules. Waves of sound energy move outward in all directions from the source. **Sound waves** consist of **compressions** (particles are forced together) and **rarefactions** (particles move farther apart and their density decreases). A wavelength consists of one compression and one rarefaction. Different sounds have different wavelengths. Sound is a form of kinetic energy.

Pitch, Loudness, Timbre, and Oscillation

- **Pitch**: Pitch is the quality of sound determined by frequency. For example, a musical note can be tuned to a specific frequency. Humans can detect frequencies between about 20 Hz to 20,000 Hz.
- **Loudness**: Loudness is a human's perception of sound intensity.
- Sound intensity: Sound intensity is measured as the sound power per unit area, and can be expressed in decibels.
- **Timbre**: This is a human's perception of the type or quality of sound.
- **Oscillation**: This is a measurement, usually of time, against a basic value, equilibrium, or rest point.

Doppler Effect

The **Doppler effect** refers to the effect the relative motion of the source of the wave and the location of the observer has on waves. The Doppler effect is easily observable in sound waves. What a person hears when a train approaches or a car honking its horn passes by are examples of the Doppler effect. The pitch of the sound is different not because the *emitted frequency* has changed, but because the *received frequency* has changed. The frequency is higher (as is the pitch) as the train approaches, the same as emitted just as it passes, and lower as the train moves away. This is because the wavelength changes. A **redshift** occurs when light or radiation is increased in wavelength. A **blueshift** is a decrease in wavelength.

Electromagnetic Spectrum

The **electromagnetic spectrum** is defined by frequency (f) and wavelength (λ). Frequency is typically measured in hertz and wavelength is usually measured in meters. Because light travels at a fairly constant speed, **frequency** is inversely proportional to **wavelength**, a relationship expressed by the formula $f = c/\lambda$, where c is the speed of light (about 300 million meters per second). Frequency multiplied by wavelength equals the speed of the wave; for electromagnetic waves, this is the speed of light, with some variance for the medium in which it is traveling. Electromagnetic waves include (from largest to smallest wavelength) radio waves, microwaves, infrared radiation (radiant heat), visible light, ultraviolet radiation, x-rays, and gamma rays. The energy of electromagnetic waves is carried in packets that have a magnitude inversely proportional to the wavelength. **Radio waves** have a range of wavelengths, from about 10^{-3} to 10^{5} meters, while their frequencies range from about 10^{3} to 10^{11} Hz.

Review Video: Electromagnetic Radiation Waves
Visit mometrix.com/academy and enter code: 135307

Review Video: Electromagnetic Spectrum
Visit mometrix.com/academy and enter code: 771761

Visible Light

Light is the portion of the electromagnetic spectrum that is visible because of its ability to stimulate the **retina**. It is absorbed and emitted by electrons, atoms, and molecules that move from one energy level to another. **Visible light** interacts with matter through molecular electron excitation (which occurs in the human retina) and through plasma oscillations (which occur in metals). Visible light is between ultraviolet and infrared light on the spectrum. The wavelengths of visible light cover a range from 380 nm (violet) to 760 nm (red). Different wavelengths correspond to different colors. **Dispersion** is the action of distributing radiation according to wavelength, such as light into colors.

Review Video: Light
Visit mometrix.com/academy and enter code: 900556

Color in Rainbows

A rainbow is an example of the separation of light. The water molecules act as a separator, relying on both *refraction* and *reflection*. Rainbows include the colors of the visible light spectrum: red, orange, yellow, green, blue, indigo, and violet, which can be remembered using the acronym Roy G. Biv. The observer is at the center of the rainbow with the sun at his back, but only an arc of the rainbow circle is visible from the ground.

Perception of Color

The human brain interprets or perceives visible light, which is emitted from the sun and other stars, as **color**. For example, when the entire wavelength reaches the retina, the brain perceives the color white. When no part of the wavelength reaches the retina, the brain perceives the color black. The particular color of an object depends upon what is **absorbed** and what is **transmitted** or **reflected**. For example, a leaf consists of chlorophyll molecules, the atoms of which absorb all wavelengths of the visible light spectrum except for green, which is why a leaf appears green. Certain wavelengths of visible light can be absorbed when they interact with matter. Wavelengths that are not absorbed can be transmitted by transparent materials or reflected by opaque materials.

Light and Solid Objects

When light waves encounter an object, the light waves are reflected, transmitted, or absorbed. If the light is **reflected** from the surface of the object, the angle at which it contacts the surface will be the same as the angle at which it leaves, on the other side of the perpendicular. If the ray of light is perpendicular to the surface, it will be reflected back in the direction from which it came. When light is **transmitted** through the object, its direction may be altered upon entering the object. This is known as refraction. When light waves are refracted, or bent, an image can appear distorted. The degree to which the light is refracted depends on the speed at which light travels in the object. Light that is neither reflected nor transmitted will be **absorbed** by the surface and stored as heat energy. Nearly all instances of light hitting an object will involve a combination of two or even all three of these.

Review Video: Reflection, Transmission, and Absorption of Light
Visit mometrix.com/academy and enter code: 109410

Diffraction

Diffraction refers to the bending of waves around small objects and the spreading out of waves past small openings. The narrower the opening, the greater the level of diffraction will be. Larger wavelengths also increase diffraction. A **diffraction grating** can be created by placing a number of slits close together, and is used more frequently than a prism to separate light. Different wavelengths are diffracted at different angles.

Review Video: Diffraction of Light Waves
Visit mometrix.com/academy and enter code: 785494

Light Waves and Changing Media

When light waves pass from water to air, the frequency stays the same even though the speed and wavelength increase. This is because frequency is equal to speed (velocity) divided by wavelength ($f = v/\lambda$). In this case, there are two different mediums (water and air), which have different **refractive indexes**. Air has a smaller refractive index. The smaller the refractive index, the faster light moves through the medium. The refractive index of a medium can affect the speed and direction of travel of transmitted light. In air, both the speed and wavelength of the light increase, but the frequency (the number of cycles in a given unit of time) is the same. The **speed** of a wave is equal to its frequency times its wavelength ($v = f \times \lambda$). **Nodes** of a wave are the points at which the amplitude is at its minimum. **Wavelength** is measured as the distance between nodes.

Applications of the Properties of Light

The various properties of light have numerous **real life applications**. For example, polarized sunglasses have lenses that help reduce glare, while non-polarized sunglasses reduce the total amount of light that reaches the eyes. Polarized lenses consist of a chemical film of molecules aligned in parallel. This allows the lenses to block wavelengths of light that are intense, horizontal, and reflected from smooth, flat surfaces. The "fiber" in fiber optics refers to a tube or pipe that channels light. Because of the composition of the fiber, light can be transmitted greater distances before losing the signal. The fiber consists of a core, cladding, and a coating. Fibers are bundled, allowing for the transmission of large amounts of data.

Geometric Optics

Geometric optics uses the concept of rays to determine how light will propagate. **Ray diagrams** can illustrate the path of light through a lens. Different types of lenses refract light, either convergently or divergently, to form images. After passing through a lens, rays converge at a focal point. **Collimated rays** are nearly parallel, and can be thought of as having no focal point. There are many types and combinations of lenses. **Convergent lenses**, also called positive lenses, are thicker in the middle and thinner at the edges. Rays are focused to a point. **Divergent lenses**, also called negative lenses, are thicker at the ends and thinner in the middle. Rays are spread apart, or diverged. A **convex lens** is bowed outward, either at one vertical surface or both. A convex lens with two convex surfaces may also be termed biconvex or double convex. A **concave lens** is bowed inward, while a planar lens is flat.

Theory of Relativity

Albert Einstein proposed two theories of relativity: the general theory of relativity (1916) and the special theory of relativity (1905). **Special relativity** is based on two basic premises. The first is that the laws of physics are the same for all observers in uniform motion relative to one another. This is also known as the principle of relativity. The second is that the speed of light in a vacuum is also the same for all observers and their relative motion or the motion of the source of the light does not affect this. **General relativity** is the generally accepted explanation of gravity as a property of space and time, or spacetime. Einstein was born in Germany in 1879 and received the Nobel Prize in Physics in 1921. He died in April of 1955.

Heat and Temperature

Heat is energy transfer (other than direct work) from one body or system to another due to thermal contact. Everything tends to become less organized and less orderly over time (entropy). In all energy transfers, therefore, the overall result is that the energy is spread out uniformly. This transfer of heat energy from hotter to cooler objects is accomplished by conduction, radiation, or convection. **Temperature** is a measurement of an object's stored heat energy. More specifically, temperature is the average kinetic energy of an object's particles. When the temperature of an object increases and its atoms move faster, kinetic energy also increases. Temperature is not energy since it changes and is not conserved. Thermometers are used to measure temperature.

Important Thermodynamics Terminology

- **Thermodynamics**: This refers to a branch of physics that studies the conversion of energy into work and heat. It is especially concerned with variables such as temperature, volume, and pressure.
- **Thermodynamic equilibrium**: This refers to objects that have the same temperature because heat is transferred between them to reach equilibrium.
- An **open system** is capable of interacting with a surrounding environment and can exchange heat, work (energy), and matter outside their system boundaries.
- A **closed system** can exchange heat and work, but not matter.
- An **isolated system** cannot exchange heat, work, or matter with its surroundings. Its total energy and mass stay the same.
- **Surrounding environment**: In physics, this term refers to everything outside a thermodynamic system (system). The terms "surroundings" and "environment" are also used. The term "boundary" refers to the division between the system and its surroundings.

- **Calorie**: This is the amount of energy it takes to raise the temperature of a gram of water by one degree Celsius. A **kilocalorie** refers to the amount of energy it takes to raise the temperature of a kilogram of water by one degree Celsius. A calorie is equal to 4.184 joules.
- **Calorimeter**: This is a measurement device with a thermometer in which chemical or physical processes take place. The resulting change in temperature and the heat capacity can then be determined. Specific heat capacities have already been identified for many materials, and can be viewed in table form.
- **BTU**: This stands for British Thermal Unit. It is a measurement of the amount of energy it takes to raise the temperature of a pound of water by one degree Fahrenheit. A BTU is equal to 252 calories or 1.054 kilojoules (kJ).
- **Gibbs free energy**: This value is similar to the available energy or maximum work of a closed system.
- **Enthalpy**: This is a measure of heat content in a system. It is usually assumed that the system is closed and the pressure is constant. Enthalpy is represented by the symbol H. The heat of a reaction is the difference between the heat stored in the reactants and in the products. It is represented by ΔH.

Review Video: Enthalpy
Visit mometrix.com/academy and enter code: 233315

The Laws of Thermodynamics

The **laws of thermodynamics** are generalized principles dealing with energy and heat.

- The **zeroth law of thermodynamics** states that two objects in thermodynamic equilibrium with a third object are also in equilibrium with each other. Being in thermodynamic equilibrium basically means that different objects are at the same temperature.
- The **first law of thermodynamics** deals with conservation of energy. It states that neither mass nor energy can be destroyed; only converted from one form to another.
- The **second law of thermodynamics** states that the entropy (the amount of energy in a system that is no longer available for work or the amount of disorder in a system) of an isolated system can only increase. The second law also states that heat is not transferred from a lower-temperature system to a higher-temperature one unless additional work is done.
- The **third law of thermodynamics** states that as temperature approaches absolute zero, entropy approaches a constant minimum. It also states that a system cannot be cooled to absolute zero.

First Law of Thermodynamics

The laws of thermodynamics state that energy can be exchanged between physical systems as heat or work, and that systems are affected by their surroundings. It can be said that the total amount of energy in the universe is constant. The **first law** is mainly concerned with the **conservation of energy** and related concepts, which include the statement that energy can only be transferred or converted, not created or destroyed. The formula used to represent the first law is $\Delta U = Q - W$, where ΔU is the change in total internal energy of a system, Q is the heat added to the system, and W is the work done by the system. Energy can be transferred by conduction, convection, radiation, mass transfer, and other processes such as collisions in chemical and nuclear reactions. As transfers occur, the matter involved becomes less ordered and less useful. This tendency towards disorder is also referred to as **entropy**.

Review Video: First Law of Thermodynamics
Visit mometrix.com/academy and enter code: 340643

Second Law of Thermodynamics

The **second law of thermodynamics** explains how energy can be used. In particular, it states that heat will not transfer spontaneously from a cold object to a hot object. Another way to say this is that heat transfers occur from higher temperatures to lower temperatures. Also covered under this law is the concept that systems not under the influence of external forces tend to become more disordered over time. This type of disorder can be expressed in terms of entropy. Another principle covered under this law is that it is impossible to make a heat engine that can extract heat and convert it all to useful work. A thermal bottleneck occurs in machines that convert energy to heat and then use it to do work. These types of machines are less efficient than ones that are solely mechanical.

Review Video: The Second Law of Thermodynamics
Visit mometrix.com/academy and enter code: 251848

Conduction

Conduction is a form of heat transfer that occurs at the molecular level. It is the result of molecular agitation that occurs within an object, body, or material while the material stays motionless. An example of this is when a frying pan is placed on a hot burner. At first, the handle is not hot. As the pan becomes hotter due to conduction, the handle eventually gets hot too. In this example, energy is being transferred down the handle toward the colder end because the higher speed particles collide with and transfer energy to the slower ones. When this happens, the original material becomes cooler and the second material becomes hotter until equilibrium is reached. **Thermal conduction** can also occur between two substances such as a cup of hot coffee and the colder surface it is placed on. Heat is transferred, but matter is not.

Review Video: Heat Transfer at the Molecular Level
Visit mometrix.com/academy and enter code: 451646

Convection and Radiation

- **Convection** refers to heat transfer that occurs through the movement or circulation of fluids (liquids or gases). Some of the fluid becomes or is hotter than the surrounding fluid, and is less dense. Heat is transferred away from the source of the heat to a cooler, denser area. Examples of convection are boiling water and the movement of warm and cold air currents in the atmosphere and the ocean. **Forced convection** occurs in convection ovens, where a fan helps circulate hot air.
- **Radiation** is heat transfer that occurs through the emission of electromagnetic waves, which carry energy away from the emitting object. All objects with temperatures above absolute zero radiate heat.
- **Latent heat** refers to the amount of heat required for a substance to undergo a phase (state) change (from a liquid to a solid, for example).

Temperature Scales

There are three main scales for measuring temperature. **Celsius** uses the base reference points of water freezing at 0 degrees and boiling at 100 degrees. **Fahrenheit** uses the base reference points of water freezing at 32 degrees and boiling at 212 degrees. Celsius and Fahrenheit are both relative temperature scales since they use water as their reference point.

The **Kelvin** temperature scale is an absolute temperature scale. Its zero mark corresponds to absolute zero. Water's freezing and boiling points are 273.15 Kelvin and 373.15 Kelvin, respectively. Where Celsius and Fahrenheit are measured is degrees, Kelvin does not use degree terminology.

- Converting Celsius to Fahrenheit: $°F = \frac{9}{5}°C + 32$
- Converting Fahrenheit to Celsius: $°C = \frac{5}{9}(°F - 32)$
- Converting Celsius to Kelvin: $K = °C + 273.15$
- Converting Kelvin to Celsius: $°C = K - 273.15$

Heat Capacity and Specific Heat

- **Heat capacity**, also known as thermal mass, refers to the amount of heat energy required to raise the temperature of an object, and is measured in Joules per Kelvin or Joules per degree Celsius. The equation for relating heat energy to heat capacity is $Q = C\Delta T$, where Q is the heat energy transferred, C is the heat capacity of the body, and ΔT is the change in the object's temperature.
- **Specific heat capacity**, also known as specific heat, is the heat capacity per unit mass. Every element and compound has its own specific heat. For example, it takes different amounts of heat energy to raise the temperature of the same amounts of magnesium and lead by one degree. The equation for relating heat energy to specific heat capacity is $Q = mc\Delta T$, where m represents the mass of the object, and c represents its specific heat capacity.

Review Video: Specific Heat Capacity
Visit mometrix.com/academy and enter code: 736791

Properties of Matter

Matter refers to substances that have **mass** and occupy **space** (or volume). The traditional definition of matter describes it as having three states: solid, liquid, and gas. These different states are caused by differences in the distances and angles between molecules or atoms, which result in differences in the energy that binds them. **Solid** structures are rigid or nearly rigid and have strong bonds. Molecules or atoms of **liquids** move around and have weak bonds, although they are not weak enough to readily break. Molecules or atoms of **gases** move almost independently of each other, are typically far apart, and do not form bonds. The current definition of matter describes it as having four states. The fourth is **plasma**, which is an ionized gas that has some electrons that are described as free because they are not bound to an atom or molecule.

The following table shows similarities and differences between solids, liquids, and gases:

	Solid	**Liquid**	**Gas**
Shape	Fixed shape	No fixed shape (assumes shape of container)	No fixed shape (assumes shape of container)
Volume	Fixed	Fixed	Changes to assume shape of container
Fluidity	Does not flow easily	Flows easily	Flows easily
Compressibility	Hard to compr ess	Hard to compress	Compresses

- **Mass**: Mass is a measure of the amount of substance in an object.
- **Weight**: Weight is a measure of the gravitational pull of Earth on an object.
- **Volume**: Volume is a measure of the amount of space occupied. There are many formulas to determine volume. For example, the volume of a cube is the length of one side cubed (a^3) and the volume of a rectangular prism is length times width times height ($l \cdot w \cdot h$). The volume of an irregular shape can be determined by how much water it displaces.
- **Density**: Density is a measure of the amount of mass per unit volume. The formula to find density is mass divided by volume ($D=m/V$). It is expressed in terms of mass per cubic unit, such as grams per cubic centimeter (g/cm^3).
- **Specific gravity**: This is a measure of the ratio of a substance's density compared to the density of water.

Both physical changes and chemical reactions are everyday occurrences. **Physical changes** do not result in different substances. For example, when water becomes ice it has undergone a physical change, but not a chemical change. It has changed its form, but not its composition. It is still H_2O. **Chemical properties** are concerned with the constituent particles that make up the physicality of a substance. Chemical properties are apparent when chemical changes occur. The chemical properties of a substance are influenced by its electron configuration, which is determined in part by the number of protons in the nucleus (the atomic number). Carbon, for example, has 6 protons and 6 electrons. It is an element's outermost valence electrons that mainly determine its chemical properties. **Chemical reactions** may release or consume energy.

Atomic Charge

Atomic theory is concerned with the characteristics and properties of atoms that make up matter. It deals with matter on a microscopic level as opposed to a macroscopic level. Atomic theory, for instance, discusses the kinetic motion of atoms in order to explain the properties of macroscopic quantities of matter. **John Dalton** (1766-1844) is credited with making many contributions to the field of atomic theory that are still considered valid. This includes the notion that all matter consists of **atoms** and that atoms are indestructible. In other words, atoms can be neither created nor destroyed. This is also the theory behind the **conservation of matter**, which explains why chemical reactions do not result in any detectable gains or losses in matter. This holds true for chemical reactions and smaller scale processes. When dealing with large amounts of energy, however, atoms can be destroyed by **nuclear reactions.** This can happen in particle colliders or atom smashers.

Most atoms are **neutral** since the positive charge of the protons in the nucleus is balanced by the negative charge of the surrounding electrons. Electrons are transferred between atoms when they come into contact with each other. This creates a molecule or atom in which the number of electrons does not equal the number of protons, which gives it a positive or negative charge. A **negative ion** is created when an atom gains electrons, while a **positive ion** is created when an atom loses electrons. An **ionic bond** is formed between ions with opposite charges. The resulting compound is neutral. **Ionization** refers to the process by which neutral particles are ionized into charged particles. Gases and plasmas can be partially or fully ionized through ionization.

Review Video: Nuclear and Chemical Reactions
Visit mometrix.com/academy and enter code: 572819

Energy Transfer

Atoms interact by **transferring** or sharing the electrons furthest from the nucleus. Known as the **outer** or **valence electrons**, they are responsible for the chemical properties of an element. Bonds between atoms are created when electrons are paired up by being transferred or shared. If electrons are transferred from one atom to another, the bond is **ionic.** If electrons are shared, the bond is **covalent.** Atoms of the same element may bond together to form molecules or crystalline solids. When two or more different types of atoms bind together chemically, a **compound** is made. The physical properties of compounds reflect the nature of the interactions among their molecules. These interactions are determined by the structure of the molecule, including the atoms they consist of and the distances and angles between them.

Electrons in an atom can orbit different **levels** around the nucleus. They can absorb or release energy, which can change the location of their orbit or even allow them to break free from the atom. The outermost layer is the **valence layer**, which contains the valence electrons. The valence layer tends to have or share eight electrons. Molecules are formed by a chemical bond between atoms, a bond which occurs at the valence level. Two basic types of bonds are covalent and ionic. A **covalent bond** is formed when atoms share electrons. An **ionic bond** is formed when an atom transfers an electron to another atom. A **hydrogen bond** is a weak bond between a hydrogen atom of one molecule and an electronegative atom (such as nitrogen, oxygen, or fluorine) of another molecule. The **Van der Waals force** is a weak force between molecules. This type of force is much weaker than actual chemical bonds between atoms.

Review Video: John Dalton
Visit mometrix.com/academy and enter code: 565627

Composition of the Universe

Aside from dark energy and dark matter, which are thought to account for all but four percent of the universe, the two most abundant **elements** in the universe are hydrogen (H) and helium (He). After hydrogen and helium, the most abundant elements are oxygen, neon, nitrogen, carbon, silicon, and magnesium. The most abundant **isotopes** in the solar system are hydrogen-1 and helium-4. Measurements of the masses of elements in the Earth's crust indicate that oxygen (O), silicon (Si), and aluminum (Al) are the most abundant on Earth. Hydrogen in its plasma state is the most abundant chemical element in stars in their main sequences, but is relatively rare on planet Earth.

Combustion and Species

Combustion, or burning, is a sequence of chemical reactions involving fuel and an oxidant that produces heat and sometimes light. There are many types of combustion, such as rapid, slow, complete, turbulent, microgravity, and incomplete. **Fuels** and **oxidants** determine the compounds formed by a combustion reaction. For example, when rocket fuel consisting of hydrogen and oxygen combusts, it results in the formation of water vapor. When air and wood burn, resulting compounds include nitrogen, unburned carbon, and carbon compounds. Combustion is an **exothermic process**, meaning it releases energy. **Exothermic energy** is commonly released as heat, but can take other forms, such as light, electricity, or sound.

In chemistry, **species** is a generic term that can be used to refer to any type of particle, such as atoms, ions, molecules, molecular fragments, or specific forms of elements.

Review Video: Combustion
Visit mometrix.com/academy and enter code: 592219

Important Terminology

- **Elements**: These are substances that consist of only one type of atom.
- **Compounds**: These are substances containing two or more elements. Compounds are formed by chemical reactions and frequently have different properties than the original elements. Compounds are decomposed by a chemical reaction rather than separated by a physical one.
- **Solutions**: These are homogeneous mixtures composed of two or more substances that have become one.
- **Mixtures**: Mixtures contain two or more substances that are combined but have not reacted chemically with each other. Mixtures can be separated using physical methods, while compounds cannot.
- **Heat**: Heat is the transfer of energy from a body or system as a result of thermal contact. Heat consists of random motion and the vibration of atoms, molecules, and ions. The higher the temperature is the greater the atomic or molecular motion will be.
- **Energy**: Energy is the capacity to do work.

- **Work**: Work is the quantity of energy transferred by one system to another due to changes in a system that is the result of external forces, or macroscopic variables. Another way to put this is that work is the amount of energy that must be transferred to overcome a force. Lifting an object in the air is an example of work. The opposing force that must be overcome is gravity. Work is measured in joules (J).
- **Power**: The rate at which work is performed.
- **Thermal energy**: Thermal energy is the energy present in a system due to temperature.
- **Thermal contact** refers to energy transferred to a body by a means other than work a system in thermal contact with another can exchange energy with it through the process of heat transfer. Thermal contact does not necessarily involve direct physical contact. Heat is energy that can be transferred from one body or system to another without work being done. Everything tends to become less organized and less useful over time (entropy) in all energy transfers, therefore, the overall result is that the heat is spread out so that objects are in thermodynamic equilibrium and the heat can no longer be transferred without additional work.

Structure of Atoms

All matter consists of **atoms**. Atoms consist of a nucleus and electrons. The **nucleus** consists of protons and neutrons. The properties of these are measurable; they have mass and an electrical charge. The nucleus is positively charged due to the presence of protons. **Electrons** are negatively charged and orbit the nucleus. The nucleus has considerably more mass than the surrounding electrons. Atoms can bond together to make **molecules**. Atoms that have an equal number of protons and electrons are electrically neutral. If the number of protons and electrons in an atom is not equal, the atom has a positive or negative charge and is an **ion**.

Atoms are extremely small. A **hydrogen atom** is about 5×10^{-8} mm in diameter. According to some estimates, five trillion hydrogen atoms could fit on the head of a pin. **Atomic radius** refers to the average distance between the nucleus and the outermost electron. Models of atoms that include the proton, nucleus, and electrons typically show the electrons very close to the nucleus and revolving around it, similar to how the Earth orbits the sun. However, another model relates the Earth as the nucleus and its atmosphere as electrons, which is the basis of the term "**electron cloud.**" Another description is that electrons swarm around the nucleus. It should be noted that these atomic models are not to scale. A more accurate representation would be a nucleus with a diameter of about 2 cm in a stadium. The electrons would be in the bleachers.

Atom: The atom is one of the most basic units of matter. An atom consists of a central nucleus surrounded by electrons.

Nucleus: The nucleus of an atom consists of protons and neutrons. It is positively charged, dense, and heavier than the surrounding electrons. The plural form of nucleus is nuclei.

Electrons: These are atomic particles that are negatively charged and orbit the nucleus of an atom.

Protons: Along with neutrons, protons make up the nucleus of an atom. The number of protons in the nucleus determines the atomic number of an element. Carbon atoms, for example, have six protons. The atomic number of carbon is 6. The number of protons also indicates the charge of an atom. The number of protons minus the number of electrons indicates the charge of an atom.

Atomic number (proton number): The atomic number of an element refers to the number of protons in the nucleus of an atom. It is a unique identifier. It can be represented as Z. Atoms with a neutral charge have an atomic number that is equal to the number of electrons.

Neutrons: Neutrons are the uncharged atomic particles contained within the nucleus. The number of neutrons in a nucleus can be represented as "N."

Nucleon: This refers collectively to the neutrons and protons.

Element: An element is matter with one particular type of atom. It can be identified by its atomic number, or the number of protons in its nucleus. There are approximately 117 elements currently known, 94 of which occur naturally on Earth. Elements from the periodic table include hydrogen, carbon, iron, helium, mercury, and oxygen.

Atomic mass: This is also known as the mass number. The atomic mass is the total number of protons and neutrons in the nucleus of an atom. It is referred to as "A." The atomic mass (A) is equal to the number of protons (Z) plus the number of neutrons (N). This can be represented by the equation $A = Z + N$. The mass of electrons in an atom is basically insignificant because it is so small.

Atomic weight: This may sometimes be referred to as "relative atomic mass," but should not be confused with atomic mass. Atomic weight is the ratio of the average mass per atom of a sample (which can include various isotopes of an element) to 1/12 of the mass of an atom of carbon-12.

Review Video: Structure of Atoms
Visit mometrix.com/academy and enter code: 905932

Review Video: Reading Nuclear Equations
Visit mometrix.com/academy and enter code: 688890

Nuclear Reactions

The particles of an atom's nucleus (the protons and neutrons) are bound together by **nuclear force**, also known as **residual strong force**. Unlike chemical reactions, which involve electrons, nuclear reactions occur when two nuclei or nuclear particles collide. This results in the release or absorption of energy and products that are different from the initial particles. The energy released in a nuclear reaction can take various forms, including the release of kinetic energy of the product particles and the emission of very high energy photons known as **gamma rays**. Some energy may also remain in the nucleus. **Radioactivity** refers to the particles emitted from nuclei as a result of nuclear instability. There are many nuclear isotopes that are unstable and can spontaneously emit some kind of radiation. The most common types of radiation are alpha, beta, and gamma radiation, but there are several other varieties of radioactive decay.

Atomic Models and Theories

There have been many theories regarding the **structure** of atoms and their particles. Part of the challenge in developing an understanding of matter is that atoms and their particles are too small to be seen. It is believed that the first conceptualization of the atom was developed by **Democritus** in 400 B.C. Some of the more notable models are the solid sphere or billiard ball model postulated by **John Dalton**, the plum pudding or raisin bun model by **J.J. Thomson**, the planetary or nuclear model by **Ernest Rutherford**, the Bohr or orbit model by **Niels Bohr**, and the electron cloud or quantum mechanical model by **Louis de Broglie** and **Erwin Schrodinger**. Rutherford directed the alpha scattering experiment that discounted the plum pudding model. The shortcoming of the Bohr model was the belief that electrons orbited in fixed rather than changing ecliptic orbits.

Review Video: Atomic Models
Visit mometrix.com/academy and enter code: 434851

Radioactivity

Radioisotopes: Also known as radionuclides or radioactive isotopes, radioisotopes are atoms that have an unstable nucleus. This is a nucleus that has excess energy and the potential to make radiation particles within the nucleus (subatomic particles) or undergo radioactive decay, which can result in the emission of gamma rays. Radionuclides may occur naturally but can also be artificially produced.

Radioactive decay: This occurs when an unstable atomic nucleus spontaneously loses energy by emitting ionizing particles and radiation. Decay is a form of energy transfer, as energy is lost. It also results in different products. Before decay there is one type of atom, called the **parent nuclide**. After decay there are one or more different products, called the **daughter nuclide(s)**.

Radioactivity: This refers to particles that are emitted from nuclei as a result of nuclear instability.

Review Video: Radioactivity
Visit mometrix.com/academy and enter code: 537142

Radioactive half-life is the time it takes for half of the radioactive nuclei in a sample to undergo radioactive decay. Radioactive decay rates are usually expressed in terms of half-lives. The different types of radioactivity lead to different decay paths, which transmute the nuclei into other chemical elements. **Decay products** (or daughter nuclides) make radioactive dating possible. **Decay chains** are a series of decays that result in different products. for example, uranium-238 is often found in granite. Its decay chain includes 14 daughter products. It eventually becomes a stable isotope of lead, which is why lead is often found with deposits of uranium ore. Its first half-life is equivalent to the approximate age of the earth, about 4.5 billion years. One of its products is radon, a radioactive gas. **Radiation** is when energy is emitted by one body and absorbed by another. Nuclear weapons, nuclear reactors, and radioactive substances are all examples of things that involve ionizing radiation. Acoustic and electromagnetic radiation are other types of radiation.

Stable isotopes: Isotopes that have not been observed to decay are stable, or non-radioactive, isotopes. It is not known whether some stable isotopes may have such long decay times that observing decay is not possible. Currently, 80 elements have one or more stable isotopes. There are 256 known stable isotopes in total. Carbon, for example, has three isotopes. Two (carbon-12 and carbon-13) are stable and one (carbon-14) is radioactive.

Radioactive isotopes: These have unstable nuclei and can undergo spontaneous nuclear reactions, which results in particles or radiation being emitted. It cannot be predicted when a specific nucleus will decay, but large groups of identical nuclei decay at predictable rates. Knowledge about rates of decay can be used to estimate the age of materials that contain radioactive isotopes.

Ionizing radiation is that which can cause an electron to detach from an atom. It occurs in radioactive reactions and comes in three types: alpha (α), beta (β), and gamma (γ). Alpha rays are positive, beta rays are negative, and gamma rays are neutral. **Alpha particles** are larger than beta particles and can cause severe damage if ingested. Because of their large mass, however, they can be stopped easily. Even paper can protect against this type of radiation. **Beta particles** can be beta-minus or beta-plus. Beta-minus particles contain an energetic electron, while beta-plus particles are emitted by positrons and can result in gamma photons. Beta particles can be stopped with thin metal. **Gamma rays** are a type of high energy electromagnetic radiation consisting of photons. Gamma radiation rids the decaying nucleus of excess energy after it has emitted either alpha or beta radiation. Gamma rays can cause serious damage when absorbed by living tissue, and it takes thick lead to stop them. Alpha, beta, and gamma radiation can also have positive applications.

Nuclear fission and nuclear fusion are similar in that they occur in the nucleus of an atom, can release great amounts of energy, and result in the formation of different elements (known as nuclear transmutation). They are different in that one breaks apart a nucleus and the other joins nuclei. **Nuclear fission** is the splitting of a large nucleus into smaller pieces. **Nuclear fusion** is the joining of two nuclei, which occurs under extreme temperatures and pressures. Fusion occurs naturally in stars, and is the process responsible for the release of great amounts of energy. When fusion occurs, many atomic nuclei with like charges are joined together, forming a heavier nucleus. When this occurs, energy can be absorbed and/or released.

Review Video: Nuclear Fusion
Visit mometrix.com/academy and enter code: 381782

Radioactive waste is a waste product that is considered dangerous because of either low levels or high levels of radioactivity. Radioactive waste could include discarded clothing that was used as protection against radiation or decay products of substances used to create electricity through nuclear fission. Small amounts of radioactive material can be ingested as a method of tracing how the body distributes certain elements. Other radioactive materials are used as light sources because they glow when heated. Uncontrolled radiation or even small amounts of radioactive material can cause sickness and cancer in humans. **Gamma wave radiation** is fast moving radiation that can cause cancer and damage genetic information by crashing into DNA molecules or other cells. Low-level radiation also occurs naturally. When related to everyday occurrences, radiation is measured in millirems per hour (mrem/hr). Humans can be exposed to radiation from stone used to build houses, cosmic rays from space, x-rays and other medical devices, and nuclear energy products.

Electronegativity

Electronegativity is a measure of how capable an atom is of attracting a pair of bonding electrons. It refers to the fact that one atom exerts slightly more force in a bond than another, creating a **dipole**. If the electronegative difference between two atoms is small, the atoms will form a **polar covalent bond**. If the difference is large, the atoms will form an **ionic bond**. When there is no electronegativity, a **pure nonpolar covalent bond** is formed.

Electronegativity can be discussed as a trend in the periodic table. Fluorine (F) has the greatest electronegativity, and elements to the left and below fluorine have lower levels of electronegativity. This property of elements is often measured using the **Pauling scale**, which ranges from 4.0 (fluorine) to 0.7 (francium). Elements with high electronegativity are highly reactive because they can capture electrons. The symbols δ^+ (delta plus) and δ^- (delta minus) stand for fractional charges.

Electrons

Electrons are subatomic particles that orbit the nucleus at various levels commonly referred to as layers, shells, or clouds. The orbiting electron or electrons account for only a fraction of the atom's mass. They are much smaller than the nucleus, are negatively charged, and exhibit wave-like characteristics. Electrons are part of the **lepton** family of elementary particles. Electrons can occupy orbits that are varying distances away from the nucleus, and tend to occupy the lowest energy level they can. If an atom has all its electrons in the lowest available positions, it has a **stable electron arrangement**. The outermost electron shell of an atom in its uncombined state is known as the **valence shell**. The electrons there are called **valence electrons**, and it is their number that determines bonding behavior. Atoms tend to react in a manner that will allow them to fill or empty their valence shells.

Electrons Shells

Chemical bonds involve a negative-positive attraction between an electron or electrons and the nucleus of an atom or nuclei of more than one atom. The attraction keeps the atom cohesive, but also enables the formation of bonds among other atoms and molecules. Each of the seven energy levels (or shells) of an atom has a maximum number of electrons it can contain. The farther away from the nucleus an electron is, the more energy it has. The first shell, or K-shell, holds a maximum of 2 electrons; the second, L, holds 8; the third, M, holds 18; the fourth, N, holds 32; the fifth, O, holds 60; the sixth, P, holds 82; the seventh, Q, holds 108. The shells also have subshells. Chemical bonds form and break between atoms when atoms gain, lose, or share an electron in the outer (valence) shell.

Isotopes

The number of **protons** in an atom determines the element of that atom. for instance, all helium atoms have exactly two protons, and all oxygen atoms have exactly eight protons. If two atoms have the same number of protons, then they are the same element. However, the number of **neutrons** in two atoms can be different without the atoms being different elements. **Isotope** is the term used to distinguish between atoms that have the same number of protons but a different number of neutrons. The names of isotopes have the element name with the mass number. Recall that the **mass number** is the number of protons plus the number of neutrons. for example, carbon-12 refers to an atom that has 6 protons, which makes it carbon, and 6 neutrons. In other words, 6 protons + 6 neutrons = 12. Carbon-13 has six protons and seven neutrons, and carbon-14 has six protons and eight neutrons. Isotopes can also be written with the mass number in superscript before the element symbol. for example, carbon-12 can be written as ^{12}C.

Oxidation State and Oxidation Number.

Oxidation state and oxidation number are usually the same number. Even though they have different meanings, they are frequently used interchangeably. **Oxidation numbers** are Roman numerals in parentheses that are used as part of the naming scheme for inorganic compounds. **Oxidation state** refers to the hypothetical charge on an atom if all of its bonds are 100 percent ionic. They are integers that can occasionally be fractional numbers. Oxidation state is increased through oxidation (loss of electrons) and decreased through reduction (gain of electrons). The number for an oxidation state refers to a single atom or ion, and is a way to keep track of electrons. When using **Lewis diagrams**, shared electrons are generally assigned to the more electronegative element. In bonds involving two atoms of the same element, electrons are split between them. Lone pairs of electrons are assigned to the atom they are with.

Cathode Rays

The discovery of **cathode rays** in the late 1800s was basically the discovery of electrons. It was also discovered that electrons carry the negative charge of the atom and that the atom consists of smaller particles. Various scientists used different variations of cathode ray tubes containing no air or varying amounts of air. A cathode ray consists of a cathode, a negative electrode, and an anode, which has a positive charge. Modern cathode ray tubes heat a filament on the cathode end of the tube, which excites the electrons and separates them from their atoms. They travel in straight lines through the tube to the anode and back to the cathode through an electrical wire. The rays are invisible, but early scientists discovered fluorescence when the walls of the glass glowed when electrons hit them. Cathode rays are also known as **electron beams**.

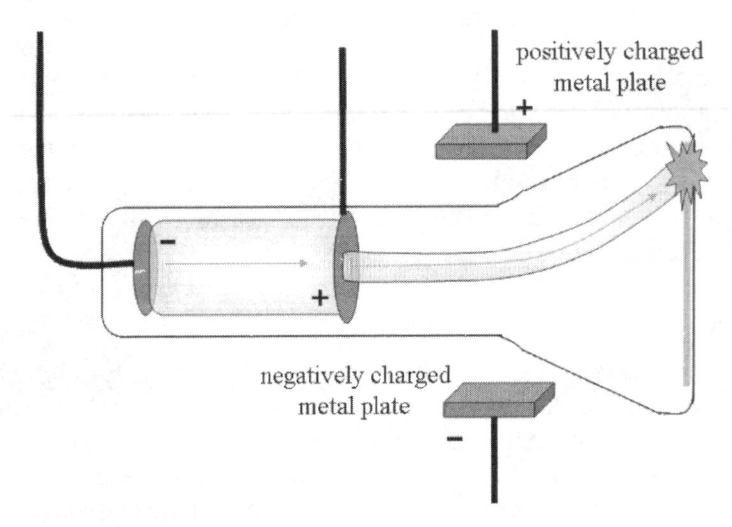

Helium Atom Vs. Hydrogen Atom

In the periodic table of elements, a **period** (also known as a row) is organized in such a way that atomic numbers (which indicate the number of protons) increase from left to right. In a single row, the number of electrons in the outermost shell is the same for all elements. In a single row, atomic radii decrease from left to right. In elements with more protons, the electrons are pulled in by the greater nuclear charge and the atoms become smaller because their atomic radii are shorter. Hydrogen and helium are in the same period. The most common isotope of **hydrogen** has one proton and one electron, but no neutron. **Helium** has two electrons and two protons. The higher number of protons exerts a greater force on the electrons, which is why a helium atom is smaller than a hydrogen atom.

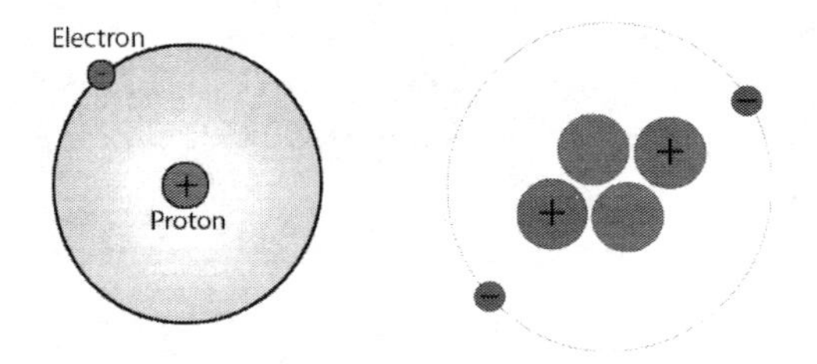

Review Video: Nuclear Charge
Visit mometrix.com/academy and enter code: 412575

Review Video: Order of Electron Filling in the Periodic Table
Visit mometrix.com/academy and enter code: 761477

Spectral Lines

Atomic spectral lines indicate change in the electrical level of an atom. This usually occurs when an electron transitions from one orbit to another. During this process, photons are absorbed or emitted. for example, an **emission line** is formed when an electron transitions to a lower energy level and a photon is emitted. An **absorption line** is formed when an electron transfers to a higher energy level and a photon is absorbed. A **photon** is an elementary particle thought to be the basic unit, or quantum, of light. When viewed in comparison to a visible spectrum, an emission line is bright and an absorption line is dark. Spectral lines can be used to help identify atoms and determine the chemical composition of a material. Gas is usually used in spectral analysis.

Conservation of Mass Number and Charge

Mass number is the sum of neutrons and protons in the nucleus (A = N + Z). The conservation of mass number is a concept related to nuclear reactions. Two conditions are required to balance a nuclear reaction. They are **conservation of mass number** and **conservation of nuclear charge**. In a nuclear equation, the mass numbers should be equal on each side of the arrow. In this type of equation, the mass number is in superscript in front of the element and the atomic number is in subscript. The total number of nucleons is the same even though the product elements are different. for example, when a specific isotope of uranium decays into thorium and helium, the original mass number of uranium is 238. After the reaction, the mass number of thorium is 234 and the mass number of helium is 4 (238 = 234 + 4). The mass number is the same on both sides of the equation.

Atomic Radius and Ionic Radius

Atomic size is typically measured in Angstroms (A) or picometers, where 1 Angstrom is equal to 10^{-10} of a meter, or 100 picometers (pm). The **atomic radius** of a chemical element refers to the distance from the nucleus to the boundary of an electron cloud or half the distance between two bonded nuclei. It may also refer to an isolated atom, but this can be confusing since atoms can share electrons, electron clouds can overlap, and electrons may be in motion. The trend across a period is for the atomic radius to decrease since as the atomic number (number of protons) increases across a row, electrons tend to be added in the same outermost shell, which increases nuclear charge and contracts the atom. The **ionic radius** is based upon nuclei when the ions are in a crystal lattice, meaning the atoms are organized in a specific manner.

Alpha Decay of Radon

The **alpha decay of radon** (Rn) to polonium (Po), which is part of the uranium-238 decay chain, is a good example of conservation of mass number. Two protons and two neutrons are lost when a nucleus emits an alpha particle, meaning the mass number will be four less and the atomic number (Z), protons, will be 2 less. When the atomic number (Z) and mass number (A) are diagrammed in a formula, the mass number is in superscript in front of the symbol for the element and the atomic number is in subscript. When Rn, with a mass number of 222 and an atomic number of 86, emits an alpha particle, it loses four from its mass number. It becomes polonium, which has a mass number of 218 and an atomic number of 84. Since an alpha particle with two protons and two neutrons is also a result of the reaction, the mass number is **conserved**.

One rule for calculating **oxidation state** is that the oxidation state is 0 for atoms in elemental form (only one kind of atom is present and its charge is 0). for example, both S_8 and Fe have an oxidation state of 0. for a monatomic ion, the oxidation state is equal to its charge. for example, the oxidation state is -2 for S^{2-} and +3 for Al^{3+}. for all Group 1A (alkali) metals, the oxidation state is +1. It is +2 for all Group 2A (alkaline earth) metals unless they are in elemental form. Hydrogen has an oxidation state of +1 when it is bonded to a nonmetal. It can be -1 when bonded to a metal. Oxygen almost always has an oxidation state of -2, but in peroxides it is -1. There are other exceptions as well. The oxidation state for fluorine is always -1. In a neutral compound, the sum of all atoms or ions must equal zero. In a polyatomic ion, its charge is equal to the sum of all oxidation state numbers.

Important Terminology

Nuclide: A nuclide is a more inclusive term than isotope. Generally, the term nuclide refers to all the atomic nuclei containing a specified number of protons and neutrons, while isotopes are forms of a particular atom that vary in terms of the number of protons and neutrons. In other words, all the isotopes of all the elements are nuclides.

Isotone: This refers to nuclides that have the same number of neutrons but a different number of protons. for example, carbon-14, nitrogen-15, and oxygen-16 all have eight neutrons in the nucleus. Therefore, they are all isotones of each other.

Isobar: This refers to nuclides that have the same mass number (the same number of nucleons) but differing numbers of protons and neutrons. In other words, isobars have the same total number of protons and neutrons (collectively known as the nucleon) but different numbers of each. for example, the isotopes argon-40 (which has 18 protons and 22 neutrons) and calcium-40 (which has 20 protons and 20 neutrons) are isobars.

Nuclear isomers: Atomic nuclei are long-lived, have an equal number of protons and neutrons, and differ in energy content. Nuclear isomers are excited states of atomic nuclei. Nuclear isomers are different from chemical isomers.

Review Video: Basics of Isomers
Visit mometrix.com/academy and enter code: 809623

Allotropes: Allotropes are different structures of an element. Atoms of some elements have the ability to bond to each other in more than one way. This enables an element to have multiple arrangements of atoms, which are known as allotropes. Easily recognizable allotropes of carbon are the diamond and graphite. The carbon atoms of a diamond are bonded in a tetrahedral structure. In graphite, carbon atoms are bonded in hexagonal sheets.

Review Video: Allotropes
Visit mometrix.com/academy and enter code: 259488

Quarks: Quarks are considered basic particles and fundamental components of matter. Various flavors of quarks combine to form hadrons, such as the protons and neutrons of atomic nuclei. The six flavors of quarks are up, down, charm, strange, top, and bottom.

Periodic Table

The **periodic table** groups elements with similar chemical properties together. The grouping of elements is based on **atomic structure**. It shows periodic trends of physical and chemical properties and identifies families of elements with similar properties. It is a common model for organizing and understanding elements. In the periodic table, each element has its own cell that includes varying amounts of information presented in symbol form about the properties of the element. Cells in the table are arranged in **rows** (periods) and **columns** (groups or families). A cell includes the symbol for the element and its atomic number. The cell for hydrogen, which appears first in the upper left corner, includes an "H" and a "1" above the letter. Elements are ordered by **atomic number**, left to right, top to bottom.

In the periodic table, the columns numbered 1 through 18 group elements with similar **outer electron shell configurations**. Since the configuration of the outer electron shell is one of the primary factors affecting an element's chemical properties, elements within the same group have similar chemical properties. Previous naming conventions for groups have included the use of Roman numerals and uppercase letters. Currently, the periodic table groups are: Group 1, alkali metals; Group 2, alkaline earth metals; Groups 3-12, transition metals; Group 13, boron family; Group 14, carbon family; Group 15, pnictogens; Group 16, chalcogens; Group 17, halogens; Group 18, noble gases.

Review Video: Periodic Table
Visit mometrix.com/academy and enter code: 154828

Review Video: Metals in the Periodic Table
Visit mometrix.com/academy and enter code: 506502

Review Video: Noble Gases
Visit mometrix.com/academy and enter code: 122067

In the periodic table, there are seven **periods** (rows), and within each period there are **blocks** that group elements with the same outer electron subshell. The number of electrons in that outer shell determines which group an element belongs to within a given block. Each row's number (1, 2, 3, etc.) corresponds to the highest number electron shell that is in use. For example, row 2 uses only electron shells 1 and 2, while row 7 uses all shells from 1-7.

Atomic radii will decrease from left to right across a period (row) on the periodic table. In a group (column), there is an increase in the atomic radii of elements from top to bottom. Ionic radii will be smaller than the atomic radii for metals, but the opposite is true for non-metals. From left to right, **electronegativity**, or an atom's likeliness of taking another atom's electrons, increases. In a group, electronegativity decreases from top to bottom. **Ionization energy** or the amount of energy needed to get rid of an atom's outermost electron, increases across a period and decreases down a group. **Electron affinity** will become more negative across a period but will not change much within a group. The **melting point** decreases from top to bottom in the metal groups and increases from top to bottom in the non-metal groups.

Group→ ↓Period	1	2	3	4	5	6	7	8	9	10	11	12	13	14	15	16	17	18
1	1 H																	2 He
2	3 Li	4 Be											5 B	6 C	7 N	8 O	9 F	10 Ne
3	11 Na	12 Mg											13 Al	14 Si	15 P	16 S	17 Cl	18 Ar
4	19 K	20 Ca	21 Sc	22 Ti	23 V	24 Cr	25 Mn	26 Fe	27 Co	28 Ni	29 Cu	30 Zn	31 Ga	32 Ge	33 As	34 Se	35 Br	36 Kr
5	37 Rb	38 Sr	39 Y	40 Zr	41 Nb	42 Mo	43 Tc	44 Ru	45 Rh	46 Pd	47 Ag	48 Cd	49 In	50 Sn	51 Sb	52 Te	53 I	54 Xe
6	55 Cs	56 Ba	*	72 Hf	73 Ta	74 W	75 Re	76 Os	77 Ir	78 Pt	79 Au	80 Hg	81 Tl	82 Pb	83 Bi	84 Po	85 At	86 Rn
7	87 Fr	88 Ra	**	104 Rf	105 Db	106 Sg	107 Bh	108 Hs	109 Mt	110 Ds	111 Rg	112 Cn	113 Uut	114 Fl	115 Uup	116 Lv	117 Uus	118 Uuo
		*	57 La	58 Ce	59 Pr	60 Nd	61 Pm	62 Sm	63 Eu	64 Gd	65 Tb	66 Dy	67 Ho	68 Er	69 Tm	70 Yb	71 Lu	
		**	89 Ac	90 Th	91 Pa	92 U	93 Np	94 Pu	95 Am	96 Cm	97 Bk	98 Cf	99 Es	100 Fm	101 Md	102 No	103 Lr	

Molar Mass, Charles's Law, and Boyle's Law

- **Molar mass**: This refers to the mass of one mole of a substance (element or compound), usually measured in grams per mole (g/mol). This differs from molecular mass in that molecular mass is the mass of one molecule of a substance relative to the atomic mass unit (amu).

- **Charles's law**: This states that gases expand when they are heated. It is also known as the law of volumes.
- **Boyle's law**: This states that gases contract when pressure is applied to them. It also states that if temperature remains constant, the relationship between absolute pressure and volume is inversely proportional. When one increases, the other decreases. Considered a specialized case of the ideal gas law, Boyle's law is sometimes known as the Boyle-Mariotte law.

Kinetic Theory of Gases

The **kinetic theory of gases** assumes that gas molecules are small compared to the distances between them and that they are in constant random motion. The attractive and repulsive forces between gas molecules are negligible. Their kinetic energy does not change with time as long as the temperature remains the same. The higher the temperature is, the greater the motion will be. As the temperature of a gas increases, so does the kinetic energy of the molecules. In other words, gas will occupy a greater volume as the temperature is increased and a lesser volume as the temperature is decreased. In addition, the same amount of gas will occupy a greater volume as the temperature increases, but pressure remains constant. At any given temperature, gas molecules have the same average kinetic energy.

Ideal Gas Law

The **ideal gas law** is used to explain the properties of a gas under ideal pressure, volume, and temperature conditions. It is best suited for describing monatomic gases (gases in which atoms are not bound together) and gases at high temperatures and low pressures. It is not well-suited for instances in which a gas or its components are close to their condensation point. All collisions are perfectly elastic and there are no intermolecular attractive forces at work. The ideal gas law is a way to explain and measure the macroscopic properties of matter. It can be derived from the kinetic theory of gases, which deals with the microscopic properties of matter. The equation for the ideal gas law is **PV = nRT**, where *P* is absolute **pressure**, *V* is absolute **volume**, and *T* is absolute **temperature**. *R* refers to the **universal gas constant**, which is 8.3145 J/mol Kelvin, and *n* is the number of **moles**.

Review Video: Ideal Gas Law
Visit mometrix.com/academy and enter code: 381353

Review Video: Ideal Gas vs Real Gas
Visit mometrix.com/academy and enter code: 619477

Atoms and Molecules

An **element** is matter with one particular type of atom. Elements from the periodic table such as hydrogen, carbon, iron, helium, mercury, and oxygen are atoms. **Atoms** combine to form **molecules**. For example, two atoms of hydrogen (H) and one atom of oxygen (O) combine to form one molecule of water (H_2O).

Compounds

Compounds are substances containing two or more elements. Compounds are formed by chemical reactions and frequently have different properties than the original elements. Compounds are decomposed by a chemical reaction rather than separated by a physical one.

Binary Compounds

Binary compounds refer to compounds that contain only two elements. They can be ionic or covalent. **Binary ionic compounds** are formed by **cations** (metallic positive ions) and **anions** (nonmetal negative ions). Ionic compounds are not molecules. The suffix "ide" is used if there is one anion, as in the case of cuprous oxide, for example. Another example is that fluorine is an element, while fluoride is the negative ion of fluorine. The binary compound barium fluoride would be written as BaF_2. This is because one barium ion has a charge of +2 and one fluoride ion has a charge of -1, so it would take two fluoride ions to balance out the one barium ion. If there is no charge symbol, it is assumed that the charge is 1. The suffixes "ate" or "ite" are used when there is more than one anion, as in the case of mercurous nitrate, for example. A **ternary compound** is one formed of three elements.

Hydrogen Bonds

Hydrogen bonds are weaker than covalent and ionic bonds, and refer to the type of attraction in an electronegative atom such as oxygen, fluorine, or nitrogen. Hydrogen bonds can form within a single molecule or between molecules. A water molecule is **polar**, meaning it is partially positively charged on one end (the hydrogen end) and partially negatively charged on the other (the oxygen end). This is because the hydrogen atoms are arranged around the oxygen atom in a close tetrahedron. Hydrogen is **oxidized** (its number of electrons is reduced) when it bonds with oxygen to form water. Hydrogen bonds tend not only to be weak, but also short-lived. They also tend to be numerous. Hydrogen bonds give water many of its important properties, including its high specific heat and high heat of vaporization, its solvent qualities, its adhesiveness and cohesiveness, its hydrophobic qualities, and its ability to float in its solid form. Hydrogen bonds are also an important component of proteins, and nucleic acids.

Molecular Formula

Elements are represented by uppercase letters. If there is no subscript, it indicates there is only one atom of the element. Otherwise, the subscript indicates the number of atoms. In molecular formulas, elements are organized according to the **Hill system**. Carbon is first, hydrogen comes next, and the remaining elements are listed in alphabetical order. If there is no carbon, all elements are listed alphabetically. There are a couple of exceptions to these rules. First, oxygen is usually listed last in oxides. Second, in ionic compounds the positive ion is listed first, followed by the negative ion. In CO_2, for example, C indicates 1 atom of carbon and O_2 indicates 2 atoms of oxygen. The compound is carbon dioxide. The formula for ammonia (an ionic compound) is NH_3, which is one atom of nitrogen and three of hydrogen. H_2O is two atoms of hydrogen and one of oxygen. Sugar is $C_6H_{12}O_6$, which is 6 atoms of carbon, 12 of hydrogen, and 6 of oxygen.

Ionization Energy, Electron Affinity, and Polar Bond

- **Ionization energy**: Ionization energy is the energy required for an electron to free itself from the grip of its neutral atom. Ionization energy increases across a row. Groups on the left of the table have fewer valence electrons and noble gases have the maximum number of valence electrons (a filled outer shell). Ionization energy can be measured in kilojoules (kJ) per mole or electron volts (eV) per atom (1 kJ/mol = 0.010364 eV/atom). Elements with low ionization energies are highly reactive because they can easily give up electrons.
- **Electron affinity**: This is a way to measure the change in energy when a negative ion is formed by adding an electron to a neutral atom.
- **Polar bond**: This refers to a covalent type of bond with a separation of charge. One end is negative and the other is positive. The hydrogen-oxygen bond in water is one example of a polar bond.

Review Video: Ionization Energy
Visit mometrix.com/academy and enter code: 862908

Electron Configuration

Electron configuration is a trend whereby electrons fill shells and subshells in an element in a particular order and with a particular number of electrons. The chemical properties of the elements reflect their electron configurations. **Energy levels** (shells) do not have to be completely filled before the next one begins to be filled. An example of electron configuration notation is $1s^22s^22p^5$, where the first number is the row (period), or shell. The letter refers to the subshell of the shell, and the number in superscript is the number of electrons in the subshell. A common shorthand method for electron configuration notation is to use a **noble gas** (in a bracket) to abbreviate the shells that elements have in common. For example, the electron configuration for neon is $1s^22s^22p^6$. The configuration for phosphorus is $1s^22s^22p^63s^23p^3$, which can be written as $[Ne]3s^23p^3$. Subshells are filled in the following manner: 1s, 2s, 2p, 3s, 3p, 4s, 3d, 4p, 5s, 4d, 5p, 6s, 4f, 5d, 6p, 7s, 5f, 6d, and 7p.

Electron Shells

There are seven **electron shells**. One is closest to the nucleus and seven is the farthest away. Electron shells can also be identified with the letters K, L, M, N, O, P, and Q. Traditionally, there were four subshells identified by the first letter of their descriptive name: s (sharp), p (principal), d (diffuse), and f (fundamental). The maximum number of electrons for each subshell is as follows: s is 2, p is 6, d is 10, and f is 14. Every shell has an **s subshell**, the second shell and those above also have a **p subshell**, the third shell and those above also have a **d subshell**, and so on. Each subshell contains atomic orbitals, which describes the wave-like characteristics of an electron or a pair of electrons expressed as two angles and the distance from the nucleus. **Atomic orbital** is a concept used to express the likelihood of an electron's position in accordance with the idea of wave-particle duality.

Valence Shell, the Aufbau Principle, and the Pauli Exclusion Principle

- **Valence shell**: This is the highest occupied electron shell, and contains the valence electrons.
- **Aufbau principle**: This states that the electrons of an atom occupy quantum levels or orbitals starting at the lowest energy level and proceeding to the highest. Each orbital can only contain a maximum of two paired electrons that have opposite spins.
- **Pauli exclusion principle**: This states that no more than two electrons can be in the same quantum state in one energy level. This affects how electrons are configured.

Review Video: Aufbau Principle
Visit mometrix.com/academy and enter code: 852758

Organic Compounds

The main trait of **organic compounds** is that they contain carbon *and* hydrogen. An example is urea ($CO(NH_2)_2$). Even though urea does not contain carbon-carbon bonds or carbon-hydrogen bonds, it is considered organic because it contains both carbon and hydrogen. Carbon can form long chains, double and triple bonds, and rings. While inorganic compounds tend to have high melting points, organic compounds tend to melt at temperatures below 300° C.

Inorganic Compounds

The main trait of **inorganic compounds** is that they do not contain carbon and hydrogen. An example is carbon dioxide. Even though carbon dioxide contains carbon, it is considered inorganic because it does not contain carbon **and** hydrogen. Inorganic compounds also include mineral salts, metals and alloys, non-metallic compounds such as phosphorus, and metal complexes.

Nomenclature refers to the manner in which a compound is named. First, it must be determined whether the compound is **ionic** (formed through electron transfer between cations and anions) or **molecular** (formed through electron sharing between molecules). When dealing with an ionic compound, the name is determined using the standard naming conventions for ionic compounds. This involves indicating the **positive element** first (the charge must be defined when there is more than one option for the valency) followed by the **negative element** plus the appropriate suffix. The rules for naming a molecular compound are as follows: write elements in order of increasing group number and determine the prefix by determining the number of atoms. Exclude mono for the first atom. The name for CO_2, for example, is carbon dioxide. The end of oxygen is dropped and "ide" is added to make oxide, and the prefix "di" is used to indicate there are two atoms of oxygen.

Review Video: Ionic Compounds
Visit mometrix.com/academy and enter code: 255084

Naming Systems

The four naming systems are for acids, organic compounds, binary ionic compounds, and binary molecular compounds. General rules are as follows:

- **Acids**: Compounds that start with H and contain only one other element (except H_2O) use "hydro-," the "element," and "-ic." HCl, for instance, would be hydrochloric acid. A compound consisting of H and a polyatomic ion with the suffix "-ate" is named using the "element" and "-ic." H_2SO_4, for instance, would be sulfuric acid. Similarly, a compound consisting of H and a polyatomic ion with the suffix "-ite" is named using the "element" and "-ous." H_2SO_3, for example, would be sulfurous acid.
- **Binary molecular compounds**: These start with a nonmetal other than H or C and contain a combination of nonmetals in close proximity on the periodic table. These compounds use the "-ide" suffix. The prefix is based on the subscript found in the formula, and may be mono-, di-, tri-, tetra-, penta-, hexa-, hepta-, octa-, nona-, deca-, undeca-, dodeca-, etc.

Review Video: Naming of Alcohols
Visit mometrix.com/academy and enter code: 737321

Review Video: Naming of Organic Acids
Visit mometrix.com/academy and enter code: 663668

Lewis Formulas and Kekulé Diagrams

- **Lewis formulas**: These show the bonding or nonbonding tendency of specific pairs of valence electrons. **Lewis dot diagrams** use dots to represent valence electrons. Dots are paired around an atom. When an atom forms a covalent bond with another atom, the elements share the dots as they would electrons. Double and triple bonds are indicated with additional adjacent dots. Methane (CH_4), for instance, would be shown as a C with 2 dots above, below, and to the right and left and an H next to each set of dots. In structural formulas, the dots are single lines.

- **Kekulé diagrams**: Like Lewis dot diagrams, these are two-dimensional representations of chemical compounds. Covalent bonds are shown as lines between elements. Double and triple bonds are shown as two or three lines and unbonded valence electrons are shown as dots.

Review Video: What are Covalent Bonds
Visit mometrix.com/academy and enter code: 482899

Atomic Mass Unit, Moles, and Avogadro's Number

Atomic mass unit (amu) is the smallest unit of mass, and is equal to 1/12 of the mass of the carbon isotope carbon-12. A **mole (mol)** is a measurement of molecular weight that is equal to the molecule's amu in grams. For example, carbon has an amu of 12, so a mole of carbon weighs 12 grams. One mole is equal to about 6.02×10^{23} elementary entities, which are usually atoms or molecules. This amount is also known as the Avogadro constant or **Avogadro's number (NA)**. Another way to say this is that one mole of a substance is the same as one Avogadro's number of that substance. One mole of chlorine, for example, is 6.02×10^{23} chlorine atoms. The charge on one mole of electrons is referred to as a **Faraday**.

Review Video: Avogadro's Law
Visit mometrix.com/academy and enter code: 360197

Review Video: Mole Concept
Visit mometrix.com/academy and enter code: 593205

Crystals

A **crystal** is considered to be a well-organized, repeating configuration of atoms, ions, or molecules. The strong attractive forces between oppositely-charged ions are responsible for the repeating patterns in **solid crystals**. These arrangements of repeating patterns can occur as a liquid cools to form a solid, as is seen with cubes of salt or ice. Crystalline structures occur across all classes of materials and form from all types of bonding. Salt is an example of a crystal formed with ionic bonds. A diamond is formed with covalent bonds. The majority of naturally occurring and artificially prepared solids have crystalline structures. Solids that do not are called **amorphous solids** because they have random arrangements.

The **symmetry** of a crystal is used to determine its classification. Crystal systems are grouped in accordance with their **axial systems** (there are three axes). The unique systems of crystals are cubic, hexagonal, rhombohedral, orthorhombic, monoclinic, and triclinic. Crystals in the cubic system are the most symmetric. The **unit cell** is the spatial arrangement of atoms. The spacing between unit cells is known as the **lattice parameters**.

Review Video: Shapes of Crystalline Solids
Visit mometrix.com/academy and enter code: 561128

Intermolecular Forces

Intermolecular forces are weaker than ionic and covalent bonds. They occur between stable molecules or functional groups of macromolecules. **Macromolecules** are large molecules that are usually created by polymerization and sometimes distinguished by their lack of covalent bonds. London dispersion force, dipole-dipole interactions, and hydrogen bonding are all examples of intermolecular forces. London dispersion force is also known as instantaneous dipole-induced dipole force because the force is caused by a change in dipole (a separation of the positive and negative charges in an atom). These forces are weak and the attractions are quickly formed and broken. An electron from one atom affects another atom, resulting in a force that dissipates as soon as an electron moves. Dipole-dipole (Keesom) interactions occur within atoms that are already covalently bonded and have permanent dipoles. These atoms have a different amount of electronegativity (attraction of electrons). One atom attracts another, electrostatic forces are generated, and molecules align to increase this attraction.

Chemical Reactions

Chemical reactions measured in human time can take place quickly or slowly. They can take fractions of a second or billions of years. The rates of chemical reactions are determined by how frequently reacting atoms and molecules interact. Rates are also influenced by the temperature and various properties (such as shape) of the reacting materials. **Catalysts** accelerate chemical reactions (decrease activation energy), while **inhibitors** decrease reaction rates (increase activation energy). Some types of reactions release energy in the form of heat and light. Some types of reactions involve the transfer of either electrons or hydrogen ions between reacting ions, molecules, or atoms. In other reactions, chemical bonds are broken down by heat or light to form reactive radicals with electrons that will readily form new bonds. Processes such as the formation of ozone and greenhouse gases in the atmosphere and the burning and processing of fossil fuels are controlled by radical reactions.

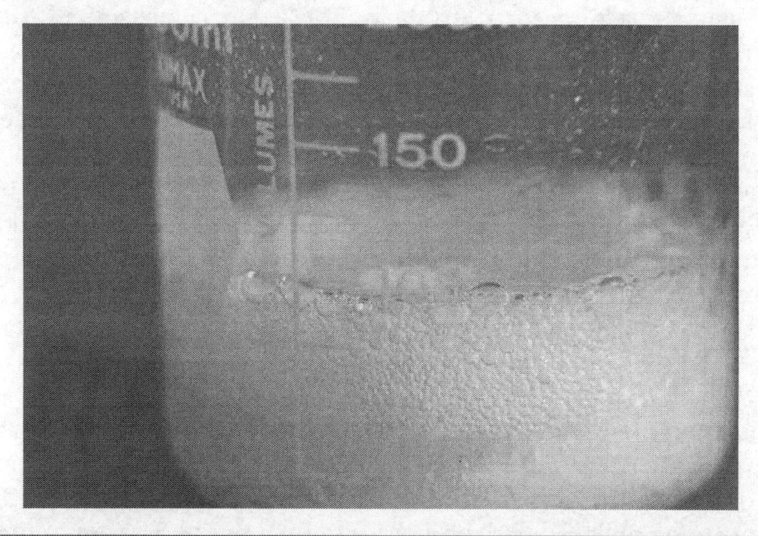

Review Video: Chemical Reactions
Visit mometrix.com/academy and enter code: 579876

Review Video: Catalysts
Visit mometrix.com/academy and enter code: 288189

Chemical Equations

Chemical equations describe chemical reactions. The **reactants** are on the left side before the arrow and the **products** are on the right side after the arrow. The arrow indicates the reaction or change. The **coefficient**, or stoichiometric coefficient, is the number before the element, and indicates the ratio of reactants to products in terms of moles. The equation for the formation of water from hydrogen and oxygen, for example, is $2H_2$ (g) + O_2 (g) → $2H_2O$ (l). The 2 that precedes hydrogen and water is the coefficient, which means there are 2 moles of hydrogen and 2 of water. There is 1 mole of oxygen, which does not have to be indicated with the number 1. In parentheses, g stands for gas, l stands for liquid, s stands for solid, and aq stands for aqueous solution (a substance dissolved in water). **Charges** are shown in superscript for individual ions, but not for ionic compounds. **Polyatomic ions** are separated by parentheses so the ion will not be confused with the number of ions.

Balancing Chemical Equations

An **unbalanced equation** is one that does not follow the law of conservation of mass, which states that matter can only be changed, not created. If an equation is unbalanced, the numbers of atoms indicated by the stoichiometric coefficients on each side of the arrow will not be equal. Start by writing the formulas for each species in the reaction. Count the atoms on each side and determine if the number is equal. Coefficients must be whole numbers. Fractional amounts, such as half a molecule, are not possible. Equations can be balanced by multiplying the coefficients by a constant that will produce the smallest possible whole number coefficient. $H_2 + O_2 \rightarrow H_2O$ is an example of an unbalanced equation. The balanced equation is $2H_2 + O_2 \rightarrow 2H_2O$, which indicates that it takes two moles of hydrogen and one of oxygen to produce two moles of water.

Review Video: Balanced Chemical Equations
Visit mometrix.com/academy and enter code: 839820

Types of Reactions

One way to organize chemical reactions is to sort them into two categories: **oxidation/reduction reactions** (also called redox reactions) and **metathesis reactions** (which include acid/base reactions). Oxidation/reduction reactions can involve the transfer of one or more electrons, or they can occur as a result of the transfer of oxygen, hydrogen, or halogen atoms. The species that loses electrons is oxidized and is referred to as the reducing agent. The species that gains electrons is reduced and is referred to as the oxidizing agent. The element undergoing oxidation experiences an increase in its oxidation number, while the element undergoing reduction experiences a decrease in its oxidation number. **Single replacement reactions** are types of oxidation/reduction reactions. In a single replacement reaction, electrons are transferred from one chemical species to another. The transfer of electrons results in changes in the nature and charge of the species.

Single Substitution, Displacement, and Replacement Reactions

Single substitution, **displacement**, or **replacement reactions** are when one reactant is displaced by another to form the final product ($A + BC \rightarrow AB + C$). Single substitution reactions can be cationic or anionic. When a piece of copper (Cu) is placed into a solution of silver nitrate ($AgNO_3$), the solution turns blue. The copper appears to be replaced with a silvery-white material. The equation is $2AgNO_3 + Cu \rightarrow Cu(NO_3)_2 + 2Ag$. When this reaction takes place, the copper dissolves and the silver in the silver nitrate solution precipitates (becomes a solid), resulting in copper nitrate and silver. Copper and silver have switched places in the nitrate.

Double displacement, **double replacement**, **substitution**, **metathesis**, or **ion exchange reactions** are when ions or bonds are exchanged by two compounds to form different compounds ($AC + BD \rightarrow AD + BC$). An example of this is that silver nitrate and sodium chloride form two different products (silver chloride and sodium nitrate) when they react. The formula for this reaction is $AgNO_3 + NaCl \rightarrow AgCl + NaNO_3$.

Combination and Decomposition Reactions

Combination, or **synthesis, reactions**: In a combination reaction, two or more reactants combine to form a single product ($A + B \rightarrow C$). These reactions are also called synthesis or **addition reactions**. An example is burning hydrogen in air to produce water. The equation is $2H_2\ (g) + O_2\ (g) \rightarrow 2H_2O\ (l)$. Another example is when water and sulfur trioxide react to form sulfuric acid. The equation is $H_2O + SO_3 \rightarrow H_2SO_4$.

Decomposition (or desynthesis, decombination, or deconstruction) reactions: In a decomposition reaction, a reactant is broken down into two or more products ($A \rightarrow B + C$). These reactions are also called analysis reactions. **Thermal decomposition** is caused by heat. **Electrolytic decomposition** is due to electricity. An example of this type of reaction is the decomposition of water into hydrogen and oxygen gas. The equation is $2H_2O \rightarrow 2H_2 + O_2$.

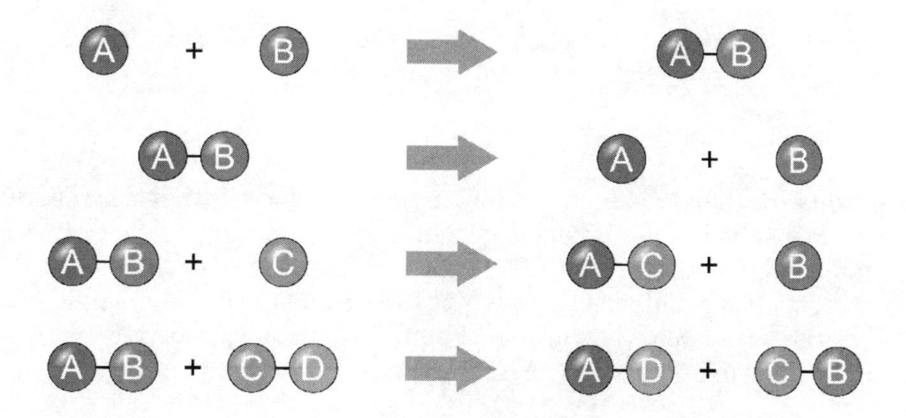

Acid/Base Reactions

In **acid/base reactions**, an **acid** is a compound that can donate a proton, while a **base** is a compound that can accept a proton. In these types of reactions, the acid and base react to form a salt and water. When the proton is donated, the base becomes water and the remaining ions form a salt. One method of determining whether a reaction is an oxidation/reduction or a metathesis reaction is that the oxidation number of atoms does not change during a metathesis reaction.

Review Video: Reactions of Acids, Bases and Oxides
Visit mometrix.com/academy and enter code: 773459

Isomerization and Neutralization Reactions

Isomerization, or **rearrangement**, is the process of forming a compound's isomer. Within a compound, bonds are reformed. The reactant and product have the same molecular formula, but different structural formulas and different properties ($A \rightarrow B$ or $A \rightarrow A'$). For example, butane (C_4H_{10}) is a hydrocarbon consisting of four carbon atoms in a straight chain. Heating it to 100° C or higher in the presence of a catalyst forms isobutane (methylpropane), which has a branched-chain structure. Boiling and freezing points are greatly different for butane and isobutane. A rearrangement reaction occurs within the molecule.

Review Video: Two Structural Formulas for Butane
Visit mometrix.com/academy and enter code: 307520

A **neutralization**, **acid-base**, or **proton transfer reaction** is when one compound acquires H^+ from another. These types of reactions are also usually double displacement reactions. The acid has an H^+ that is transferred to the base and neutralized to form a salt.

Catalysts

Catalysts can increase reaction rates by decreasing the number of steps it takes to form products. The mass of the catalyst should be the same at the beginning of the reaction as it is at the end. The **activation energy** is the minimum amount required to get a reaction started. Activation energy causes particles to collide with sufficient energy to start the reaction. A catalyst enables more particles to react, which lowers the activation energy. Examples of catalysts in reactions are manganese oxide (MnO_2) in the decomposition of hydrogen peroxide, iron in the manufacture of ammonia using the Haber process, and concentrate of sulfuric acid in the nitration of benzene.

Review Video: Haber Process for Making Ammonia
Visit mometrix.com/academy and enter code: 213059

Endothermic and Exothermic Reactions

Endothermic reactions are chemical reactions that absorb heat and **exothermic reactions** are chemical reactions that release heat. The heat difference between endothermic and exothermic reactions is caused by bonds forming and breaking. If more energy is needed to break the reactant bonds than is released when they form, the reaction is endothermic. Heat is absorbed and the environmental temperature decreases. If more energy is released when product bonds form than is needed to break the reactant bonds, the reaction is exothermic. Heat is released and the environmental temperature increases.

Factors Affecting Reactions

Endergonic: This is a chemical reaction in which it takes more energy to instigate the reaction than is produced by it.

Exergonic: This is a chemical reaction in which the net amount of Gibbs free energy is less than zero.

The **collision theory** states that for a chemical reaction to occur, atoms or molecules have to collide with each other with a certain amount of energy. A certain amount of energy is required to breach the activation barrier. Heating a mixture will raise the energy levels of the molecules and the rate of reaction (the time it takes for a reaction to complete). Other factors that can affect the rate of reaction are surface area, concentration, pressure, and the presence of a catalyst.

Chemiluminescence, Phosphorescence, and Luminescence

Phosphorescence and **luminescence** occur because energy is absorbed by a substance (charged) and light is re-emitted comparatively slowly.

These processes are different from **chemiluminescence**, in which an excited state is created by a chemical reaction and transferred to another molecule. A glow stick is an example of chemiluminescence.

LeChatelier's Principle

When a system at equilibrium is subjected to a change in the concentration of products or reactants, the system will counteract to establish a **new equilibrium**. This relationship is known as **Le Chatelier's principle**.

Consider the following system at equilibrium: $CO\ (g) + NO_2\ (g) \leftrightharpoons CO_2\ (g) + NO\ (g)$

If NO_2 or CO (reactants) are added to the system, the result will be the formation of additional CO_2 and NO (products) until a new equilibrium is established. Conversely, if CO or NO_2 are removed from the system, the result will be the formation of additional CO and NO_2 until a new equilibrium is established.

Review Video: Le Châtelier's Principle
Visit mometrix.com/academy and enter code: 360187

Solutions

A **solution** is a homogeneous mixture. A **mixture** is two or more different substances that are mixed together, but not combined chemically. **Homogeneous mixtures** are those that are uniform in their composition. Solutions consist of a **solute** (the substance that is dissolved) and a **solvent** (the substance that does the dissolving). An example is sugar water. The solvent is the water and the solute is the sugar. The intermolecular attraction between the solvent and the solute is called **solvation**. **Hydration** refers to solutions in which water is the solvent. Solutions are formed when the forces of the molecules of the solute and the solvent are as strong as the individual molecular forces of the solute and the solvent. An example is that salt (NaCl) dissolves in water to create a solution. The Na^+ and the Cl^- ions in salt interact with the molecules of water and vice versa to overcome the individual molecular forces of the solute and the solvent.

Review Video: Solutions
Visit mometrix.com/academy and enter code: 995937

Review Video: Stoichiometry
Visit mometrix.com/academy and enter code: 801833

Properties of Solutions

Properties of solutions include:

- they have a maximum particle size of one nm,
- they do not separate when allowed to stand or when poured through a fiber filter,
- they are clear and do not scatter light, and
- their boiling points increase while their melting points decrease when the amount of solute is increased.

Components of Solutions

A **syrup** is a solution of water and sugar. A **brine** is a solution of table salt, or sodium chloride (NaCl), and water. A **saline solution** is a sterilized solution of sodium chloride in water. A **seltzer** is a solution of carbon dioxide in water.

The term **dilute** is used when there is less solute. Adding more solvent is known as diluting a solution, as is removing a portion of the solute. **Concentrated** is the term used when there is more solute. Adding more solute makes a solution more concentrated, as does removing a portion of the solvent.

Concentration and Molarity

Concentration can be measured in molarity, molality, or parts per million (ppm). **Molarity** is a measure of the number of moles of solute in a liter of solution. One mole per liter is a 1 M solution. **Molality** is a measure of the number of moles of solute in a kilogram of solution. **Parts per million** is a way of measuring very dilute solutions. One ppm is equal to one gram of solute per one million grams of solution (or, 1 mg/L of water).

Review Video: Molarity of a Solution
Visit mometrix.com/academy and enter code: 810121

Important Terminology

- A **mixture** is a combination of two or more substances that are not bonded.
- **Suspensions** are mixtures of heterogeneous materials. Particles are usually larger than those found in true solutions. Dirt mixed vigorously with water is an example of a suspension. The dirt is temporarily suspended in water, but the two separate once the mixing is ceased.
- A mixture of large (1 nm to 500 nm) particles is called a **colloidal suspension**.
- The particles are termed **dispersants** and the dispersing medium is similar to the solvent in a solution.
- **Sol** refers to a liquid or a solid that also has solids dispersed through it, such as milk or gelatin. An aerosol spray is a colloid suspension of gas and the solid or liquid being dispersed.
- An **emulsion** refers to a liquid or a solid that has a liquid dispersed through it.
- A **foam** is a liquid that has gas dispersed through it.
- An **Immiscible** is a substance that cannot be blended or used to form a homogeneous substance. It will stay separated or will separate into layers.
- The antonym of immiscible is **miscible**, which refers to a substance that can be mixed.

Polar and Nonpolar Solvents

For **solvation** to occur, bonds of similar strength must be broken and formed. Nonpolar substances are usually **soluble** in nonpolar solvents. Ionic and polar matter is usually soluble in polar solvents. Water is a polar solvent. Oil is nonpolar. Therefore, the saying "oil and water don't mix" is quite true. Heptane (C_7H_{16}) is another nonpolar liquid that is said to be immiscible in water, meaning it can't combine with water. The hydrogen bonds of the water molecules are stronger than the London dispersion forces of the heptane. Polar molecules such as NH_3 (ammonia), SO_2 (sulfur dioxide), and H_2S (hydrogen sulfide) are termed hydrophilic, meaning they readily combine with water. Nonpolar molecules, including the noble gases and other gases such as He (helium), Ne (neon), and CO_2 (carbon dioxide) are termed hydrophobic, meaning they repel or do not readily combine with water. One way to remember this is that "like dissolves like." Polar solvents dissolve polar solutes, while nonpolar solvents dissolve nonpolar solutes.

Review Video: Hydrogen Sulfide
Visit mometrix.com/academy and enter code: 552628

Effects of Temperature and Pressure on Solubility

- **Solids** tend to dissolve faster with increased temperature or agitation rate. Solubility will also increase with decreasing size of solute particles. Solubility tends to increase for solids being dissolved in water as the temperature approaches 100 °C, but at higher temperatures ionic solutes tend to become less soluble.
- **Gas** solubility in liquids tends to decrease at higher temperatures.

- A solution may become "**supersaturated**" at high temperatures, meaning that it contains a higher concentration of solute than it would contain at normal temperatures. As a supersaturated solution is cooled, the solute will **precipitate** (return to solid form) and "fall out of the solution."
- **Melting points** can be lowered by using a solvent such as salt on icy roads, which lowers the freezing point of ice. Adding salt to water when making ice cream also lowers the melting point of the water. A solution's melting point is usually lower than the melting point of the solvent alone.
- **Pressure** has little effect on the solubility of solids or liquids. In gas solutions, an increase in pressure increases solubility, and vice versa. But the solubility of a gas will increase if the pressure of the gas above a solution is increased.

Review Video: Melting Points
Visit mometrix.com/academy and enter code: 424075

Electrolytes and Electrolysis

- **Electrolyte**: This refers to a substance that is ionized in water. **Strong electrolytes** are completely ionized and are good conductors of electricity. Salts are examples of strong electrolytes. Compounds that dissolve in water without completely ionizing are **weak electrolytes**. Acids and bases are examples of weak electrolytes. **Nonelectrolytes** are those that dissolve with no ionization.
- **Electrolysis**: This refers to the decomposition of a substance by electric current. For example, when electric current is passed through melted NaCl (sodium chloride), sodium (Na), a metal, and chlorine gas (Cl_2) are formed.

pH and pH Scale

The **potential of hydrogen (pH)** is a measurement of the concentration of hydrogen ions in a substance in terms of the number of moles of H^+ per liter of solution. A lower pH indicates a higher H^+ concentration, while a higher pH indicates a lower H^+ concentration. Pure water has a neutral pH, which is 7. Anything with a pH lower than water (less than 7) is considered **acidic**. Urine, stomach acid, citric acid, vinegar, hydrochloric acid, and battery acid are acids. Anything with a pH higher than water (greater than 7) is a **base**. Drain cleaner, soap, baking soda, ammonia, egg whites, and sea water are common bases.

Acid-Base Reactions

When combined, acids and bases neutralize each other's properties and produce a **salt**. The H^+ cation of the acid combines with the OH^- anion of the base to form water. The cation of the base and the anion of the acid form a salt compound. An example is that hydrochloric acid and sodium hydroxide react to form table salt. The equation for the reaction is $HCl + NaOH \rightarrow H_2O + NaCl$.

The theories related to the classification of acids and bases are the Arrhenius theory, the Brønsted-Lowry theory, and the Lewis theory. The **Arrhenius acid-base theory** states that substances that can ionize to form positive hydrogen ions (H^+) or hydronium ions in an aqueous solution are acids and substances that produce hydroxide ions (OH^-) are bases. The **Brønsted-Lowry theory** states that substances that can act as a proton donor are acids and those that can act as a proton acceptor are bases. The **Lewis theory** states that acids are electron-pair acceptors and bases are electron-pair donors.

Properties of Acids and Bases

Some properties of **acids** are that they conduct electricity, change blue litmus paper to red, have a sour taste, react with bases to neutralize them, and react with active metals to free hydrogen. A **weak acid** is one that does not donate all of its protons or disassociate completely. **Strong acids** include hydrochloric, hydriodic, hydrobromic, perchloric, nitric, and sulfuric. They ionize completely. **Superacids** are those that are stronger than 100 percent sulfuric acid. They include fluoroantimonic, magic, and perchloric acids. Acids can be used in pickling, a process used to remove rust and corrosion from metals. They are also used as catalysts in the processing of minerals and the production of salts and fertilizers. Acids may be added to foods as preservatives or to add taste.

Some properties of **bases** are that they conduct electricity, change red litmus paper to blue, feel slippery, and react with acids to neutralize their properties. A **weak base** is one that does not completely ionize in an aqueous solution, and usually has a low pH. **Strong bases** can free protons in very weak acids. Examples of strong bases are hydroxide compounds such as potassium, barium, and lithium hydroxides. Most are in the first and second groups of the periodic table. A **superbase** is extremely strong compared to sodium hydroxide and cannot be kept in an aqueous solution. Superbases are organized into organic, organometallic, and inorganic classes. Bases are used as insoluble catalysts in heterogeneous reactions and as catalysts in hydrogenation.

Review Video: Properties of Acids
Visit mometrix.com/academy and enter code: 645283

Buffers

A **buffer** is a solution whose pH remains relatively constant when a small amount of an acid or a base is added. It is usually made of a weak acid and its conjugate base (proton receiver) or one of its soluble salts. It can also be made of a weak base and its conjugate acid (proton donator) or one of its salts. A constant pH is necessary in living cells because some living things can only live within a certain pH range. If that pH changes, the cells could die. Blood is an example of a buffer. A **pK_a** is a measure of acid dissociation or the acid dissociation constant. Buffer solutions can help keep enzymes at the correct pH. They are also used in the fermentation process, in dyeing fabrics, and in the calibration of pH meters. An example of a buffer is HC_2H_3O (a weak acid) and $NaC_2H_3O_2$ (a salt containing the $C_2H_3O_2^-$ ion).

Review Video: Buffer
Visit mometrix.com/academy and enter code: 389183

pH Indicators

A **pH indicator** is a substance that acts as a detector of hydrogen or hydronium ions. It is halochromic, meaning it changes color to indicate that hydrogen or hydronium ions have been detected. Examples include phenolphthalein, pH paper, and litmus paper.

Properties of Salts

Some properties of **salts** are that they are formed from acid base reactions, are ionic compounds consisting of metallic and nonmetallic ions, dissociate in water, and are comprised of tightly bonded ions. Some common salts are sodium chloride (NaCl), sodium bisulfate, potassium dichromate ($K_2Cr_2O_7$), and calcium chloride ($CaCl_2$). Calcium chloride is used as a drying agent, and may be used to absorb moisture when freezing mixtures. Potassium nitrate (KNO_3) is used to make fertilizer and in the manufacture of explosives. Sodium nitrate ($NaNO_3$) is also used in the making of fertilizer. Baking soda (sodium bicarbonate) is a salt, as are Epsom salts [magnesium sulfate ($MgSO_4$)].

Cell Structure and Processes

Prokaryotic and Eukaryotic Cells

Cells can be broadly characterized as prokaryotic and eukaryotic. The main difference is that **eukaryotic cells** have a nucleus and **prokaryotic cells** do not. In eukaryotic cells, DNA is mostly contained in chromosomes in the nucleus, although there is some DNA in mitochondria and chloroplasts. In prokaryotic cells, the genetic material aggregates in the cytoplasm in a nucleoid.

There are other differences. Eukaryotic cells are considered more complex than prokaryotic cells. Eukaryotic cells have membrane-bound organelles that perform various functions and contribute to the complexity of these types of cells. Prokaryotic cells do not contain membrane-bound organelles. Prokaryotic cells usually divide by binary fission and are haploid. Eukaryotic cells divide by mitosis and are diploid.

Plant and animal cells are eukaryotic. **Bacteria** are prokaryotic.

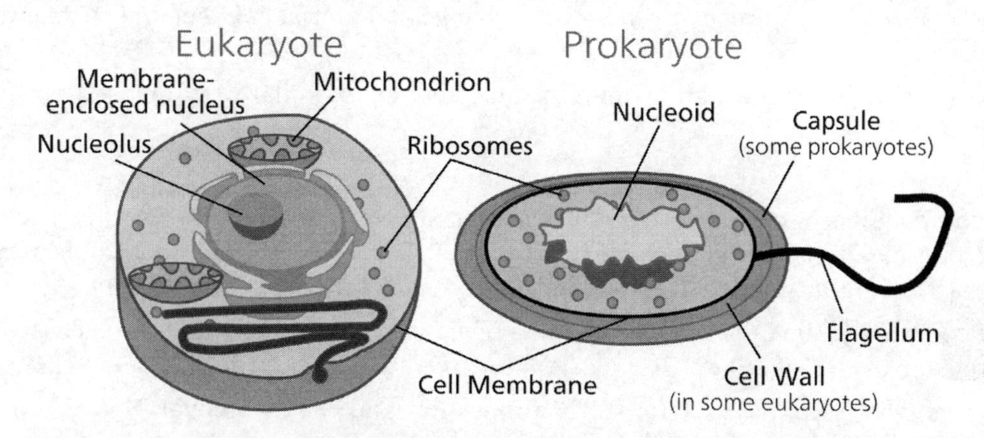

Review Video: Eukaryotic and Prokaryotic
Visit mometrix.com/academy and enter code: 231438

Plant and Animal Cells

The main difference between plant and animal cells is that **plant cells** have a cell wall made of cellulose that can handle high levels of pressure within the cell, which can occur when liquid enters a plant cell. Also, plant cells have chloroplasts that are used during the process of photosynthesis, which is the conversion of sunlight into food. Plant cells usually have one large vacuole, whereas **animal cells** can have many smaller ones. During cellular reproduction, plant cells build a cell plate between the two new cells, while animal cells make a cleavage furrow and pinch in half. Plant cells also tend to be larger than animal cells.

Animal and plant cells are similar in that they are eukaryotic and have cell membranes, cytoplasm, and vacuoles. Both plant and animal cells duplicate genetic material, separate it, and then divide in half to reproduce.

Review Video: Plant and Animal Cells
Visit mometrix.com/academy and enter code: 115568

Nuclear Parts of a Cell

- **Nucleus** (pl. nuclei): This is a small structure that contains the chromosomes and regulates the DNA of a cell. The nucleus is the defining structure of eukaryotic cells, and all eukaryotic cells have a nucleus. The nucleus is responsible for the passing on of genetic traits between generations. The nucleus contains a nuclear envelope, nucleoplasm, a nucleolus, nuclear pores, chromatin, and ribosomes.
- **Chromosomes**: These are highly condensed, threadlike rods of DNA. Short for deoxyribonucleic acid, DNA is the genetic material that stores information.
- **Chromatin**: This consists of the DNA and protein that make up chromosomes.
- **Nucleolus** (nucleole): This structure contained within the nucleus consists of protein. It is small, round, does not have a membrane, is involved in protein synthesis, and synthesizes and stores RNA (ribonucleic acid).
- **Nuclear envelope**: This encloses the structures of the nucleus. It consists of inner and outer membranes made of lipids.
- **Nuclear pores**: These are involved in the exchange of material between the nucleus and the cytoplasm.
- **Nucleoplasm**: This is the liquid within the nucleus, and is similar to cytoplasm.

Cell Structure

- **Ribosomes**: Ribosomes are involved in synthesizing proteins from amino acids. They are numerous, making up about one quarter of the cell. Some cells contain thousands of ribosome. Some are mobile and some are embedded in the rough endoplasmic reticulum.
- **Golgi complex** (Golgi apparatus): This is involved in synthesizing materials such as proteins that are transported out of the cell. It is located near the nucleus and consists of layers of membranes.
- **Vacuoles**: These are sacs used for storage, digestion, and waste removal. There is one large vacuole in plant cells. Animal cells have small, sometimes numerous vacuoles.
- **Vesicle**: This is a small organelle within a cell. It has a membrane and performs varying functions, including moving materials within a cell.
- **Cytoskeleton**: This consists of microtubules that help shape and support the cell.
- **Microtubules**: These are part of the cytoskeleton and help support the cell. They are made of protein.
- **Cytosol**: This is the liquid material in the cell. It is mostly water, but also contains some floating molecules.
- **Cytoplasm**: This is a general term that refers to cytosol and the substructures (organelles) found within the plasma membrane, but not within the nucleus.
- **Cell membrane** (plasma membrane): This defines the cell by acting as a barrier. It helps keeps cytoplasm in and substances located outside the cell out. It also determines what is allowed to enter and exit the cell. Some cell membranes are composed of a phospholipid bilayer.
- **Endoplasmic reticulum**: The two types of endoplasmic reticulum are rough (has ribosomes on the surface) and smooth (does not have ribosomes on the surface). It is a tubular network that comprises the transport system of a cell. It is fused to the nuclear membrane and extends through the cytoplasm to the cell membrane.

- **Mitochondrion** (pl. mitochondria): These cell structures vary in terms of size and quantity. Some cells may have one mitochondrion, while others have thousands. This structure performs various functions such as generating ATP, and is also involved in cell growth and death. Mitochondria contain their own DNA that is separate from that contained in the nucleus.

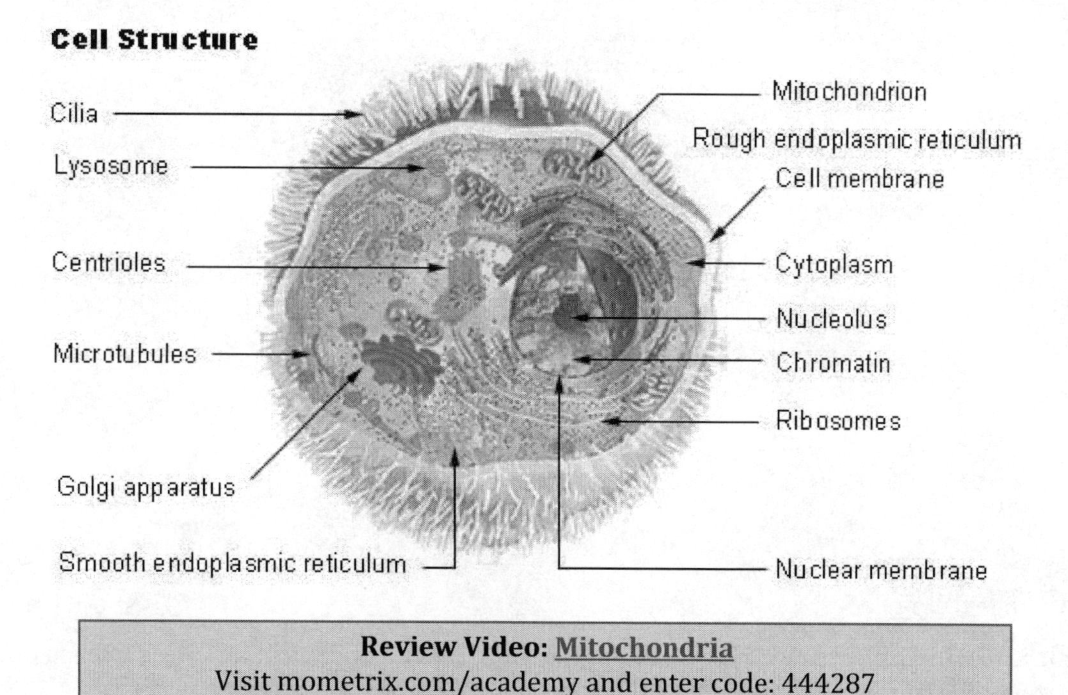

Review Video: Mitochondria
Visit mometrix.com/academy and enter code: 444287

Plant Cell Structure

- **Cell wall**: Made of cellulose and composed of numerous layers, the cell wall provides plants with a sturdy barrier that can hold fluid within the cell. The cell wall surrounds the cell membrane.
- **Chloroplast**: This is a specialized organelle that plant cells use for photosynthesis, which is the process plants use to create food energy from sunlight. Chloroplasts contain **chlorophyll**, which has a green color.
- **Plastid**: This is a membrane-bound organelle found in plant cells that is used to make chemical compounds and store food. It can also contain pigments used during photosynthesis. Plastids can develop into more specialized structures such as chloroplasts, chromoplasts (make and hold yellow and orange pigments), amyloplasts (store starch), and leucoplasts (lack pigments, but can become differentiated).
- **Plasmodesmata** (sing. plasmodesma): These are channels between the cell walls of plant cells that allow for transport between cells.

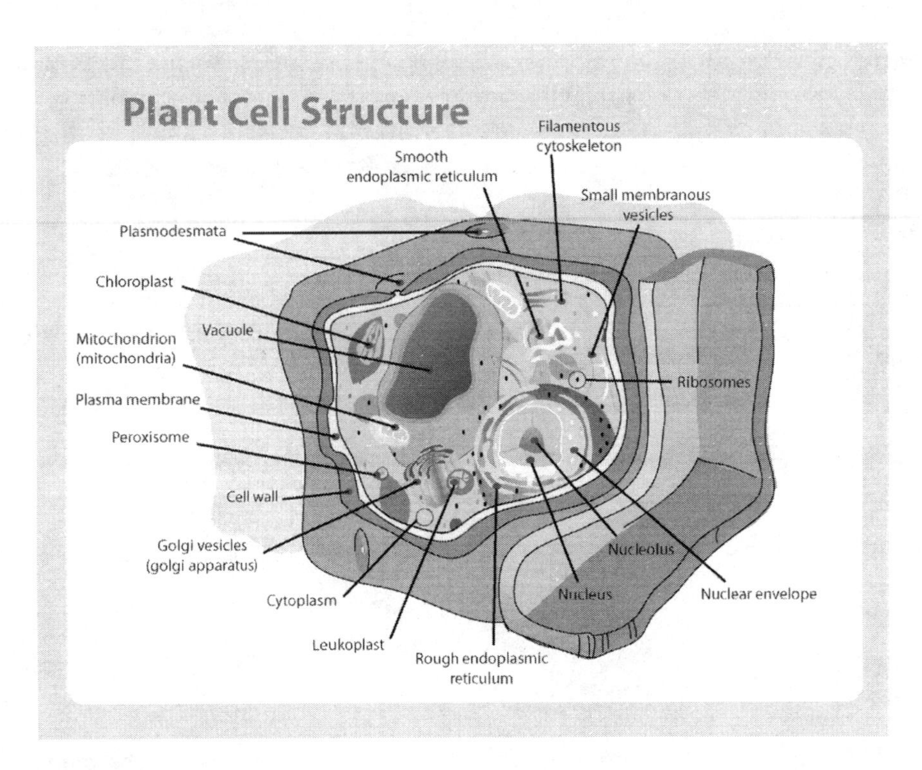

Animal Cell Structure

- **Centrosome**: This is comprised of the pair of centrioles located at right angles to each other and surrounded by protein. The centrosome is involved in mitosis and the cell cycle.
- **Centriole**: These are cylinder-shaped structures near the nucleus that are involved in cellular division. Each cylinder consists of nine groups of three microtubules. Centrioles occur in pairs.
- **Lysosome**: This digests proteins, lipids, and carbohydrates, and also transports undigested substances to the cell membrane so they can be removed. The shape of a lysosome depends on the material being transported.
- **Cilia** (singular: cilium): These are appendages extending from the surface of the cell, the movement of which causes the cell to move. They can also result in fluid being moved by the cell.
- **Flagella**: These are tail-like structures on cells that use whip-like movements to help the cell move. They are similar to cilia, but are usually longer and not as numerous. A cell usually only has one or a few flagella.

Lipids, Organelles, RNA, Polymers, Monomers, Nucleotides, and Nucleoids

- **Lipids**: molecules that are hydrophobic or amphiphilic (having hydrophilic and hydrophobic properties) in nature. Examples include fats, triglycerides, steroids, and waxes. Lipids take many forms and have varying functions, such as storing energy and acting as a building block of cell membranes. Lipids are produced by anabolysis.
- **Organelle**: This is a general term that refers to an organ or smaller structure within a cell. Membrane-bound organelles are found in eukaryotic cells.
- **RNA**: RNA is short for ribonucleic acid, which is a type of molecule that consists of a long chain (polymer) of nucleotide units.
- **Polymer**: This is a compound of large molecules formed by repeating monomers.

- **Monomer**: A monomer is a small molecule. It is a single compound that forms chemical bonds with other monomers to make a polymer.
- **Nucleotides**: These are molecules that combine to form DNA and RNA.
- **Nucleoid**: This is the nucleus-like, irregularly-shaped mass of DNA that contains the chromatin in a prokaryotic cell.

> **Review Video: Polymers**
> Visit mometrix.com/academy and enter code: 481202

Mitochondria Functions

Four functions of **mitochondria** are: the production of cell energy, cell signaling (how communications are carried out within a cell, cellular differentiation (the process whereby a non-differentiated cell becomes transformed into a cell with a more specialized purpose), and cell cycle and growth regulation (the process whereby the cell gets ready to reproduce and reproduces). Mitochondria are numerous in eukaryotic cells. There may be hundreds or even thousands of mitochondria in a single cell. Mitochondria can be involved in many functions, their main one being supplying the cell with **energy**. Mitochondria consist of an inner and outer membrane. The inner membrane encloses the matrix, which contains the mitochondrial DNA (mtDNA) and ribosomes. Between the inner and outer membranes are folds (cristae). Chemical reactions occur here that release energy, control water levels in cells, and recycle and create proteins and fats. Aerobic respiration also occurs in the mitochondria.

Cellular Respiration

Cellular respiration refers to a set of metabolic reactions that convert chemical bonds into energy stored in the form of ATP. Respiration includes many oxidation and reduction reactions that occur thanks to the electron transport system within the cell. Oxidation is a loss of electrons and reduction is a gain of electrons. Electrons in C-H (carbon/hydrogen) and C-C (carbon/carbon) bonds of molecules such as carbohydrates are donated to oxygen atoms. Processes involved in cellular respiration include glycolysis, the Krebs cycle, the electron transport chain, and chemiosmosis. The two forms of respiration are aerobic and anaerobic. **Aerobic respiration** is very common, and oxygen is the final electron acceptor. In **anaerobic respiration**, the final electron acceptor is not oxygen. Aerobic respiration results in more ATP than anaerobic respiration. **Fermentation** is another process by which energy is converted.

> **Review Video: Aerobic Respiration**
> Visit mometrix.com/academy and enter code: 770290

Photosynthesis

Photosynthesis is the conversion of sunlight into energy in plant cells, and also occurs in some types of bacteria and protists. Carbon dioxide and water are converted into glucose during photosynthesis, and light is required during this process. Cyanobacteria are thought to be the descendants of the first organisms to use photosynthesis about 3.5 billion years ago. Photosynthesis is a form of **cellular respiration**. It occurs in chloroplasts that use thylakoids, which are structures in the membrane that contain light reaction chemicals. **Chlorophyll** is a pigment that absorbs light. During the process, water is used and oxygen is released. The equation for the chemical reaction that occurs during photosynthesis is

$6H_2O + 6CO_2 \rightarrow C_6H_{12}O_6 + 6O_2$. During photosynthesis, six molecules of water and six molecules of carbon dioxide react to form one molecule of sugar and six molecules of oxygen.

Review Video: Photosynthesis in Biology
Visit mometrix.com/academy and enter code: 402602

Cell Transport Mechanisms

Active transport mechanisms include exocytosis and endocytosis. Active transport involves transferring substances from areas of lower concentration to areas of higher concentration. Active transport requires energy in the form of ATP. **Endocytosis** is the ingestion of large particles into a cell, and can be categorized as phagocytosis (ingestion of a particle), pinocytosis (ingestion of a liquid), or receptor mediated. Endocytosis occurs when a substance is too large to cross a cell membrane. Endocytosis is a process by which eukaryotes ingest food particles. During phagocytosis, cell-eating vesicles used during ingestion are quickly formed and unformed. **Exocytosis** is the opposite of endocytosis. It is the expulsion or discharge of substances from a cell. A lysosome digests particles with enzymes, and can be expelled through exocytosis. A vacuole containing the substance to be expelled attaches to the cell membrane and expels the substance.

Passive Transport Mechanisms

Transport mechanisms allow for the movement of substances through membranes. **Passive transport mechanisms** include simple and facilitated diffusion and osmosis. They do not require energy from the cell. **Diffusion** is when particles are transported from areas of higher concentration to areas of lower concentration. When equilibrium is reached, diffusion stops. Examples are gas exchange (carbon dioxide and oxygen) during photosynthesis and the transport of oxygen from air to blood and from blood to tissue. **Facilitated diffusion** is when specific molecules are transported by a specific carrier protein. Carrier proteins vary in terms of size, shape, and charge. Glucose and amino acids are examples of substances transported by carrier proteins. Osmosis is the diffusion of water through a semi-permeable membrane from an area of higher concentration to one of lower concentration. Examples of osmosis include the absorption of water by plant roots and the alimentary canal. Plants lose and gain water through osmosis. A plant cell that swells because of water retention is said to be **turgid**.

Cell Cycle

The term **cell cycle** refers to the process by which a cell reproduces, which involves cell growth, the duplication of genetic material, and cell division. Complex organisms with many cells use the cell cycle to replace cells as they lose their functionality and wear out. The entire cell cycle in animal cells can take 24 hours. The time required varies among different cell types. Human skin cells, for example, are constantly reproducing. Some other cells only divide infrequently. Once neurons are mature, they do not grow or divide. The two ways that cells can reproduce are through meiosis and mitosis. When cells replicate through **mitosis**, the "daughter cell" is an exact replica of the parent cell. When cells divide through **meiosis**, the daughter cells have different genetic coding than the parent cell. Meiosis only happens in specialized reproductive cells called gametes.

Biological Importance of Chemicals

Water molecules are important for many reasons, including:

- Water is a strong solvent for ionic compounds such as salts,
- Water acts as a transport medium for polar solutes,

- Metabolic reactions happen in solutions that contain water,
- Water can act as a temperature buffer for enzyme-catalyzed reactions,
- Water is used in photosynthesis, and
- Water molecules are used or formed in oxidation and reduction reactions.

Carbon dioxide is used by plants during photosynthesis, which produces oxygen. Oxygen is used by organisms during respiration. Nitrogen is also used by organisms. Nitrogen is a nutrient for plants, and is also used in the formation of proteins and nucleic acids.

Cell Division

- **Cell division** is performed in organisms so they can grow and replace cells that are old, worn out, or damaged.
- **Chromatids**: During cell division, the DNA is replicated, and chromatids are the two identical replicated pieces of chromosome that are joined at the centromere to form an "X."
- **Gametes**: These are cells used by organisms to reproduce sexually. Gametes in humans are haploid, meaning they contain only half of the organism's genetic information (23 chromosomes). Other human cells contain all 46 chromosomes.
- **Haploid**: Haploid means there is one set of chromosomes.
- **Diploid**: Diploid means there are two sets of chromosomes (one set from each parent).

Homeostasis, Gene Expression, Transcription, Translation, And Cellular Differentiation

- **Homeostasis**: This describes the ability and tendency of an organism, cell, or body to adjust to environmental changes to maintain equilibrium.
- **Gene expression**: This refers to the use of information in a gene to make a protein or nucleic acid product. Examples of nucleic acid products are tRNA or rRNA.
- **Transcription**: This refers to the synthesis of RNA from DNA.
- **Translation**: Synthesizing a protein from an mRNA strand.
- **Cellular differentiation**: This is the process by which a cell changes to a new cell type.

Sizes of Organelles

The size of the **nucleus** in a eukaryotic cell is about 6 micrometers (µm). It occupies about 10 percent of the cell. A **chloroplast** is about 1 µm. **Plant and animal** cell sizes range from about 10 µm to 100 µm, while the sizes of **bacteria** range from about 1 µm to 10 µm. **Atoms** have a size of about 0.1 nanometers.

- Mitosis
- **Interphase**: The cell prepares for division by replicating its genetic and cytoplasmic material. Interphase can be further divided into G_1, S, and G_2.
- **Prophase**: The chromatin thickens into chromosomes and the nuclear membrane begins to disintegrate. Pairs of centrioles move to opposite sides of the cell and spindle fibers begin to form. The mitotic spindle, formed from cytoskeleton parts, moves chromosomes around within the cell.
- **Metaphase**: The spindle moves to the center of the cell and chromosome pairs align along the center of the spindle structure.
- **Anaphase**: The pairs of chromosomes, called sisters, begin to pull apart, and may bend. When they are separated, they are called daughter chromosomes. Grooves appear in the cell membrane.

- **Telophase**: The spindle disintegrates, the nuclear membranes reform, and the chromosomes revert to chromatin. In animal cells, the membrane is pinched. In plant cells, a new cell wall begins to form.
- **Cytokinesis**: This is the physical splitting of the cell (including the cytoplasm) into two cells. Cytokinesis begins during anaphase, as the cell begins to furrow, and is completed following telophase.

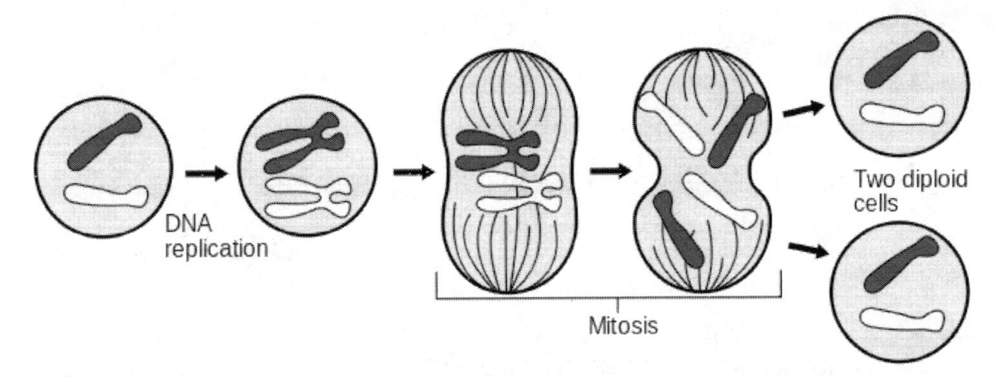

Review Video: Mitosis
Visit mometrix.com/academy and enter code: 849894

Meiosis

Meiosis has the same phases as mitosis, but they happen twice. In addition, different events occur during some phases of meiosis than mitosis. The events that occur during the first phase of meiosis are interphase (I), prophase (I), metaphase (I), anaphase (I), telophase (I), and cytokinesis (I). During this first phase of meiosis, chromosomes cross over, genetic material is exchanged, and tetrads of four chromatids are formed. The nuclear membrane dissolves. Homologous pairs of chromatids are separated and travel to different poles. At this point, there has been one cell division resulting in two cells. Each cell goes through a second cell division, which consists of prophase (II), metaphase (II), anaphase (II), telophase (II), and cytokinesis (II). The result is four daughter cells with different sets of chromosomes.

The daughter cells are **haploid**, which means they contain half the genetic material of the parent cell. The second phase of meiosis is similar to the process of mitosis. Meiosis encourages **genetic diversity**.

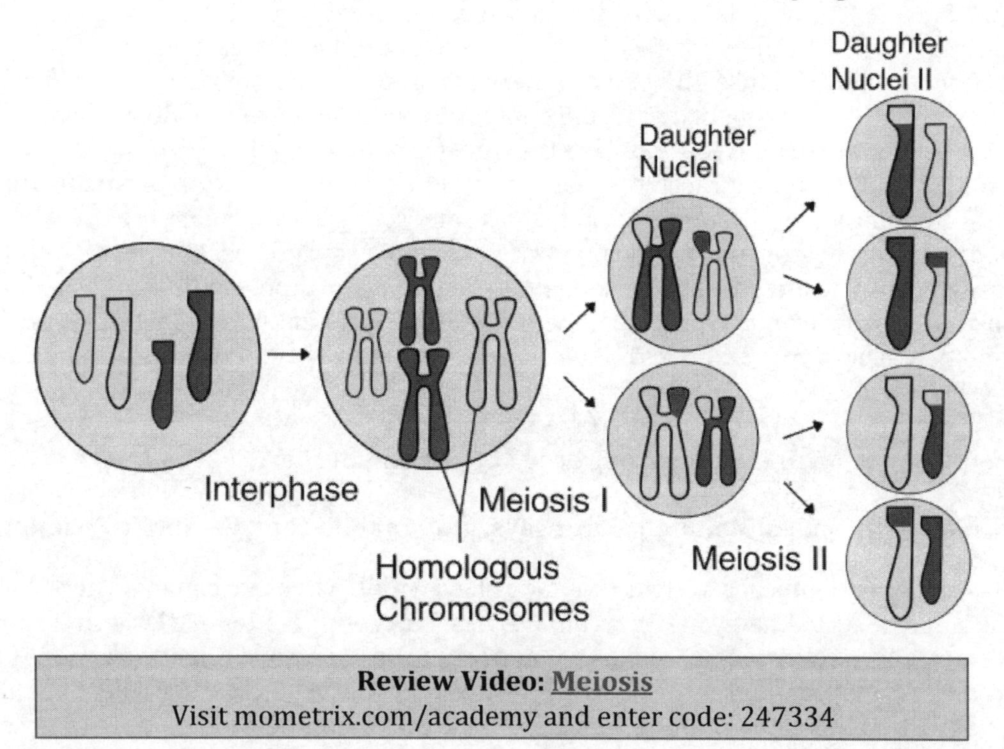

Review Video: Meiosis
Visit mometrix.com/academy and enter code: 247334

Cancerous Cells

In **cancerous cells**, the DNA or gene structure is disrupted. Abnormal numbers of chromosomes can develop. Cancer cells can have a defective Krebs cycle, resorting to glycolysis for energy production. Normal cells get about 70% of their energy from the Krebs cycle and about 20% from glycolysis. In addition, normal cells usually use **oxygen** during energy production, while cancer cells mainly produce energy without using oxygen. Normal cells have a built-in **blood vessel system**, but cancer cells must construct their own. Cancer cells over-populate and are very active, making more demands on system resources. The enzymes and hormones involved with cancer cells tend to be overactive or underactive, which can lead to other problems.

Cell Theory

The basic tenets of **cell theory** are that all living things are made up of cells and that cells are the basic units of life. Cell theory has evolved over time and is subject to interpretation. The development of cell theory is attributed to **Matthias Schleiden** and **Theodor Schwann**, who developed the theory in the early 1800s. Early cell theory was comprised of four statements: all organisms (living things) are made of cells; new cells are formed from pre-existing cells; all cells are similar; and cells are the most basic units of life. Other concepts related to classic and modern cell theory include statements such as: cells provide the basic units of functionality and structure in living things; cells are both distinct stand-alone units and basic building blocks; energy flow occurs within cells; cells contain genetic information in the form of DNA; and all cells consist of mostly the same chemicals.

Review Video: Cell Theory
Visit mometrix.com/academy and enter code: 736687

Enzymes

Enzymes can be divided into six classes: oxidoreductase, transferase, hydrolase, lyase, isomerase, and ligase. These classes end with the suffix "ase," which is true of most enzymes. Each enzyme catalyzes a chemical reaction. **Oxidoreductase enzymes** catalyze oxidation reduction (redox) reactions, during which hydrogen and oxygen are gained or lost. Examples include cytochrome oxidase, lactate, and dehydrogenase. **Transferase enzymes** catalyze the transfer of functional groups, such as the amino or phosphate group. Examples include acetate kinase and alanine deaminase. **Hydrolase enzymes** break chemical bonds by using water. Examples include lipase and sucrase. **Lyase enzymes** break chemical bonds or remove groups of atoms without using water. Examples include oxalate decarboxylase and isocitrate lyase. **Isomerase enzymes** catalyze the rearrangement of atoms within a molecule. Examples include glucose-phosphate isomerase and alanine racemase. **Ligase enzymes** join two molecules by forming a bond between atoms. Examples of ligases are acetyl-CoA synthetase and DNA ligase.

Review Video: Enzymes
Visit mometrix.com/academy and enter code: 656995

Metabolism, Macromolecules, Metabolic Pathways, and Anabolic and Catabolic Reactions

Metabolism is all of the chemical reactions that take place within a living organism. These chemical changes convert nutrients to energy and macromolecules. **Macromolecules** are large and complex, and play an important role in cell structure and function. **Metabolic pathways** refer to a series of reactions in which the product of one reaction is the substrate for the next. These pathways are dependent upon enzymes that act as catalysts. An **anabolic reaction** is one that builds larger and more complex molecules (macromolecules) from smaller ones. **Catabolic reactions** are the opposite. Larger molecules are broken down into smaller, simpler molecules. Catabolic reactions release energy, while anabolic ones require energy. The four basic organic macromolecules produced by anabolic reactions are carbohydrates (polysaccharides), nucleic acids, proteins, and lipids. The four basic building blocks involved in catabolic reactions are monosaccharides (i.e. glucose), amino acids, fatty acids (i.e. glycerol), and nucleotides.

Catabolism

Catabolism is the biosynthetic process by which macromolecules are broken down into smaller molecules. During this process, both energy and molecules that are used in anabolic processes are produced. The four main groups of molecules produced through catabolism are monosaccharides (glucose), amino acids, fatty acids (glycerol), and nucleotides. **Carbohydrates** (polysaccharides) are broken down into sugars or glucose. It is the oxidation of carbohydrates that provides the cells with most of their energy. **Glucose** can be further broken down by respiration or fermentation by glycolysis. The first step of **glycolysis** breaks down pyruvic acid with the byproducts of NADH and ATP. Pyruvic acid can then be used in the Krebs cycle or in fermentation. Glycolysis occurs in the cytoplasm of eukaryotic cells. **Fatty acids** are long chains that are oxidized to acetyl-CoA, which provides energy to cells. **Nucleic acids** consist of nucleotides. **Nucleotide triphosphates** such as ATP carry energy. They also release energy when their bonds are broken.

Review Video: Carbohydrates
Visit mometrix.com/academy and enter code: 601714

Anabolism

Anabolism is a form of biosynthesis. It usually involves a series of steps, or pathways, where the product of one reaction is used in the next. Anabolism uses smaller molecules to build carbohydrates (polysaccharides), nucleic acids, proteins, and lipids. Energy is used and stored during this process. Anabolic reactions can form a variety of macromolecules. An example of **polysaccharide biosynthesis** in animals and bacteria is gluconeogenesis, the formation of glucose from pyruvate with covalent bonds. Examples of **nucleic acid synthesis** include the formation of DNA, RNA, ATP, and other macromolecules. It can be achieved by either the pentose phosphate or Entner Doudoroff pathways. **Protein biosynthesis** uses amino acids, which are intermediate products of the Krebs cycle. **Lipid biosynthesis** uses fatty acids, which are formed from acetyl CoA (coenzyme A) during the Krebs cycle, and glycerol, which is derived from dihydroxyacetone phosphate and glycolysis.

Amino Acids

Amino acids are the building blocks of proteins. Structurally, amino acids consist of a central carbon atom that is bound to an amino group ($-NH_3$), a carboxylic acid group (-COOH), a side chain ("R" group), and a hydrogen atom (H).

Each amino acid contains a different **side chain**. Amino acid side chains may be charged, polar, or hydrophobic.

Review Video: Amino Acids
Visit mometrix.com/academy and enter code: 190385

Proteins

Proteins are made up of amino acids that are linked together into a polypeptide chain that folds into a particular structure. The peptide connections are the result of condensation reactions. A condensation reaction results in a loss of water when two molecules are joined together.

Proteins have four levels of structure: primary, secondary, tertiary, and quaternary. **Primary structure** is the amino acid sequence. **Secondary structure** consists of sub-structures called alpha helices and beta sheets. These structures are formed by hydrogen bonding between polar groups in the protein background and may be stabilized by the side chains. Examples of secondary structure are alpha helices and beta sheets. **Tertiary structure** is the interaction between different elements of secondary structure to form a folded geometric shape. **Quaternary structure** is the interaction of one or more folded polypeptide chains to form a multi-subunit protein.

Review Video: Proteins
Visit mometrix.com/academy and enter code: 903713

Chemiosmosis and Enzymes

Chemiosmosis is a process by which energy is made available for ADP to form ATP. When electrons move down the electron transport chain, the energy pumps protons to one side of a membrane. The equilibrium is disrupted at this point because the concentration gradient where the protons have gathered is greater than the concentration gradient on the other side of the membrane. The protons diffuse through the membrane as a result. The energy of this process fuels **phosphorylation**.

Enzymes act as catalysts by lowering the activation energy necessary for a reaction. They are **proteins**, have specific functions, are often globular and 3-D in form, and have names that end in "-ase." An enzyme has an active site where a substrate attaches and products are formed and released. Most enzymes also need a non-protein **coenzyme** that attaches to the enzyme to form the active site.

Enzymes act as catalysts by lowering the activation energy necessary for a reaction. An enzyme has an active site where a substrate attaches and products are formed and released. Most enzymes also need a non-protein coenzyme that attaches to the enzyme to form the active site.

Most enzymes are **proteins**. Examples of non-protein enzymes are ribozymes and the ribosome.

Lipids

Lipids are molecules that are hydrophobic or amphiphilic (having hydrophilic and hydrophobic properties) in nature. In this way, they are similar to hydrocarbons (substances consisting only of carbon and hydrogen). The major roles of lipids include energy storage and structural functions. Examples of these molecules include fats, triglycerides, steroids, and waxes. Lipids have numerous C-H bonds.

Fats are made of long chains of fatty acids (three fatty acids bound to a glycerol). **Fatty acids** are chains with reduced carbon at one end and a carboxylic acid group at the other. An example is soap, which contains the sodium salts of free fatty acids. **Phospholipids** are lipids that have a phosphate group rather than a fatty acid. **Glycerides** are another type of lipid. Examples of glycerides are fats and oils. Glycerides are formed from fatty acids and glycerol (a type of alcohol).

Unlike carbohydrates, amino acids, and nucleic acids, individual lipids will not covalently bond together to form long **polymers**. But the hydrophobic portions of phospholipids may sequester together to form lipid bilayers in cells.

Review Video: Lipids
Visit mometrix.com/academy and enter code: 269746

Catabolization of Macromolecules

- **Amino acids** are **catabolized** either during glycolysis or during the Krebs cycle. Processes used to break down amino acids include transamination, which is the transfer of NH_2 (amine), decarboxylation, which is the loss of -COOH groups, and dehydrogenation of H_2.
- **Sugars** like glucose from carbohydrates usually begin to be broken down by glycolysis at the beginning of the cycle, eventually going through the Krebs cycle and then the electron transport chain. **Proteins** are broken down into amino acids and have many different entry points into the Krebs cycle and electron transport chain.
- **Carbohydrates** are responsible for providing energy. They are involved in the metabolic energy cycles of photosynthesis and respiration. Structurally, carbohydrates usually take the form of some variation of CH_2O. In respiration, glucose is completely dismantled, but is only partially broken up during fermentation. **Lipids** get broken down into glycerol for glycolysis and fatty acids enter at the Krebs cycle.

Glycolysis

In **glycolysis**, glucose is converted into pyruvate and energy stored in ATP bonds is released. Glycolysis can involve various pathways. Various intermediates are produced that are used in other processes, and the **pyruvic acid** produced by glycolysis can be further used for respiration by the Krebs cycle or in fermentation. Glycolysis occurs in both aerobic and anaerobic organisms. Oxidation of molecules produces **reduced coenzymes**, such as NADH. The coenzymes relocate hydrogens to the electron transport chain. The proton is transported through the cell membrane and the electron is transported down the chain by proteins. At the end of the chain, **water** is formed when the final acceptor releases two electrons that combine with oxygen. The protons are pumped back into the cell or organelle by the ATP synthase enzyme, which uses energy produced to add a phosphate to ADP to form **ATP**. The proton motive force is produced by the protons being moved across the membrane.

Review Video: Glycolysis
Visit mometrix.com/academy and enter code: 466815

Intermediaries of Glycolysis

Glycolysis can involve different **metabolic pathways**. The following 10 steps are based on the **Embden-Meyerhof pathway**, in which glucose is the starting product and pyruvic acid is the final product. Two molecules of ATP and two of NADH are the products of this process. To start, enzymes utilize ATP to form glucose-6-phosphate. The glucose-6-phosphate is converted to fructose-6-phosphate. Another ATP molecule and an enzyme are used to convert fructose-6-phosphate to fructose-1,6-disphosphate. Both dihydroxyacetone phosphate (DHAP) and glyceraldehyde-3-phosphate are formed from fructose-1,6-bisphosphate. It is during the preceding reactions that energy is conserved or gained. NAD conversions to NADH molecules and phosphate influx result in 1,3-diphosphoglceric acid. Then, two ADP molecules are phosphorylated to become ATP molecules, resulting in 3-phosphoglyceric acid, which forms into 2-phosphoglyceric acid. At this point, water is produced as a product and phosphoenolpyruvic acid is formed. Another set of ADP molecules are phosphorylated into ATP molecules. **Pyruvic acid** is the end result.

Glycolic Pathways

Glycolysis is a general term for the conversion of glucose into pyruvate.

- **Embden-Meyerhof pathway**: This is a type of glycolysis in which one molecule of glucose becomes two ATP and two NADH molecules. Pyruvic acid (two pyruvate molecules) is the end product.
- **Entner-Doudoroff pathway**: This is a type of glycolysis in which one glucose molecule forms into one molecule of ATP and two of NADPH, which are used for other reactions. The end product is two pyruvate molecules.
- **Pentose Phosphate pathway**: Also known as the **hexose monophosphate shunt**, this is a type of glycolysis in which one glucose molecule produces one ATP and two NADPH molecules. Five carbon sugars are metabolized during this reaction. Glucose is broken down into ribose, ribulose, and xylose, which are used during glycolysis and during the **Calvin (or Calvin-Benson) cycle** to create nucleotides, nucleic acids, and amino acids.

Monosaccharides, Disaccharides, and Starches

The simple sugars can be grouped into monosaccharides (glucose, fructose, and sucrose) and disaccharides. These are all types of carbohydrates. **Monosaccharides** have one monomer of sugar and **disaccharides** have two. Monosaccharides have a carbon:hydrogen:oxygen ratio of 1:2:1. Aldose and ketose are monosaccharides with a carbonyl functional group (oxygen atom and carbon atom joined by a double bond). The difference between aldose and ketose is that the carbonyl group in aldose is connected at an end carbon and the carbonyl group in ketose is connected at a middle carbon. Glucose is a monosaccharide containing six carbons, making it a hexose and an aldose. A disaccharide is formed from two monosaccharides with a glycosidic link. Examples include two glucoses forming a maltose, a glucose and a galactose forming a lactose, and a glucose and a fructose forming a sucrose. A **starch** is a polysaccharide consisting only of glucose monomers. Examples are amylose, amylopectin, and glycogen.

Krebs Cycle

The **Krebs cycle** is also called the citric acid cycle or the tricarboxylic acid cycle (TCA). It is a **catabolic pathway** in which the bonds of glucose and occasionally fats or lipids are broken down and reformed into ATP. It is a respiration process that uses oxygen and produces carbon dioxide, water, and ATP. Cells require energy from ATP to synthesize proteins from amino acids and replicate DNA. The cycle is acetyl CoA, citric acid, isocitric acid, ketoglutaric acid (products are amino acids and CO_2), succinyl CoA, succinic acid, fumaric acid, malic acid, and oxaloacetic acid. One of the products of the Krebs cycle is NADH, which is then used in the electron chain transport system to manufacture ATP. From glycolysis, pyruvate is oxidized in a step linking to the Krebs cycle. After the Krebs cycle, NADH and succinate are oxidized in the electron transport chain.

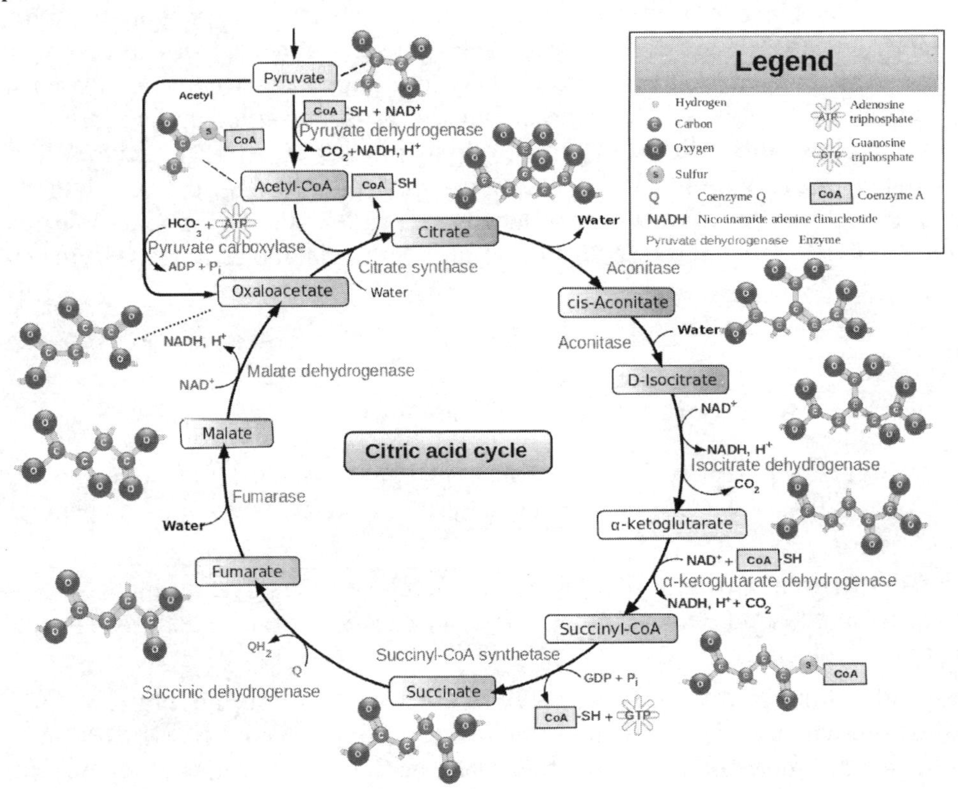

Electron Transport Chain

The **electron transport chain** is part of phosphorylation, whereby electrons are transported from enzyme to enzyme until they reach a final acceptor. The electron transport chain includes a series of oxidizing and reducing molecules involved in the release of energy. In **redox reactions**, electrons are removed from a substrate (oxidative) and H^+ (protons) can also be simultaneously removed. A substrate gains electrons during reduction. For example, when glucose is oxidized, electrons are lost and energy is released. There are enzymes in the membranes of mitochondria. The electrons are carried from one enzyme to another by a co-enzyme. Protons are also released to the other side of the membrane. For example, FAD and $FADH_2$ are used in oxidative phosphorylation. FAD is reduced to $FADH_2$. Electrons are stored there and then sent onward, and the $FADH_2$ becomes FAD again. In aerobic respiration, the final electron acceptor is O_2. In anaerobic respiration, it is something other than O_2.

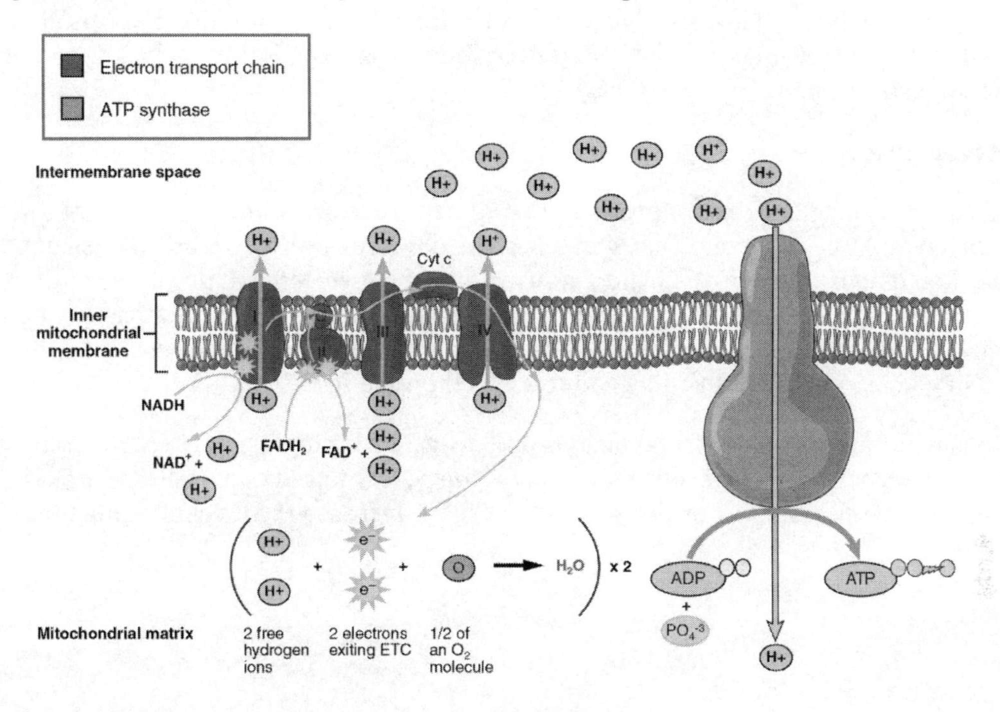

Fermentation

Fermentation is an anaerobic reaction in which glucose is only partially broken down. It releases energy through the oxidation of sugars or other types of organic molecules. Oxygen is sometimes involved, but not always. It is different from respiration in that it uses neither the Krebs cycle nor the electron transport chain and the final electron acceptor is an organic molecule. It uses **substrate-level phosphorylation** to form ATP. NAD^+ is reduced to NADH and NADH further reduces pyruvic acid to various end products. Fermentation can lead to excess waste products and is less efficient than aerobic respiration. **Homolactic fermentation** refers to lactic acid fermentation in which the sugars are converted to lactic acid only (there is one end product). In **heterolactic fermentation**, the sugars are converted to a range of products.

Examples of Fermentation

Lactic acid fermentation is the breakdown of glucose and six-carbon sugars into lactic acid to release energy. It is an anaerobic process, meaning that it does not require oxygen. It can occur in muscle cells and is also performed by streptococcus and lactobacillus bacteria. It can also be used to making yogurt and other food products.

Alcohol fermentation is the breakdown of glucose and six-carbon sugars into ethanol and carbon dioxide to release energy. It is an anaerobic process. It is performed by yeast and used in the production of alcoholic beverages.

Homeostasis and Feedback Loops

Homeostasis is the ability and tendency of an organism, cell, or body to adjust to environmental changes to maintain equilibrium. One way an organism can maintain homeostasis is through the release of **hormones**. Some hormones work in pairs. When a condition reaches an upper limit, a hormone is released to correct the condition. When a condition reaches the other end of the spectrum, another hormone is released. Hormones that work in this way are termed **antagonistic**. Insulin and glucagon are hormones that help regulate the level of glycogen in the blood. **Positive feedback loops** actually tend to destabilize systems by increasing changes. A **negative feedback loop** acts to make a system more stable by buffering changes.

Examples of Homeostasis

The hormones insulin and glucagon are involved in **negative feedback loops** in the liver's control of blood sugar levels. Alpha cells secrete glucagon when the concentration of blood glucose decreases. Glucagon is broken down and fatty acids and amino acids are converted to glucose. Once there is more glucose, glucagon secretion is reduced. Beta cells secrete insulin when the concentration of blood glucose increases. This leads to the liver absorbing glucose. Glucose is converted to glycogen, and fat and the concentration of glucose decrease. Insulin production is then reduced.

Hormones work in other ways aside from **antagonistically**. For example, follicle stimulating hormone (FSH) increases the production of estrogen. Once estrogen reaches a certain level, it suppresses FSH production. In some cases, a single hormone can increase or decrease the level of a substance.

Heredity and Evolution of Life

Theory of Evolution

Scientific evidence supporting the **theory of evolution** can be found in biogeography, comparative anatomy and embryology, the fossil record, and molecular evidence. **Biogeography** studies the geographical distribution of animals and plants. Evidence of evolution related to the area of biogeography includes species that are well suited for extreme environments. The **fossil record** shows that species lived only for a short time period before becoming extinct. The fossil record can also show the succession of plants and animals. Living fossils are existing species that have not changed much morphologically and are very similar to ancient examples in the fossil record. Examples include the horseshoe crab and ginkgo. **Comparative embryology** studies how species are similar in the embryonic stage, but become increasingly specialized and diverse as they age. Vestigial organs are those that still exist, but become nonfunctional. Examples include the hind limbs of whales and the wings of birds that can no longer fly, such as ostriches.

Rate of Evolution

The **rate of evolution** is affected by the variability of a population. **Variability** increases the likelihood of evolution. Variability in a population can be increased by mutations, immigration, sexual reproduction (as opposed to asexual reproduction), and size. Natural selection, emigration, and smaller populations can lead to decreased variability. **Sexual selection** affects evolution. If fewer genes are available, it will limit the number of genes passed on to subsequent generations. Some animal mating behaviors are not as successful as others. A male that does not attract a female because of a weak mating call or dull feathers, for example, will not pass on its genes.

Types of Evolution

Three types of evolution are divergent, convergent, and parallel. **Divergent evolution** refers to two species that become different over time. This can be caused by one of the species adapting to a different environment. **Convergent evolution** refers to two species that start out fairly different but evolve to share many similar traits. **Parallel evolution** refers to species that are not similar and do not become more or less similar over time. Mechanisms of evolution include descent (the passing on of genetic information), mutation, migration, natural selection, genetic variation, and genetic drift. The biological definition of **species** refers to a group of individuals that can mate and reproduce. Speciation refers to the evolution of a new biological species. The **biological species concept (BSC)** basically states that a species is a community of individuals that can reproduce and have a niche in nature.

Review Video: Organic Evolution
Visit mometrix.com/academy and enter code: 108959

Natural Selection, Gradualism, and Punctuated Equilibrium

Natural selection: This theory developed by Darwin states that traits that help give a species a survival advantage are passed on to subsequent generations. Members of a species that do not have the advantageous trait die before they reproduce. Darwin's four principles are:

- from generation to generation, there are various individuals within a species;
- genes determine variations;

- more individuals are born than survive to maturation; and
- specific genes enable an organism to better survive.

Gradualism: It is an idea that evolution proceeds at a steady pace and does not include sudden developments of new species or features from one generation to the next. This can be contrasted with punctuated equilibrium.

Punctuated equilibrium: This can be contrasted with gradualism. It is the idea in evolutionary biology that states that evolution involves long time periods of no change (stasis) accompanied by relatively brief periods (hundreds of thousands of years) of rapid change.

Types of Species Isolation

- **Spatial**: This refers to species that are separated by a distance that prevents them from mating.
- **Geographical**: This is when species are physically separated by a barrier. A barrier can divide a population, which is known as vicariance. If a population crosses a barrier to create two species, it is known as dispersal.
- **Habitat**: This refers to species that live in different habitats in the same area.
- **Temporal**: This refers to the fact that species reach sexual maturity at different times. An example is plants that flower at different times of the year.
- **Behavioral**: This refers to the fact that mating rituals distinguish interaction between sexes. For example, many species of crickets are morphologically (structurally) the same, yet a female of one species will only respond to the mating rituals of males within her species.
- **Mechanical**: This refers to physiological structural differences that prevent mating or the transfer of gametes.
- **Gametic isolation**: This refers to the fact that fertilization may not occur when gametes of different species are not compatible.

Allele Frequency

The **gene pool** refers to all alleles of a gene and their combinations. The **Hardy-Weinberg principle** (or Castle-Hardy Weinberg principle) postulates that the **allele frequency** for dominant and recessive alleles will remain the same in a population through successive generations if certain conditions exist. These conditions are: no mutations, large populations, random mating, no migration, and equal genotypes. Changes in the frequency and types of alleles in a gene pool can be caused by gene flow, random mutation, nonrandom mating, and genetic drift. In organisms that reproduce by sexual reproduction, **reproduction isolation** is defined as something that acts as a barrier to two species reproducing. These barriers are classified as prezygotic and postzygotic.

Random Mutations, Nonrandom Mating, and Gene Migration

- **Random mutations**: These are genetic changes caused by DNA errors or environmental factors such as chemicals and radiation. Mutations can be beneficial or harmful.
- **Nonrandom mating**: This refers to the fact that the probability of two individuals mating in a population is not the same for all pairs. Nonrandom mating can be caused by geographical isolation, small populations, and other factors. Nonrandom mating can lead to inbreeding (mating with a relative), which can lead to a decline in physical fitness as seen in a phenotype and the reduction of allele frequency and occurrence.

- **Gene migration**: Also known as gene flow, gene migration is the movement of alleles to another population. This can occur through immigration, when individuals of a species move into an area, or through emigration, when individuals of a species move out of an area.

Common Genetic Disorders

- **Cystic fibrosis**: recessive genetic disorder resulting in respiratory disorders
- **Huntington's disease**: autosomal dominant disorder resulting in the degeneration of nerve cells
- **Down syndrome**: caused by an extra copy of chromosome 21
- **Sickle cell anemia**: recessive genetic disorder resulting in deformed blood cells that can cause respiratory and circulation issues
- **Color blindness**: an X-linked recessive inheritance. Because it is X-linked recessive, it is more common in males than females.

Postzygotic Barriers to Reproduction

- **Hybrid viability**: This is when a hybrid zygote does not reach maturity.
- **Hybrid sterility**: This is also known as hybrid infertility. It occurs when two species produce a hybrid offspring that reaches maturity, but is sterile. An example of this is the mule. Mules are the result of a horse and a donkey mating. Mules, however, can not reproduce.
- **Hybrid breakdown**: This is when the first generation is not only viable, but also reaches maturity and can reproduce. Subsequent generations, however, are neither viable nor fertile.
- **Hybrid zygote abnormality**: This is when two species produce a zygote that does not survive to birth or germination, does not develop normally or reach sexual maturity, and cannot reproduce.
- **Allopatric speciation**: This refers to speciation that occurs because of geographical factors, such as physical barriers or dispersal.
- **Sympatric speciation**: This refers to speciation that happens within parent populations.
- **Parapatric speciation**: This refers to speciation that occurs because of an extreme change in habitat.

Bottleneck and Adaptive Radiation

Bottleneck: This occurs when a small percentage of a population survives a disaster or when the size of a population is greatly reduced for at least one generation. It results in reduced **allele diversity** and can even lead to entire alleles being eliminated in a species. This can lead to an increased inability to adapt to certain environmental factors. An example of a bottleneck is that hunting by humans reduced the northern elephant seal population to 20 individuals. Their population is now about 30,000, but the population's genes are much less varied than the genes of the southern elephant seal population. Another example is that a typhoon killed all but 30 people on an island in the South Pacific. One of the survivors had the recessive gene for color blindness. Currently, about 10% of the current population of 2,000 is color blind.

Adaptive radiation: This refers to the fact that speciation occurs through adapting to an environment through natural selection. It also refers to the fact that a species has a common ancestor.

Genetic Drift and Founder's Effect

Genetic drift: Easily observable in small populations, genetic drift is a change in the frequency of an allele.

Founder's effect: This occurs when a small population breaks away from a larger population and forms a smaller and isolated population. The resulting reduction in allele diversity leads to a greater expression of certain genetic traits than would be observed in a larger population. An example is the Amish in America, who are the descendants of 30 Swiss founders. The Amish are isolated by culture and breed within their population. One of the founders had Ellis-van Creveld syndrome. It is rare in larger populations, but is found at a rate of about 1 in 200 in the Amish community. It results in short stature, extra fingers and toes, and heart defects.

Abiotic Synthesis and Endosymbiotic Theory

The Earth's age is estimated to be 4.5 billion years.

Abiotic synthesis: This is related to the commonly accepted theory that life originated from inorganic matter. It refers to the making of organic molecules outside of a living body, and is believed to have been the first step in the development of life on Earth. The theory was tested by **Stanley Miller**. He combined the inorganic molecules water, hydrogen, methane, and ammonia in a closed, sterile flask and applied an electric discharge. His ingredients started as a clear mixture. After a week, he had a cloudy soup that contained amino acids and organic compounds.

Endosymbiotic theory: This is the belief that **eukaryotes** (cells with nuclei) developed from **prokaryotic cells** (those without nuclei). The theory is that chloroplasts in plant cells and mitochondria in animal cells evolved from smaller prokaryotes living within larger prokaryotes.

Molecular Oxygen

When the Earth was formed, the atmosphere did not contain **oxygen**. It is thought to have appeared in the **Paleoproterozoic era** about 2.5 to 1.6 billion years ago. First, oxygen combined with iron in oceans to form banded iron formations (thin layers of iron oxides and layers of iron poor rock). After that, oxygen began to "gas out" of the oceans slowly. One of the major events in Earth's geologic history is the **great oxygen event**, or oxygen catastrophe, during which large amounts of oxygen led to the extinction of **anaerobic organisms**. This, in turn, led to an increased number of **aerobic organisms**. Eventually, it also resulted in the development of eukaryotic cells and more complex life forms.

Origin of Life on Earth

One theory of how life originated on Earth is that life developed from nonliving materials. The first stage of this transformation happened when **abiotic (nonliving) synthesis** took place, which is the formation of **monomers** like amino acids and nucleotides. Next, monomers joined together to create **polymers** such as proteins and nucleic acids. These polymers are then believed to have formed into protobionts. The last stage was the development of the process of **heredity**. Supporters of this theory believe that RNA was the first genetic material. Another theory postulates that hereditary systems came about before the origination of nucleic acids. Another theory is that life, or the precursors for it, were transported to Earth from a meteorite or other object from space. There is no real evidence to support this theory.

Nucleotides

A **nucleotide**, whether DNA or RNA, contains three components: a phosphate group, a ringed, five-carbon sugar (deoxyribose in DNA, ribose in RNA), and a nitrogenous base. The **phosphate group** binds to one side of the **ringed, five-carbon sugar**. The **nitrogenous base** binds to the opposite side of the ringed, five-carbon sugar.

The five bases in DNA and RNA can be categorized as either pyrimidine or purine according to their structure. The **pyrimidine bases** include cytosine (C), thymine (T), and uracil (U). They are six-sided and have a single ring shape. The **purine bases** are adenine (A) and guanine (G), which consist of two attached rings.

DNA contains the bases A, T, C, and G. **RNA** contains the bases A, U, C, and G. In forming higher-order nucleotide structures, A pairs with T or U and C pairs with G.

Review Video: Nucleic Acids
Visit mometrix.com/academy and enter code: 503931

Review Video: DNA
Visit mometrix.com/academy and enter code: 639552

Nucleosides

A **nucleoside** is a nitrogenous base bound only to a sugar (no phosphate group). When combined with a sugar, any of the five bases in DNA and RNA become nucleosides. Nucleosides formed from **purine bases** end in "osine" and those formed from **pyrimidine bases** end in "idine." Adenosine and thymidine are examples of nucleosides.

Oligonucleotides

An **oligonucleotide** of DNA or RNA is formed by linking the phosphate groups of individual nucleotides. The nitrogenous bases in one strand can hydrogen bond with nitrogenous bases in the same oligonucleotide to form single-stranded structures. Alternatively, the bases in one strand can hydrogen bond with bases in a different strand to form double-stranded structures.

DNA Structure and Replication

DNA has a right-handed, double-helix shape, resembles a twisted ladder, and is compact. It consists of **nucleotides**. Nucleotides consist of a five-carbon sugar (pentose), a phosphate group, and a nitrogenous base. Two bases pair up to form the rungs of the ladder. The "side rails" or backbone consists of the covalently bonded sugar and phosphate. The bases are attached to each other with hydrogen bonds, which are easily dismantled so replication can occur. Each base is attached to a phosphate and to a sugar. There are four types of **nitrogenous bases**: adenine (A), guanine (G), cytosine (C), and thymine (T). There are about 3 billion bases in human DNA. The bases are mostly the same in everybody, but their order is different. It is the order of these bases that creates diversity in people. Adenine (A) pairs with thymine (T), and cytosine (C) pairs with guanine (G).

Pairs of chromosomes are composed of DNA, which is tightly wound to conserve space. When **replication** starts, it unwinds. The steps in DNA replication are controlled by **enzymes**. The enzyme helicase instigates the deforming of hydrogen bonds between the bases to split the two strands. The splitting starts at the A-T bases (adenine and thymine) as there are only two hydrogen bonds. The cytosine-guanine base pair has three bonds. The term "**origin of replication**" is used to refer to where the splitting starts. The portion of the DNA that is unwound to be replicated is called the replication fork. Each strand of DNA is transcribed by an mRNA. It copies the DNA onto itself, base by base, in a complementary manner. The exception is that uracil replaces thymine.

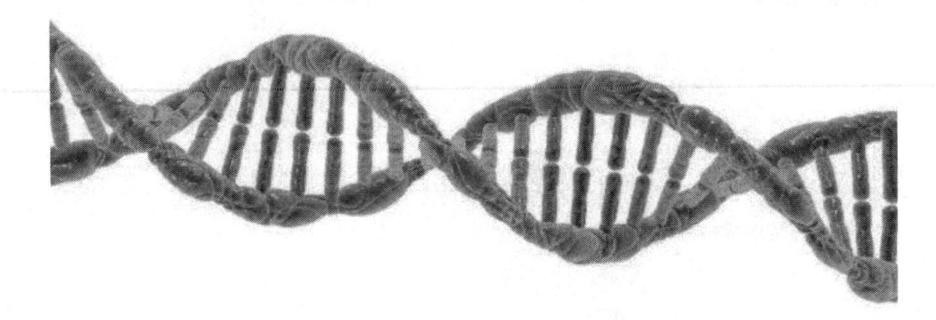

Types of DNA Replication

- **Semiconservative**: DNA replication is considered semiconservative because the two replicated copies of DNA each have one strand of the original parent DNA, or half of the original genetic material.
- **Antiparallel replication**: This refers to the fact that during DNA replication, the nucleotides (A, C, G, T, and U) on leading and lagging strands run in opposite directions. RNA synthesis is said to occur in a $5' \rightarrow 3'$ (five prime to three prime) direction. That means that the phosphate group of the nucleotide that is being added to the chain, which is 5′, is attached to the end of the chain at the end of a hydroxyl group, which is 3′.
- **Base pairing**: This explains how RNA transcribes DNA in an inverted fashion. C on DNA is inserted as a G on RNA, and A on DNA becomes U on RNA.

Function of Proteins in DNA Replication

Many **proteins** are involved in the replication of DNA, and each has a specific function. Helicase is a protein that facilitates the unwinding of the double helix structure of DNA. Single-strand binding (SSB) proteins attach themselves to each strand to prevent the DNA strands from joining back together. After DNA is unwound, there are leading and lagging strands. The **leading strand** is synthesized continuously and the **lagging strand** is synthesized in short fragments that are referred to as Okazaki fragments. Primase, an RNA polymerase (catalyzing enzyme), acts as a starting point for replication by forming short strands, or primers, of RNA. The DNA clamp, or sliding clamp, helps prevent DNA polymerase from coming apart from the strand. DNA polymerase helps form the DNA strand by linking nucleotides. As the process progresses, RNase H removes the primers. DNA ligase then links the existing shorter strands into a longer strand.

Types of RNA

Types of RNA include ribosomal RNA (rRNA), transfer RNA (tRNA), and messenger RNA (mRNA).

- **rRNA**: forms the RNA component of the ribosome. It is evolutionarily conserved, which means it can be used to study relationships in organisms.
- **mRNA**: used by the ribosome to generate proteins (translation). The mRNA contains a series of three-nucleotide "codons" that code for the amino acids in a protein sequence.
- **tRNA**: functions in translation by carrying an amino acid to the corresponding codon on the mRNA strand.

Review Video: RNA
Visit mometrix.com/academy and enter code: 888852

Differences between RNA and DNA

RNA and DNA differ in terms of structure and function. **RNA** contains ribose sugars, while **DNA** contains deoxyribose sugars. Uracil is found only in RNA and thymine in found only in DNA. RNA supports the functions carried out by DNA. It aids in gene expression, replication, and transportation.

Codons

Codons are groups of three nucleotides on the messenger RNA. A codon has the code for a single amino acid. There are 64 codons but 20 amino acids. More than one combination, or triplet, can be used to synthesize the necessary amino acids. For example, AAA (adenine-adenine-adenine) or AAG (adenine-adenine-guanine) can serve as codons for lysine. These groups of three occur in strings and might be thought of as frames. For example, AAAUCUUCGU, if read in groups of three from the beginning, would be AAA, UCU, UCG. If the same sequence was read in groups of three starting from the second position, the groups would be AAU, CUU, and so on. The resulting protein sequences would be completely different. For this reason, there are **start and stop codons** that indicate the beginning and ending of a sequence (or frame). AUG (methionine) is the start codon. UAA, UGA, and UAG are stop codons.

Mutations

Gene disorders are the result of **DNA mutations**. DNA mutations lead to unfavorable gene disorders, but also provide genetic variability. This diversity can lead to increased survivability of a species. Mutations can be neutral, beneficial, or harmful. Mutations can be hereditary, meaning they are passed from parent to child. **Polymorphism** refers to differences in humans, such as eye and hair color, that may have originally been the result of gene mutations but are now part of the normal variation of the species. Mutations can be **de novo**, meaning they happen either only in sex cells or shortly after fertilization. They can also be **acquired**, or somatic. These are the kinds that happen as a result of environmental factors or replication errors. **Mosaicism** is when a mutation happens in a cell during an early embryonic stage. The result is that some cells will have the mutation and some will not.

DNA-Level Mutations

A **DNA mutation** occurs when the normal gene sequence is altered. Mutations can happen when DNA is damaged as a result of environmental factors, such as chemicals, radiation, or ultraviolet rays from the sun. It can also happen when errors are made during DNA replication. The phosphate-sugar side rail of DNA can be damaged if the bonds between oxygen and phosphate groups are broken. **Translocation** happens when the broken bonds attempt to bond with other DNA. This repair can cause a mutation. The nucleotide itself can be altered. A cytosine, for example, might look like a thymine. During replication, the damaged cytosine is replicated as a thymine and paired with a guanine.

Translation and tRNA Molecules

A tRNA molecule contains a three-nucleotide anticodon region that is complimentary to the mRNA codons. For example, a codon that is AAA on the mRNA would be associated with the anticodon UUU on the tRNA. Each tRNA molecule is bound to the amino acid specified by its anticodon.

The **ribosome** has three tRNA binding sites—A, P, and E. Translation initiates when the ***A-site*** becomes occupied by the tRNA molecule corresponding to the mRNA start codon. The ribosome then moves the first tRNA from the *A-site* to the ***P-site***. The *A-site* is then occupied by the tRNA molecule corresponding to the second mRNA codon. The ribosome then transfers the amino acid on the *P-site* tRNA to the amino acid on the *A-site* tRNA. The first tRNA, which now has no amino acid, is moved from the *P-site* the ***E-site***. The second tRNA, complexed to a chain of two amino acids, is moved from the *A-site* to the *P-site*. The *A-site* is then occupied by the tRNA corresponding to the third mRNA codon. The *P-site* amino acid chain is transferred to the amino acid bound to the *A-site* tRNA. The first tRNA then exits from the *E-site* and the second and third tRNA molecules shift, opening the *A-site* for the next tRNA. The growing amino acid chain continues to be transferred from the *P-site* to the *A-site* until translation is complete.

Translocation

Translocation is a genetic mutation in which one piece of a chromosome is transferred to another chromosome. Burkitt's lymphoma, chronic myelogenous leukemia, and Down syndrome are all examples. Trisomy 21, or Down syndrome, occurs when a copy of chromosome 21 attaches to chromosome 14. Most Down syndrome cases are caused by a pair of chromosomes (the 21st) that does not split during meiosis. Both divided cells will have an abnormal number of chromosomes. One will have 22 and the other will have 24. When this egg gets fertilized, it will have three copies of chromosome 21 instead of two. Down syndrome can also be caused by translocation between the 14th and 21st chromosomes. In these instances, genetic material is swapped. There are 200 to 250 genes on the 21st chromosome. The overexpression of the gene results in the following Down syndrome traits: premature aging, decreased immune system function, heart defects, skeletal abnormalities, disruption of DNA synthesis and repair, intellectual disabilities, and cataracts.

Mendel's Laws

Mendel's laws are the law of segregation (first law) and the law of independent assortment (second law). The **law of segregation** states that there are two alleles and that half of the total number of alleles are contributed by each parent organism. The **law of independent assortment** states that traits are passed on randomly and are not influenced by other traits. The exception to this is linked traits. A **Punnett square** can illustrate how alleles combine from the contributing genes to form various phenotypes. One set of a parent's genes are put in columns, while the genes from the other parent are placed in rows. The allele combinations are shown in each cell. When two different alleles are present in a pair, the dominant one is expressed. A Punnett square can be used to predict the outcome of crosses.

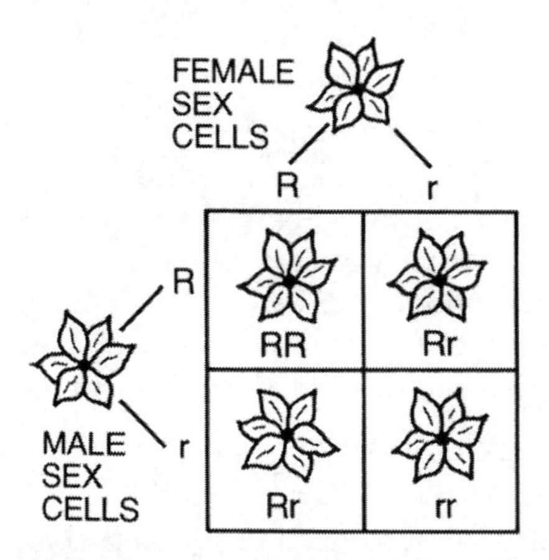

Review Video: Gene & Alleles
Visit mometrix.com/academy and enter code: 363997

Review Video: Punnett Square
Visit mometrix.com/academy and enter code: 853855

Gene, Genotype, Phenotype, and Allele

A **gene** is a portion of DNA that identifies how traits are expressed and passed on in an organism. A gene is part of the genetic code. Collectively, all genes form the **genotype** of an individual. The genotype includes genes that may not be expressed, such as recessive genes. The **phenotype** is the physical, visual manifestation of genes. It is determined by the basic genetic information and how genes have been affected by their environment.

An **allele** is a variation of a gene. Also known as a trait, it determines the manifestation of a gene. This manifestation results in a specific physical appearance of some facet of an organism, such as eye color or height. The genetic information for eye color is a gene. The gene variations responsible for blue, green, brown, or black eyes are called alleles. **Locus** (pl. loci) refers to the location of a gene or alleles.

Dominant and Recessive Genes

Gene traits are represented in pairs with an uppercase letter for the **dominant trait** (A) and a lowercase letter for the **recessive trait** (a). Genes occur in pairs (AA, Aa, or aa). There is one gene on each chromosome half supplied by each parent organism. Since half the genetic material is from each parent, the offspring's traits are represented as a combination of these. A dominant trait only requires one gene of a gene pair for it to be expressed in a phenotype, whereas a recessive requires both genes in order to be manifested. For example, if the mother's genotype is Dd and the father's is dd, the possible combinations are Dd and dd. The dominant trait will be manifested if the genotype is DD or Dd. The recessive trait will be manifested if the genotype is dd. Both DD and dd are **homozygous** pairs. Dd is **heterozygous**.

Monohybrid and Hybrid Crosses

Genetic crosses are the possible combinations of alleles, and can be represented using Punnett squares. A **monohybrid cross** refers to a cross involving only one trait. Typically, the ratio is 3:1 (DD, Dd, Dd, dd), which is the ratio of dominant gene manifestation to recessive gene manifestation. This ratio occurs when both parents have a pair of dominant and recessive genes. If one parent has a pair of dominant genes (DD) and the other has a pair of recessive (dd) genes, the recessive trait cannot be expressed in the next generation because the resulting crosses all have the Dd genotype. A **dihybrid cross** refers to one involving more than one trait, which means more combinations are possible. The ratio of genotypes for a dihybrid cross is 9:3:3:1 when the traits are not linked. The ratio for incomplete dominance is 1:2:1, which corresponds to dominant, mixed, and recessive phenotypes.

Non-Mendelian Concepts

- **Co-dominance** refers to the expression of both alleles so that both traits are shown. The ABO human blood typing system is an example of a co-dominance.
- **Incomplete dominance** is when both the dominant and recessive genes are expressed, resulting in a phenotype that is a mixture of the two. The fact that snapdragons can be red, white, or pink is a good example. The dominant red gene (RR) results in a red flower because of large amounts of red pigment. White (rr) occurs because both genes call for no pigment. Pink (Rr) occurs because one gene is for red and one is for no pigment. The colors blend to produce pink flowers. A cross of pink flowers (Rr) can result in red (RR), white (rr), or pink (Rr) flowers.

- **Complete dominance** refers to the situation in which a homozygous pair of dominant alleles (AA) and a heterozygous pair of alleles (Aa) result in the same phenotype. Dominant genes have the following characteristics: they are expressed in each generation; they are passed on to roughly half the offspring; and a parent that does not express the trait cannot pass it on to offspring. The Mendelian complete dominance concept states that one gene consisting of two alleles is the only factor involved in the creation of a phenotype. Most traits, however, are more complex.
- **Polygenic inheritance**: This goes beyond the simplistic Mendelian concept that one gene influences one trait. It refers to traits that are influenced by more than one gene, and takes into account environmental influences on development.
- **Multiple alleles**: Only two alleles make up a gene, but when there are three or more possible alleles, it is known as a multiple allele. A gene where only two alleles are possible is termed **polymorphic**.

Crossing Over, Gametes, Pedigree Analysis, and Probability Analysis

- **Crossing over**: This refers to the swapping of genetic material between homologous chromosomes. This leads to different combinations of genes showing up in a phenotype. This is part of gene recombination, which is when genes are reassembled.
- **Gametes**: These are cells that fuse with one another during sexual reproduction. Each gamete contains half the genetic information of the parent. They are haploid (having 23 chromosome pairs in humans). The resulting zygote, which is formed when the two gametes become one cell, is **diploid** (46 chromosome pairs in humans).
- **Pedigree analysis**: This involves isolating a trait in an organism and tracing its manifestation. Pedigree charts are often used for this type of analysis. A family pedigree shows how a trait can be seen throughout generations.
- **Probability analysis**: This calculates the chances of a particular trait or combination of traits being expressed in an organism.

Genetic Linkage

Genetic linkage is the tendency for genes that are close to one another to be inherited together. Linkage is the exception to independent assortment. **Sex-linked traits** are those that occur on a sex chromosome. **Autosomal** refers to non-sex chromosomes. In humans, there are 22 autosomal pairs of chromosomes and a pair of sex chromosomes. Depending on the sex, pairs are either XX (female) or XY (male). Since females don't have Y chromosomes, alleles on this gene are only manifested in males. Males can only pass on sex-linked traits on the X chromosome to their daughters since sons would not receive an X from them. **Hemizygous** means there is only one copy of a gene. Color blindness occurs more in males than females because it is a sex-linked trait on the X chromosome. Since it is recessive, females have a better chance of expressing the dominant characteristic of non-color blindness.

Lethal Alleles, Pleiotropy, Epistasis, and Karyotype

- **Lethal allele**: This is when a mutation in an essential gene results in the death of the organism. Cystic fibrosis and Tay-Sachs disease are examples of lethal recessive alleles.
- **Pleiotropy**: This refers to a gene that affects more than one trait.
- **Epistasis**: This refers to the situation in which two or more genes determine a single phenotype.
- **Karyotype**: This is a picture of genes based on a sample of blood or skin.

The non-Mendelian concept of **polygenetic inheritance** takes into account how environmental factors affect phenotypes. For example, an individual inherits genes that help determine height, but a diet lacking in certain nutrients could limit that individual's ability to reach that height. Another example is the concept of genetic disposition, which is a propensity for a certain disease that is genetically inherited, but not necessarily manifested. For example, individuals with certain skin types are more likely to develop skin cancer. If they limit their exposure to solar radiation, however, this will not necessarily occur.

Genetic Engineering, Cloning, Restriction Enzymes, And Vectors

- **Genetic engineering**: This refers to changing or manipulating an organism's genes. Other terms that may be used to refer to genetic engineering are recombinant DNA, gene splicing, cloning, and genetic modification or manipulation. Genetic engineering is different from **indirect gene manipulation**, in which breeding is controlled based on observable phenotypes. Genetic engineering refers to altering the genes themselves.
- **Cloning**: There are two definitions for cloning. The first refers to the **natural cloning** that occurs in nature when organisms reproduce asexually and make exact copies of them. This can happen in bacteria, plants, birds, and other organisms. The definition heard more in popular culture refers to cloning as the **genetic engineering** of portions of DNA, cells, or entire organisms.
- **Restriction enzymes**: These are proteins that can recognize portions of DNA strands and cleave them at certain points.
- **Vectors**: Vectors deliver DNA to a cell, and can include viruses and bacterial plasmids.

Types of Blood Cells

There are three types of blood cells: red blood cells, white blood cells, and platelets. **Red blood cells** are the most common. They are responsible for the transportation of oxygen and the removal of carbon dioxide through a mechanism involving the molecule hemoglobin. **White blood cells** are involved in the immune response. **Platelets** are small, irregularly-shaped cells involved in blood clotting.

Blood types

There are four possible **blood types**: A, B, AB, and O. These types are produced by combinations of the three **alleles**. AA and AO lead to type A blood. BB and BO lead to type B blood. AB leads to type AB blood because the alleles are co-dominant. AB has both A antigens and B antigens. The O allele is recessive. OO leads to blood type O, which lacks proteins and blood-surface antigens. Blood donors with an O blood type are known as universal donors because they do not have the type of antigens that can trigger immune system responses. Blood donors with type AB blood are known as universal recipients because they do not have the antibodies that will attack A and B antigen molecules. If parents have AB and O blood, offspring have a 50% chance of having type A blood and a 0% chance of having type O blood.

Antigens trigger a response in the immune system to help repel foreign substances. Matching blood types during medical procedures is important since the human immune system can detect and attack blood that is a different type. Specific blood types are used in transfusions, and blood types are determined based on the **proteins** (or lack of proteins) contained in the blood.

Applications of Genetic Engineering

Diagnostic and medical applications of genetic engineering include treating diabetes with insulin, producing human proteins, treating hemophilia, anemia, and blood clots, and manufacturing hepatitis B vaccine. Gene therapy has been used to replace defective alleles with normal alleles. For example, if a patient has a condition caused by an enzyme deficiency, replacing the defective allele enables the person to produce that enzyme. **Medical forensic applications** involving DNA analysis include using it to identify individuals and solve criminal cases. **Agricultural applications** include crop modification to develop types of wheat, cotton, and soybeans that resist weed controlling herbicides. Plants can be altered to make them grow bigger or vaccinated to make them resistant to plant viruses and insects.

Recombinant DNA and Gene Splicing

Recombinant DNA (rDNA) refers to manipulating sequences of DNA. One portion of DNA is removed and replaced with another. **Gene splicing** is a way to recombine DNA. In gene splicing, base pairs of DNA are chemically cleaved. **Restriction enzymes** are used to perform the cutting part of gene splicing. Once base pairs are separated, different additional genetic information can be added by a vector. **DNA ligase** (an enzyme) is used to put the pieces back together. The process of DNA recombination happens naturally and incrementally as a result of evolution. Use of recombinant DNA produced through genetic engineering has been used in medical and agricultural applications.

Human Genome Project

The **human genome project** was an international effort by scientists in 18 countries that was undertaken to gain information about human DNA. The project set out to identify all of the genes in human DNA. Other goals included: determining the sequences of the three billion base pairs comprising human DNA, inputting information collected into databases, producing tools for data analysis and making them available, and opening a discussion about the ethical, legal, and social implications of obtaining such in-depth knowledge about the genetic makeup of humans. The completed mapping and sequencing is expected to lead to further research in the fields of molecular medicine and DNA forensics. It is also expected to spur on research in related fields, such as energy source development, bioarcheology, human migration and evolution, agriculture improvement and production, livestock breeding, and bioprocessing.

Contributors to the Theory of Evolution

Georges Cuvier (1744-1829)

Cuvier was a French naturalist who used the fossil record (paleontology) to compare the anatomies of extinct species and existing species to make conclusions about extinction. He believed in the catastrophism theory more strongly than the theory of evolution.

Jean-Baptise Lamarck (1769-1832)

Lamarck was a French naturalist who believed in the idea of evolution and thought it was a natural occurrence influenced by the environment. Lamarck put forth a theory of evolution by inheritance of acquired characteristics. He theorized that organisms became more complex by moving up a ladder of progress.

Charles Robert Darwin (1809-1882)

Darwin was an English naturalist known for his belief that evolution occurred by natural selection. He believed that species descend from common ancestors.

Alfred Russell Wallace (1823-1913)

He was a British naturalist who independently developed a theory of evolution by natural selection. He believed in the transmutation of species (that one species develops into another).

Contributing Individuals to the Structure of DNA

James Watson and Francis Crick (1952)

Formulated the double-helix model of DNA and speculated about its importance in carrying and transferring genetic information.

Rosalind Franklin (1952)

Took the x-ray diffraction image that was used by James Watson and Francis Crick to develop their double-helix model of DNA.

Diversity of Life

Five-kingdom Classification System

The groupings in the **five-kingdom classification system** are kingdom, phylum/division, class, order, family, genus, and species. A memory aid for this is: King Phillip Came Over For Good Soup. The five **kingdoms** are Monera, Protista, Fungi, Plantae, and Animalia. The kingdom is the top-level classification in this system. Below that are the following groupings: phylum, class, order, family, genus, and species. The **Monera kingdom** includes about 10,000 known species of prokaryotes, such as bacteria and cyanobacteria. Members of this kingdom can be unicellular organisms or colonies. The next four kingdoms consist of **eukaryotes**. The **Protista kingdom** includes about 250,000 species of unicellular protozoans and unicellular and multicellular algae. The **Fungi kingdom** includes about 100,000 species. A recently introduced system of classification includes a three-domain grouping above kingdom. The domain groupings are Archaea, Bacteria (which both consist of prokaryotes), and Eukarya, which include eukaryotes. According to the five-kingdom classification system, humans are: kingdom Animalia, phylum Chordata, subphylum Vertebrata, class Mammalia, order Primate, family Hominidae, genus Homo, and species Sapiens.

Review Video: Kingdom Animalia
Visit mometrix.com/academy and enter code: 558413

Protista Kingdom

Organisms in the **Protista kingdom** are classified according to their methods of locomotion, their methods of reproduction, and how they get their nutrients. **Protists** can move by the use of a flagellum, cilia, or pseudopod. Flagellates have flagellum, which are long tails or whip-like structures that are rotated to help the protist move. **Ciliates** use cilia, which are smaller hair-like structures on the exterior of a cell that wiggle to help move the surrounding matter. **Amoeboids** use pseudopodia to move. **Bacteria** reproduce either sexually or asexually. Binary fission is a form of asexual reproduction whereby bacteria divide in half to produce two new organisms that are clones of the parent. In sexual reproduction, genetic material is exchanged. When kingdom members are categorized according to how they obtain nutrients, the three types of protists are photosynthetic, consumers, and saprophytes. **Photosynthetic protists** convert sunlight into energy. Organisms that use photosynthesis are considered producers. **Consumers**, also known as heterotrophs, eat or consume other organisms. **Saprophytes** consume dead or decaying substances.

Fungi Kingdom

Mycology is the study of fungi.

The **Fungi kingdom** includes about 100,000 species. They are further delineated as mushrooms, yeasts, molds, rusts, mildews, stinkhorns, puffballs, and truffles. Fungi are characterized by cell walls that have **chitin**, a long polymer of carbohydrate. Fungi are different from species in the Plant kingdom, which have cell walls consisting of cellulose. Fungi are thought to have evolved from a single ancestor. Although they are often thought of as a type of plant, they are more similar to animals than plants. Fungi are typically small and numerous, and have a diverse morphology among species.

Organisms and Microbes

An **organism** is a living thing. A **unicellular organism** is an organism that has only one cell. Examples of unicellular organisms are bacteria and paramecium. A **multicellular organism** is one that consists of many cells.

The term **microbe** refers to small organisms that are only visible through a microscope. Examples include viruses, bacteria, fungi, and protozoa. Microbes are also referred to as **microorganisms**, and it is these that are studied by microbiologists. **Bacteria** can be rod shaped, round (cocci), or spiral (spirilla). These shapes are used to differentiate among types of bacteria. Bacteria can be identified by staining them. This particular type of stain is called a **gram stain**. If bacteria are gram-positive, they absorb the stain and become purple. If bacteria are gram-negative, they do not absorb the stain and become a pinkish color.

Viruses

Viruses are microorganisms that replicate in the cells of other organisms, including plants, animals, bacteria, and other microorganisms. Viruses can be transmitted to other organisms in a number of ways, such as by insects, by air, and through direct contact. All viruses have a head. Some also have a tail consisting of protein. The tail is used to attach to a host cell and enter it. This is one way in which viruses introduce their genetic material to the host. The head of a virus, also called a protein capsid, contains **genetic material** in the form of DNA, RNA, or enzymes. The adenovirus and the herpes virus are both DNA viruses. The HIV retrovirus, influenza, and the rotavirus are RNA viruses. The number of virus types is thought to be in the millions. **Virology** is a branch of microbiology that is devoted to the study of viruses.

Review Video: Viruses
Visit mometrix.com/academy and enter code: 984455

Some scientists do not consider viruses to belong to any of the five kingdoms or to be living organisms for many reasons. Viruses do not meet the definition of a **cell**. They cannot be classified as eukaryotic or prokaryotic. They are generally smaller than and not as complex as living cells, which are the basic units of life. Viruses do not have nuclei. They are **macromolecules** consisting of long chains of genetic material (either RNA or DNA) encased in protein. Viruses also lack membrane-bound organelles, ribosomes, and cytoplasm, all of which are usually found in cells. Viruses do not perform the basic cell processes involved in the ADP/ATP cycle, and they are not capable of cellular respiration or gas exchange. They reproduce by gaining control of a host cell and making it replicate the viral DNA instead of its own.

Hormones

Hormones in animals regulate many processes, including growth, metabolism, reproduction, and fluid balance. The names of hormones tend to end in "-one." **Endocrine hormones** are proteins or steroids. **Steroid hormones** (anabolic steroids) help control the manufacture of protein in muscles and bones.

Pancreas: secretes insulin (promotes absorption of glucose) and glucagon (elevates glucose concentration in blood).

Pineal glands: secrete melatonin, which acts as a biological clock.

Pituitary gland: secretes growth hormone (stimulates tissue growth), thyroid stimulating hormone (signals the body to produce thyroxin), adrenocorticotropic hormone (signals the adrenal gland to produce cortisol), follicle-stimulating hormone (signals ovarian follicles to mature in females; helps regulate sperm cell production in males), luteinizing hormone (stimulates the production of estrogens and starts ovulation; stimulates production of testosterone), melanocyte-stimulating hormone (skin tone), and prolactin (stimulates milk let-down).

Thyroid: secretes thyroxine, triiodothyronine, and calcitonin. These are involved with brain development, reproductive tract functions, and metabolism regulation.

Thymus: secretes thymosin.

Nutritional Requirements

Carbohydrates are the primary source of energy as they can be easily converted to glucose.

Fats are needed to help process these vitamins and can also store energy. Fats have the highest calorie value per gram (9 calories).

Dietary **fiber**, or roughage, helps the excretory system. In humans, fiber can help regulate blood sugar levels, reduce heart disease, help food pass through the digestive system, and add bulk.

Dietary **minerals** are chemical elements that are involved with biochemical functions in the body.

Proteins consist of amino acids. Proteins are broken down in the body into amino acids that are used for protein biosynthesis or fuel.

Water is necessary to prevent dehydration since water is lost through the excretory system and perspiration.

Vitamins

Vitamins are compounds that are not made by the body, but obtained through the diet. Dietary vitamins can be classified as either water soluble or fat soluble. Vitamins A, D, E, and K are fat soluble. Vitamins C and B are water soluble.

- **Vitamin A** (retinol) can be found in milk, eggs, liver, and some vegetables and fruits. It plays a role in immune system function, cell growth, and eye function.
- **Vitamin B** refers to a wide class of molecules found in whole grains, potatoes, and bananas. All vitamin B molecules are enzyme cofactors or precursors to cofactors.
- **Vitamin C** (ascorbic acid) is in citrus fruits and peppers. It helps promote cell cohesiveness and healthy bones, teeth, and gums. It also improves brain function and aids in the absorption of some minerals.
- **Vitamin D** (calciferol) is found in salmon, tuna, mackerel, and fish liver oil. It promotes absorption of elements and strengthens bones.
- **Vitamin E** is found in nuts, seeds, and vegetable oils. It is an antioxidant and plays roles in enzyme catalysis.
- **Vitamin K** (phylloquinone) can be found in leafy green vegetables. It is involved in blood formation.

Dietary Elements

Dietary elements include calcium, chloride, iodine, iron, magnesium, phosphorus, potassium, and sodium.

- **Calcium** is in dairy products, nuts, and green leafy vegetables. It is involved in muscle function and bone structure.
- **Chloride** is found in salt. It is involved in cell homeostasis and neuron function.
- **Iodine** is in dairy products, eggs, and fish. It is a component of tyroid hormones.
- **Iron** is in green leafy vegetables and red meat. It is used by proteins (notably hemoglobin) and enzymes.
- **Magnesium** is in nuts and soy beans. It is involved in ATP synthesis.
- **Phosphorus** is found in protein-rich foods such as meat, nuts, and beans. It is a component of bones and nucleic acids.
- **Potassium** is involved with ATP synthesis and can be found in beans, bananas, and potatoes.
- **Sodium** is found in salt. It is involved in cell homeostasis and neuron function.

The dietary elements copper, manganese, molybdenum, selenium, and zinc are primarily involved in enzyme function. Dietary sources of these elements include the following:

	Nuts	**Whole grains**	**Beans**	**Shellfish**	**Red meat & poultry**
Copper	Yes	Yes	Yes	Yes	–
Manganese	Yes	Yes	–	–	–
Molybdenum	Yes	–	Yes	–	–
Selenium	Yes	–	–	Yes	Yes
Zinc	Yes	Yes	Yes	Yes	Yes

Reproductive Systems in Organisms

Based on whether or not and when an organism uses meiosis or mitosis, the three possible cycles of reproduction are haplontic, diplontic, and haplodiplontic. Fungi, green algae, and protozoa are **haplontic**. Animals and some brown algae and fungi are **diplontic**. Plants and some fungi are **haplodiplontic**. Diplontic organisms, like animals, have a dominant diploid life cycle. The haploid generation is simply the egg and sperm. Monoecious species are bisexual (**hermaphroditic**). In this case, the individual has both male and female organs: sperm-bearing testicles and egg-bearing ovaries. Hermaphroditic species can self-fertilize. Some worms are hermaphroditic. **Cross fertilization** is when individuals exchange genetic information. Most animal species are **dioecious**, meaning individuals are distinctly male or female.

Individuals of a species have specialized reproductive cells. These cells are responsible for **meiosis**, which typically results in motile spermatozoa in the male and non-motile, food-containing ova in the female. Before fertilization, the oocyte continues to develop in a follicle. In the female, human luteinizing hormone causes the follicle to break open and the oocyte to slowly move down the fallopian tube. Fertilization occurs when the two gametes fuse to form a zygote, which develops into an individual. Sperm needs to be deposited within five days of ovulation for fertilization to occur. The ovaries secrete estrogen and progesterone. The testes secrete testosterone. The placenta secretes chorionic gonadotropin.

Gametogenesis refers to the production of haploid gametes. **Spermatogenesis** refers to sperm production, which occurs in the testes. **Oogenesis** refers to egg formation, which takes place in the ovaries. It also produces a polar body.

Asexual Reproduction

Asexual reproduction occurs when only one parent is responsible for reproduction. Forms of this include budding, fragmentation, parthenogenesis, and self-fertilization.

- **Budding**: This occurs when the offspring start as a growth on the parent organism's body. Jellyfish and some echinoderms have buds that leave the parent. Other organisms, such as corals, continue to be attached and form colonies.
- **Fragmentation**: This is similar to budding, but after maturity the individual fragments into about eight pieces. Each fragment develops into another mature individual. Some small worms reproduce using this method.
- **Parthenogenesis**: This is also known as virgin birth because the female produces eggs that develop without being fertilized. Specific species of fish, insects, frogs, and lizards reproduce by parthenogenesis.
- **Self-fertilization**: Some species are considered hermaphroditic, meaning individuals have both male and female reproductive parts. Fertilization can be achieved within the individual.

Review Video: Parthenogenesis
Visit mometrix.com/academy and enter code: 213699

Embryonic Development

The stages of **embryonic development** are the zygote, morula, blastula, and gastrula.

- **Zygote**: diploid cell formed by the fusion two gametes during fertilization
- **Morula**: ball-like mass of 16–32 cells formed by mitotic divisions (cleavages) of the zygote
- **Blastula**: hollow, ball-like structure formed when morula cells begin to secrete fluid into the center of the morula; this is the structure that attaches to the lining of the uterus (endometrium)
- **Gastrula**: formed when cells migrate to the center of the blastula to form germ layers that differentiate to form tissues and organs

Roughly two weeks after fertilization, the embryo starts to form a yolk sac that will make blood cells, an embryonic disc, and a chorion (the placenta). By week three, the beginnings of the spinal cord, brain, muscles, bones, and face appear. After that, cardiac cells begin to beat.

Animal Kingdom Facts

The **animal kingdom** is comprised of more than one million species in about 30 divisions (the plant kingdom uses the term phyla). There about 800,000 species of insects alone, representing half of all animal species. The characteristics that distinguish members of the animal kingdom from members of other kingdoms are that they are multicellular, are heterotrophic, reproduce sexually (there are some exceptions), have cells that do not contain cell walls or photosynthetic pigments, can move at some stage of life, and can rapidly respond to the environment as a result of specialized tissues like nerve and muscle. **Heterotrophic** refers to the method of getting energy by eating food that has energy releasing substances. Plants, on the other hand, are **autotrophs**, which mean they make their own energy. During reproduction, animals have a **diploid embryo** in the blastula stage. This structure is unique to animals. The **blastula** resembles a fluid-filled ball.

Classification of Animals

As **heterotrophs**, animals can be further classified as carnivores, herbivores, omnivores, and parasites. **Predation** refers to a predator that feeds on another organism, which results in its death.

- **Detritivore** refers to heterotrophs that consume organic dead matter.
- **Carnivores** are animals that are meat eaters.
- **Herbivores** are plant eaters, and omnivores eat both meat and plants.
- **Omnivores** are animals that consume meat and plants.
- A **parasite's** food source is its host. A parasite lives off of a host, which does not benefit from the interaction.

Protostomic Phyla

Members of the **protostomic phyla** have mouths that are formed from the blastopore (a central cavity formed during early embryonic development).

- **Mollusca**: Classes include bivalvia (organisms with two shells, such as clams, mussels, and oysters), gastropoda (snails and slugs), cephalopoda (octopus, squid, and chambered nautilus), scaphopoda, amphineura (chitons), and monoplacophora.
- **Annelida**: This phylum includes the classes oligochaeta (earthworms), polychaeta (clam worms), and hirudinea (leeches). They have true coeloms enclosed within the mesoderm. They are segmented, have repeating units, and have a nerve trunk.
- **Arthropoda**: The phylum is diverse and populous. Members can be found in all types of environments. They have external skeletons, jointed appendages, bilateral symmetry, and nerve cords. They also have open circulatory systems and sense organs. Subphyla include crustacea (lobster, barnacles, pill bugs, and daphnia), hexapoda (all insects, which have three body segments, six legs, and usual wings), myriapoda (centipedes and millipedes), and chelicerata (the horseshoe crab and arachnids). Pill bugs have gills. Bees, ants, and wasps belong to the order hymenoptera. Like several other insect orders, they undergo complete metamorphosis.

Review Video: Arthropoda
Visit mometrix.com/academy and enter code: 523466

Porifera, Cnidaria, Platyhelminthes, and Nematoda Phyla

These four animal phyla lack a coelom (main body cavity) or have a pseudocoelom (central cavity not completely enclosed within the mesoderm).

- **Porifera**: These are sponges. They lack a coelom and get food as water flows through them. They are usually found in marine and sometimes in freshwater environments. They are perforated and diploblastic, meaning there are two layers of cells.
- **Cnidaria**: Members of this phylum are hydrozoa, jellyfish, and obelia. They have radial symmetry, sac-like bodies, and a polyp or medusa (jellyfish) body plan. They are diploblastic, possessing both an ectoderm and an endoderm. Food can get in through a cavity, but members of this phylum do not have an anus.

- **Platyhelminthes**: These are also known as flatworms. Classes include turbellaria (planarian) and trematoda (which include lung, liver, and blood fluke parasites). They have organs and bilateral symmetry. They have three layers of tissue: an ectoderm, a mesoderm, and an endoderm.
- **Nematoda**: These are roundworms. Hookworms and many other parasites are members of this phylum. They have a pseudocoelom, which means the coelom is not completely enclosed within the mesoderm. They also have a digestive tract that runs directly from the mouth to the anus. They are nonsegmented.

Vertebrates and Invertebrates

Invertebrates do not have a backbone, whereas **vertebrates** do. The great majority of animal species (an estimated 98 percent) are invertebrates, including worms, jellyfish, mollusks, slugs, insects, and spiders. They comprise 30 phyla in all. Vertebrates belong to the phylum chordata. The vertebrate body has two cavities. The **thoracic cavity** holds the heart and lungs and the **abdominal cavity** holds the digestive organs. Animals with **exoskeletons** have skeletons on the outside. Examples include crabs, scorpions, and insects. Animals with **endoskeletons** have skeletons on the inside. Examples are humans, tigers, birds, and reptiles. All vertebrates have endoskeletons.

Deuterostomic Phyla

Members of the **deuterostomic phyla** have anuses that are formed from blastopores.

Echinodermata: Members of this phylum have radial symmetry, are marine organisms, and have a water vascular system. Classes include echinoidea (sea urchins and sand dollars), crinoidea (sea lilies), asteroidea (starfish), ophiuroidea (brittle stars), and holothuroidea (sea cucumbers).

Chordata: This phylum includes humans and all other vertebrates, as well as a few invertebrates (urochordata and cephalochordata). Members of this phylum include agnatha (lampreys and hagfish), gnathostomata, chondrichthyes (cartilaginous sharks, skates, and rays), osteichthyes (bony fishes, including ray-finned fish that humans eat), amphibians (frogs, salamander, and newts), reptiles (lizards, snakes, crocodiles, and dinosaurs), birds, and mammals.

Animal Tissue Types

Epithelial tissue is found on body surfaces (like skin) and lining body cavities (like the stomach). Functions include protection, secretion of chemicals, absorption of chemicals, and responding to external stimuli. Epithelial cells move substances in, around, and out of the body. They can also have protective and secretory functions. Because these cells contain no blood vessels they must receive nourishment from underlying tissue. The three types of epithelial tissue are squamous (flattened), cuboidal (cube-shaped), and columnar (elongated). They can be further classified as simple (a single layer) or stratified (more than one layer). Glands comprised of epithelial tissue can be unicellular or multicellular.

Connective tissue is used to bind, support, protect, store fat, and fill space. The two kinds of connective tissue are loose and fibrous. In the human body, cartilage, bone, tendons, ligaments, blood, and protective layers are types of connective tissue.

The three types of **muscle tissue** are skeletal (striated), smooth, and cardiac.

Bone is a dense, rigid tissue that protects organs, produces blood cells, and provides structural support to the body.

Organ Systems

- **Skeletal system**: This consists of the bones and joints. The skeletal system provides support for the body through its rigid structure, provides protection for internal organs, and works to make organisms motile. Growth hormone affects the rate of reproduction and the size of body cells, and also helps amino acids move through membranes.
- **Muscular system**: This includes the muscles. The muscular system allows the body to move and respond to its environment.
- **Nervous system**: This includes the brain, spinal cord, and nerves. The nervous system is a signaling system for intrabody communications, responses to stimuli, and interaction within the environment. Signals are electrochemical. **Conscious** thoughts and memories and sense interpretation occur in the nervous system. It also controls **involuntary** muscles and functions, such as breathing and the beating of the heart.
- **Digestive system**: This includes the mouth, pharynx, esophagus, stomach, intestines, rectum, anal canal, teeth, salivary glands, tongue, liver, gallbladder, pancreas, and appendix. The system helps change food into a form that the body can process and use for energy and nutrients. Digestive processes can be **mechanical**, such as chewing food and churning it in the stomach, and **chemical**, such as secreting hydrochloric acid to kill bacteria and converting protein to amino acids. The overall system converts large food particles into molecules so the body can use them. The small intestine transports the molecules to the circulatory system. The large intestine absorbs nutrients and prepares the unused portions of food for elimination.
- **Respiratory system**: This includes the nose, pharynx, larynx, trachea, bronchi, and lungs. It is involved in gas exchange, which occurs in the alveoli. Fish have gills instead of lungs.
- **Circulatory system**: This includes the heart, blood, and blood vessels, such as veins, arteries, and capillaries. Blood transports oxygen and nutrients to cells and carbon dioxide to the lungs.
- **Skin** (integumentary): This includes skin, hair, nails, sense receptors, sweat glands, and oil glands. The skin is a sense organ, provides an exterior barrier against disease, regulates body temperature through perspiration, manufactures chemicals and hormones, and provides a place for nerves from the nervous system and parts of the circulation system to travel through. Skin has three layers: epidermis, dermis, and subcutaneous. The **epidermis** is the thin, outermost, waterproof layer. Basal cells are located in the epidermis. The **dermis** contains the sweat glands, oil glands, and hair follicles. The **subcutaneous** layer has connective tissue, and also contains adipose (fat) tissue, nerves, arteries, and veins.
- **Excretory System**: This includes the kidneys, ureters, bladder, and urethra. The excretory system helps maintain the amount of fluids in the body. Wastes from the blood system and excess water are removed in urine. The system also helps remove solid waste.
- **Immune system**: This includes the lymphatic system, lymph nodes, lymph vessels, thymus, and spleen. Lymph fluid is moved throughout the body by lymph vessels that provide protection against disease. This system protects the body from external intrusions, such as microscopic organisms and foreign substances. It also works through the production of antibodies, which mark harmful agents for destruction by binding to unique molecules (antigens) of harmful agents.
- **Endocrine system**: This includes the pituitary gland, pineal gland, hypothalamus, thyroid gland, parathyroids, thymus, adrenals, pancreas, ovaries, and testes. It controls systems and processes by secreting hormones into the blood system. **Exocrine glands** are those that secrete fluid into ducts. **Endocrine glands** secrete hormones directly into the blood stream without the use of ducts. Prostaglandin (tissue hormones) diffuses only a short distance from the tissue that created it, and influences nearby cells only. **Adrenal glands** are located above each kidney.

- The **cortex** secretes some sex hormones, as well as mineralocorticoids and glucocorticoids involved in immune suppression and stress response. The **medulla** secretes epinephrine and norepinephrine. Both elevate blood sugar, increase blood pressure, and accelerate heart rate. Epinephrine also stimulates heart muscle. The **islets of Langerhans** are clumped within the pancreas and secrete glucagon and insulin, thereby regulating blood sugar levels. The four **parathyroid glands** at the rear of the thyroid secrete parathyroid hormone.
- **Reproductive system**: In the male, this system includes the testes, vas deferens, urethra, prostate, penis, and scrotum. In the female, this system includes the ovaries, fallopian tubes (oviduct and uterine tubes), cervix, uterus, vagina, vulva, and mammary glands. Sexual reproduction helps provide genetic diversity as gametes from each parent contribute half the DNA to the zygote offspring. The system provides a method of transporting the male gametes to the female. It also allows for the growth and development of the embryo. Hormones involved are testosterone, interstitial cell stimulating hormone (ICSH), luteinizing hormone (LH), follicle stimulating hormone (FSH), and estrogen. Estrogens secreted from the ovaries include estradiol, estrone, and estriol. They encourage growth, among other things. Progesterone helps prepare the endometrium for pregnancy.

Nerve Cells

Neurons are nerve cells that transmit nerve impulses throughout the central and peripheral nervous systems for the brain to interpret. The neuron includes the cell body or soma, the dendrites, and the axons. The **soma** contains the nucleus. The **nucleus** contains the chromosomes. The dendrite extends from the cell body and resembles the branches of a tree. The dendrite receives chemical messages from other cells across the synapse, a small gap. The **axon** is a thread-like extension of the cell body, up to 3 feet long in spinal nerves. The axon transmits an electro-chemical message along its length to another cell. Axons of neurons in the **peripheral nervous system (PNS)** that deal with muscles are myelinated with fat to speed up the transmission of messages. Neurons in the PNS that deal with pain are unmyelinated because transmission does not have to be fast. Some neurons in the **central nervous system (CNS)** are myelinated by oligodendrocytes.

Muscle in Mammals

Skeletal muscle is strong, quick, and capable of voluntary contraction. Skeletal muscle fibers are striated and cylinder shaped. They have about 25 nuclei that are located to the side of the cell. Skeletal muscle consists of myofibrils that contain two types of filaments (myofilaments) made of proteins. The two types of filaments are actin and myosin. These filaments are aligned, giving the appearance of striation. During contraction, they slide against each other and become more overlapped. Smooth muscle is weak, slow, and usually contracts involuntarily. Examples in humans can be found in the gastrointestinal tract, blood vessels, bladder, uterus, hair follicles, and parts of the eye.

Smooth muscle fibers are not striated, but spindle shaped. They are somewhat long and a little wider in the center. Each cell contains one nucleus that is centrally located. Smooth muscle cells also contain myofibrils, but they are not aligned.

Cardiac muscle is strong, quick, and continuously contracts involuntarily. It is found in the myocardium of the heart. Cardiac muscle is more akin to skeletal muscle than smooth muscle.

Cardiac dysfunction is a response (a compensatory mechanism) to the heart trying to maintain normal heart function. Eventually, this causes the cardiac system to weaken. When the heart muscle contracts to pump blood out, it is referred to as **systolic blood flow**. When the heart muscle relaxes and blood flows back in, it is referred to as **diastolic blood flow**. If there are problems related to systolic and/or diastolic blood flow, the amount of blood output can be lessened. The ventricle can become stiffer and will not completely fill. Dysfunction can cause the heart to try to compensate and maintain normalcy by pumping harder.

Plant Kingdom Groupings

Only plants in the division bryophyta (mosses and liverworts) are **nonvascular**, which means they do not have xylem to transport water. All of the plants in the remaining divisions are **vascular**, meaning they have true roots, stems, leaves, and xylem. **Pteridophytes** are plants that use spores and not seeds to reproduce. They include the following divisions: Psilophyta (whisk fern), Lycophyta (club mosses), Sphenophyta (horsetails), and Pterophyta (ferns). **Spermatophytes** are plants that use seeds to reproduce. Included in this category are **gymnosperms**, which are flowerless plants that use naked seeds, and **angiosperms**, which are flowering plants that contain seeds in or on a fruit. Gymnosperms include the following divisions: cycadophyta (cycads), ginkgophyta (maidenhair tree), gnetophyta (ephedra and welwitschia), and coniferophyta (which includes pinophyta conifers). Angiosperms comprise the division anthophyta (flowering plants).

Plant Phyla

Chlorophyta are green algae. Bryophyta are nonvascular mosses and liverworts. They have root-like parts called rhizoids. Since they do not have the vascular structures to transport water, they live in moist environments. Lycophyta are club mosses. They are vascular plants. They use spores and need water to reproduce. Equisetopsida (sphenophyta) are horsetails. Like lycophyta, they need water to reproduce with spores. They have rhizoids and needle-like leaves. The pteridophytes (filicopsida) are ferns. They have stems (rhizomes). Spermatopsida are the seed plants. Gymnosperms are a conifer, which means they have cones with seeds that are used in reproduction. Plants with seeds require less water. Cycadophyta are cone-bearing and look like palms. Gnetophyta are plants that live in the desert. Coniferophyta are pine trees, and have both cones and needles. Ginkgophyta are ginkgos. Anthophyta is the division with the largest number of plant species, and includes flowering plants with true seeds.

Processes and Systems of Plants

Plants are **autotrophs**, which mean they make their own food. in a sense, they are self sufficient. Three major processes used by plants are photosynthesis, transpiration, and respiration. **Photosynthesis** involves using sunlight to make food for plants. **Transpiration** evaporates water out of plants. **Respiration** is the utilization of food that was produced during photosynthesis.

Two major systems in plants are the shoot and the root system. The **shoot system** includes leaves, buds, and stems. It also includes the flowers and fruits in flowering plants. The shoot system is located above the ground. The **root system** is the component of the plant that is underground, and includes roots, tubers, and rhizomes.

Review Video: Photosynthesis
Visit mometrix.com/academy and enter code: 227035

Plant Transpiration

The rate of **transpiration** is affected by light, temperature, humidity, wind, and the saturation of the soil. Leaves contain structures called **stomata** that regulate gas exchange. Light causes stomata to open, and water is lost more quickly than in the dark. Since water evaporates quicker in higher temperatures, the rate of transpiration increases as the temperature increases. If an area is humid, the rate of transpiration is decreased. The opposite is true for areas of lower humidity. This is explained by the principle of

diffusion. The greater the difference in humidity or concentrations of substances in two regions, the greater the rate of diffusion between them will be. Water in the soil replaces water that has been lost through transpiration. If water in the soil is not replaced, the rate of transpiration decreases. Photosynthesis also slows, the stomata close, and the plant wilts when it loses turgor as water is lost from cells.

> **Review Video: Diffusion and Graham's Law of Diffusion**
> Visit mometrix.com/academy and enter code: 385707

Transpiration, Respiration, and Phylogenetic

- **Transpiration** is the movement of water through a vascular plant. It is also the method by which water is evaporated out of plants. Transpiration mainly happens during the process of photosynthesis, when water and minerals travel up through the xylem and water is released through stomata. During transpiration, water is drawn up a plant. This process also helps cool leaves.
- **Respiration**: This refers to the process of metabolizing sugars to provide plants with the energy they need for growth and reproduction. The chemical equation is $C_6H_{12}O_6 + 6O_2 \rightarrow 6CO_2 + 6H_2O +$ energy. During the process of respiration, sugars are burned, energy is released, oxygen is used, and water and carbon dioxide are produced. Respiration can occur as a light or dark reaction.
- **Phylogenetic**: This refers to organisms that are related because of their evolutionary history.

Vascular and Nonvascular Plants

Vascular plants have vascular tissue in the form of xylem and phloem. These make up the parts of the plants, such as the roots, stems, and leaves that are involved in transporting minerals and water throughout the plant. This capability enables vascular plants to grow tall. Food/energy that is produced by photosynthesis in the leaves is brought down to the roots, while water is brought to the top of the plant. **Nonvascular** (or avascular) plants lack true leaves, stems, and roots. Nonvascular plants do not develop vascular tissue, such as xylem and phloem. They tend to be small, and individual cells are adjacent to their environment.

Plant Alternation of Generations

Alternation of generations refers to the fact that the two processes used during sexual reproduction alternate. These processes are meiosis and fertilization. in **meiosis**, sex cells divide and genetic material is reduced by half, which results in a gamete. Two gametes are joined during **fertilization**, and the resulting cell is diploid. This occurs in both plants and animals. Plants have a gametophyte and a sporophyte generation. The **gametophyte generation** starts with the production of a haploid spore. More haploid spores are produced through mitosis. Sexual reproduction occurs during this stage, which results in a zygote. This is the start of the second generation, which is known as the **sporophyte generation**. A primary difference between plant and animal sexual reproduction is that plants can undergo mitosis with haploid cells. Cells can be controlled with this single set of chromosomes.

Plant Root Systems

Plant roots include zones where cell differentiation, elongation and division, and meristem formation occur. **Primary meristems** include protoderms, ground meristems, procambiums, and apical meristems. There is also a root cap. A tuber is an underground stem that is enlarged and used for food storage. A rhizome is an underground stem of sorts that sends out roots and shoots from its nodes (bulging or swelling points). Vascular tissues include xylem and phloem. **Xylem** can be scattered throughout a pith or formed into rings. **Phloem** allows for food transport down a plant. The food travels from where it was produced through photosynthesis to other structures, such as roots, that require the food. Phloem can be made up of bundles of sieve tubes. It is usually located outside the xylem.

Meristems in Vegetative Growth

The **meristems** of plants are where new cells are formed through mitosis. These cells then differentiate into specific tissue types, which may form part of the root system or increase a plant's girth, height, or length. **Cambiums** are meristems that are responsible for secondary growth, which increases girth. Flowering plants go through cycles of vegetative growth, or propagation. They use flowers to reproduce sexually. **Vegetative propagation** occurs at the apical meristems located on the tip of the stem. These start as undifferentiated cells that can form into more stems, leaves, and secondary meristems (or lateral buds), which form branches. **Nodes** are areas where leaves can develop. The area between nodes is termed **internodal**. On a stem, the apical meristem on the end is the **terminal bud**. Sometimes, this can become a flower bud. **Lenticels** allow for the diffusion of oxygen and carbon dioxide gas.

Reproduction in Flowering Plants

There are at least 230,000 species of flowering plants. They represent about 90 percent of all plants. **Angiosperms** have a sexual reproduction phase that includes flowering. When growing plants, one may think they develop in the following order: seeds, growth, flowers, and fruit. The reproductive cycle has the following order: flowers, fruit, and seeds. in other words, **seeds** are the products of successful reproduction. The colors and scents of flowers serve to attract pollinators. Flowers and other plants can also be pollinated by wind. When a pollen grain meets the ovule and is successfully fertilized, the ovule develops into a seed. A seed consists of three parts: the embryo, the endosperm, and a seed coat. The **embryo** is a small plant that has started to develop, but this development is paused. Germination is when the embryo starts to grow again. The **endosperm** consists of proteins, carbohydrates, or fats. It typically serves as a food source for the embryo. The **seed coat** provides protection from disease, insects, and water.

Sexual Parts of Flowering Plants

Flowering plants can be categorized sexually according to which organs they have. Flowers can be bisexual or unisexual. Species can be **dioecious**, which means male and female flowers are contained on different individual plants. **Monoecious** means that both male and female flowers are on one individual. **Bisexual** flowers are those that have all of the following: sepal, petal, stamen, and pistil. If they have all of these parts, they are considered complete. They have both the male stamen and the female counterpart, the pistil. **Unisexual** flowers only have a pistil or a stamen, not both. Incomplete flowers do not have all four parts. The flower rests upon a pedicel and is contained with the receptacle. The carpal is made up of the stigma at the tip, a style, and the ovary at the base. The ovary contains the ovules (eggs). Carpels are sometimes formed as a single pistil. The stamen includes the anther and the filament, and produces the male pollen.

Pollination in Flowering Plants

The anthers of the stamens (male parts) have microsporangia that form into a **pollen** grain, which consists of a small germ cell within a larger cell. The pollen grain is released and lands on a **stigma** (female) portion of the pistil. It grows a pollen tube the length of the style and ends up at the **ovule**. The pollen grain releases the sperm and fertilization occurs. in double fertilization, one of the sperm joins with the egg to become a diploid zygote. The other sperm becomes the endosperm nucleus. Seeds are formed. One cotyledon (**monocot**) or two cotyledons (**dicot**) also form to store food and surround the embryo. Correspondingly, monocots produce one seed leaf, while dicots produce two. The seed matures and becomes dormant, and fruits typically form.

Fruits in Flowering Plants

The three main types of **fruits** in flowering plants are simple fruits, aggregate fruits, and multiple fruits.

- **Simple fruits** are formed from one ovary. Simple fruits that develop from one flower are called botanical fruits. Simple fruits can also have fruits that are dry.
- **Aggregate fruits** are produced by many ovaries in one flower. Each ovary is separately fertilized and forms the aggregate fruit. Examples of these are raspberries, blackberries, and strawberries.
- **Multiple fruits** are produced by many flowers on a single structure. Examples are pineapples and figs.

Seeds can be located within the fruit (i.e., tomatoes, cherries, and apples) or on the outside of the fruit (i.e., corn and strawberries).

Review Video: Fruits in Flowering Plants
Visit mometrix.com/academy and enter code: 867090

Reproduction in Seedless Plants

Bryophytes are seedless plants. They include liverworts, hornworts, and mosses. They use spores that form into gametophytes to reproduce. Sperm are flagellated, meaning they require at least some water to swim to the egg. Some bryophytes are plants that are one sex or the other, but other bryophytes have both sexes on the same plant.

Ferns also have flagellated sperm and require water for the same reason as bryophytes. Both ferns and bryophytes undergo alternation of generations. These plants spend about half of their reproductive cycles as sporophytes, making haploid spores through meiosis during this stage. The other half of the cycle is spent as a haploid gametophyte. At this point, male and female gametes join to form one zygote.

Photoperiodism.

Photoperiodism refers to the fact that plants are affected by seasons, particularly by the amount of daylight that occurs in each season. The amount of daylight triggers processes such as flowering, growth in roots and stems, and leaves falling off of trees. **Long day plants**, like the name implies, do not need many night time hours to instigate flowering. **Short day plants** tend to flower as days get shorter. Long day plants tend to flower when days get longer. Other plants are considered to be **day neutral**. Examples of **long day obligate plants** (meaning long days are essential) are oats, clover, and carnations. Examples of **long day facultative plants** (meaning long days are desirable, but not essential) are turnip, lettuce, wheat, and barley. Examples of **short day obligate plants** are tobacco, strawberries, and coffee. Examples of **short day facultative plants** are cotton, sugar cane, and rice.

Monocot and Dicot Structures

The diversity of plants leads to an abundance of **plant structures**. Not all structures are found in all plants, and many plants have different structures that perform similar functions. **Monocots** and **dicots** are both flowering plants. The bark of a woody dicot (tree) is structurally very different than the exterior rind of a monocot corn stem, even though both serve as the outermost layer. Within both are the vascular tissues phloem and xylem. in a woody dicot, the tree trunk is made of xylem. When water is abundant, such as during the spring, the xylem vessels that are made are large. Those made later in the summer are narrower since there is less water. When viewed in cross section, these two layers form the ring of a tree's trunk, which is why they can be used to calculate a tree's age.

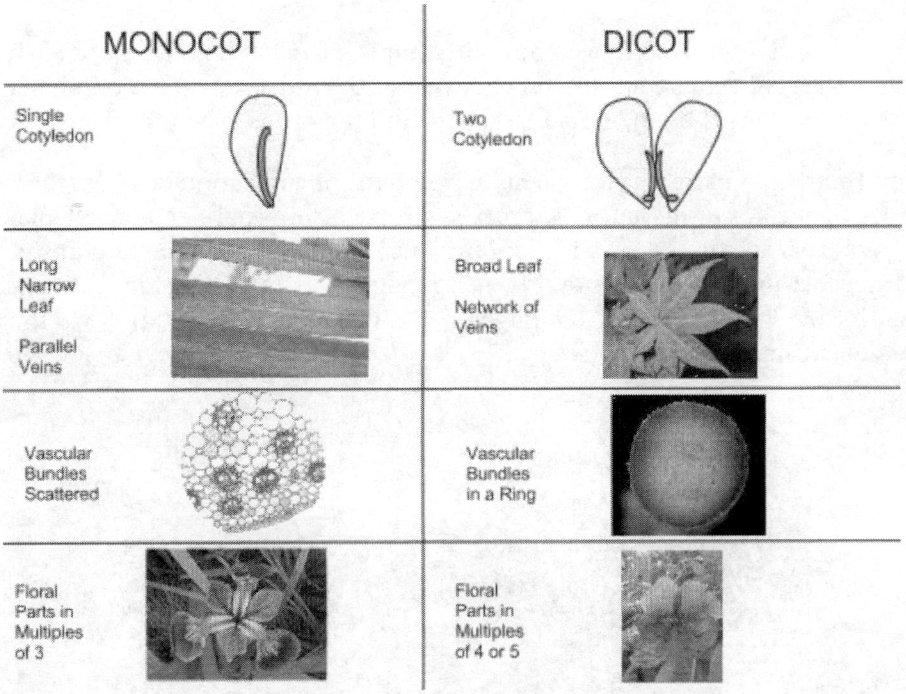

MONOCOT	DICOT
Single Cotyledon	Two Cotyledon
Long Narrow Leaf Parallel Veins	Broad Leaf Network of Veins
Vascular Bundles Scattered	Vascular Bundles in a Ring
Floral Parts in Multiples of 3	Floral Parts in Multiples of 4 or 5

Tropism in Plants

Tropism refers to the fact that plants grow in response to specific stimuli. Seeds are **geotropic** (or gravitropic), meaning they grow as a response to gravity. Roots are positively geotropic and grow towards gravity. Stems are negatively geotropic and grow away from the force of gravity. **Plagiotropic** refers to the fact that secondary branches and roots grow at right angles to gravity. **Phototropism** refers to the fact that a plant bends or grows toward a light source. **Thigmotropism** refers to how plants respond to contact.

Plant Hormones

Plant hormones are organic compounds that usually influence changes in plants. They can cause fruit to ripen or instigate plant growth. Five major groups of hormones are auxins, gibberellins, ethylenes, cytokinins, and abscisic acids. **Auxins** occur naturally and can be synthesized. They affect plant cell elongation, apical dominance, and rooting. **Gibberellins** affect plant height. **Ethylenes** help fruit ripen. **Cytokinins** are involved in cell division. **Abscisic acids** inhibit other hormones.

Interdependence of Life and Environmental Systems

Food Chains and Biomagnification

A **food chain** is a linking of organisms in a community that is based on how they use each other as food sources. Each link in the chain consumes the link above it and is consumed by the link below it. The exceptions are the organism at the top of the food chain and the organism at the bottom.

Biomagnification (bioamplification) refers to an increase in concentration of a substance within a food chain. Examples are pesticides or mercury. Mercury is emitted from coal-fired power plants and gets into the water supply, where it is eaten by a fish. A larger fish eats smaller fish, and humans eat fish. The concentration of mercury in humans has now risen. Biomagnification is affected by the persistence of a chemical, whether it can be broken down and negated, food chain energetics, and whether organisms can reduce or negate the substance.

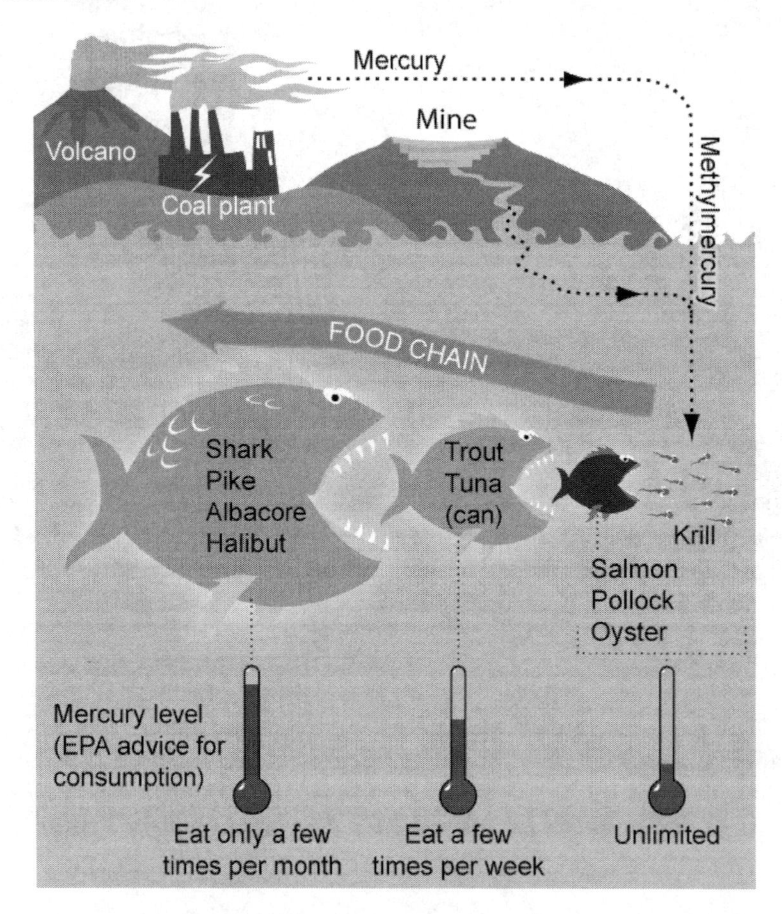

Ecosystem Stability and Ecologic Succession

Ecosystem stability: This is a concept that states that a stable ecosystem is perfectly efficient. Seasonal changes or expected climate fluctuations are balanced by **homeostasis**. It also states that interspecies interactions are part of the balance of the system. Four principles of ecosystem stability are that waste disposal and nutrient replenishment by recycling is complete, the system uses sunlight as an energy source, biodiversity remains, and populations are stable in that they do not over consume resources.

Ecologic succession: This is the concept that states that there is an orderly progression of change within a community. An example of **primary succession** is that over hundreds of years bare rock decomposes to sand, which eventually leads to soil formation, which eventually leads to the growth of grasses and trees. **Secondary succession** occurs after a disturbance or major event that greatly affects a community, such as a wild fire or construction of a dam.

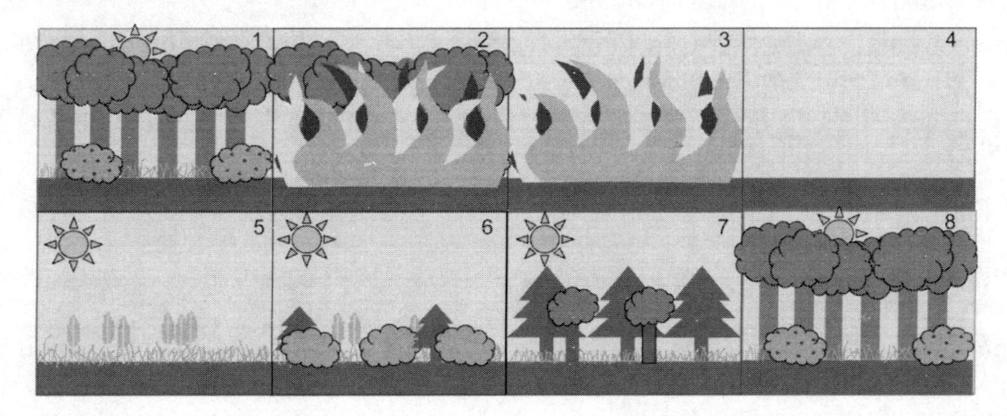

Food Webs

A **food web** consists of interconnected food chains in a community. The organisms can be linked to show the direction of energy flow. **Energy flow** in this sense is used to refer to the actual caloric flow through a system from trophic level to trophic level. **Trophic level** refers to a link in a food chain or a level of nutrition. The 10% rule is that from trophic level to level, about 90% of the energy is lost (in the form of heat, for example). The lowest trophic level consists of primary producers (usually plants), then primary consumers, then secondary consumers, and finally tertiary consumers (large carnivores). The final link is decomposers, which break down the consumers at the top. Food chains usually do not contain more than six links. These links may also be referred to as **ecological pyramids**.

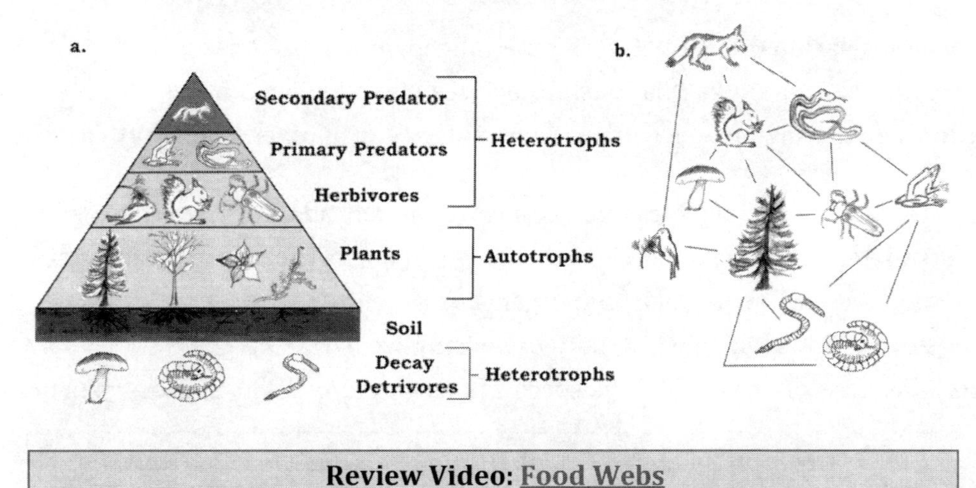

Review Video: Food Webs
Visit mometrix.com/academy and enter code: 853254

Review Video: Foodweb in a Freshwater System
Visit mometrix.com/academy and enter code: 532599

Social Behaviors

- **Territoriality**: This refers to members of a species protecting areas from other members of their species and from other species. Species members claim specific areas as their own.

- **Dominance**: This refers to the species in a community that is the most populous.
- **Altruism**: This is when a species or individual in a community exhibits behaviors that benefit another individual at a cost to itself. In biology, altruism does not have to be a conscious sacrifice.
- **Threat display**: This refers to behavior by an organism that is intended to intimidate or frighten away members of its own or another species.
- **Competitive exclusion**: This principle states that if there are limited or insufficient resources and species are competing for them, these species will not be able to co-exist. The result is that one of the species will become extinct or be forced to undergo a behavioral or evolutionary change. Another way to say this is that "complete competitors cannot coexist."

Population

- **Population** is a measure of how many individuals exist in a specific area. It can be used to measure the size of human, plant, or animal groups.
- **Population growth** depends on many factors. Factors that can limit the number of individuals in a population include lack of resources such as food and water, space, habitat destruction, competition, disease, and predators. Exponential growth refers to an unlimited rising growth rate. This kind of growth can be plotted on a chart in the shape of a J.
- **Carrying capacity** is the population size that can be sustained. The world's population is about 6.8 billion and growing. The human population has not yet reached its carrying capacity.
- **Population dynamics** refers to how a population changes over time and the factors that cause changes. An S-shaped curve shows that population growth has leveled off.
- **Biotic potential** refers to the maximum reproductive capacity of a population given ideal environmental conditions.

Relationships Between and Within Species

- **Intraspecific relationships**: relationships among members of a species.
- **Interspecific relationships**: relationships between members of different species.
- **Predation**: relationship in which one individual feeds on another (the prey), causing the prey to die.
- **Parasitism**: relationship in which one organism benefits and the other is harmed.
- **Commensalism**: interspecific relationships in which one of the organisms benefits.
- **Mutualism**: relationship in which both organisms benefit.
- **Competition**: relationship in which both organisms are harmed.
- **Biomass**: the mass of one or all of the species (species biomass) in an ecosystem or area.

Review Video: Mutualism, Commensalism, and Parasitism
Visit mometrix.com/academy and enter code: 757249

Community

A **community** is any number of species interacting within a given area. A **niche** is the role of a species within a community. **Species diversity** refers to the number of species within a community and their populations.

- **Biome**: an area in which species are associated because of climate. The six major biomes in North America are desert, tropical rain forest, grassland, coniferous forest, deciduous forest, and tundra.
- **Biotic factors**: the living factors, such as other organisms, that affect a community or population.
- **Abiotic factors**: the nonliving factors that affect a community or population, such as facets of the environment.
- **Ecology**: the study of plants, animals, their environments, and how they interact.
- **Ecosystem**: a community of species and all of the environmental factors that affect them.

Biochemical Cycles

Biochemical cycles are how chemical elements required by living organisms cycle between living and nonliving organisms. Elements that are frequently required are phosphorus, sulfur, oxygen, carbon, gaseous nitrogen, and water. Elements can go through gas cycles, sedimentary cycles, or both. Elements circulate through the air in a gas cycle and from land to water in a sedimentary one.

Mimicry

Mimicry is an adaptation developed as a response to predation. It refers to an organism that has a similar appearance to another species, which is meant to fool the predator into thinking the organism is more dangerous than it really is. Two examples are the drone fly and the io moth. The fly looks like a bee but cannot sting. The io moth has markings on its wings that make it look like an owl. The moth can startle predators and gain time to escape. Predators can also use mimicry to lure their prey.

Earth's History and the Structure and Function of Earth Systems

Radioactive Dating

Radioactive dating, also known as **radiometric dating**, is a technique that can be used to determine the **age** of rocks and even the Earth itself. The process compares the amount of radioactive material in a rock to the amount of material that has "decayed." **Decay** refers to the fact that the nuclide of an element loses subatomic particles over time. The process includes a parent element that undergoes changes to create a daughter element, also known as the decay product. The daughter element can also be unstable and lose particles, creating another daughter element. This is known as a **decay chain**. Decay occurs until all the elements are stable. Three types of dating techniques are radiocarbon dating, potassium-argon dating, and uranium-lead dating. These techniques can be used to date a variety of natural and manmade materials, including archaeological artifacts.

Theory of Mass Extinction

Mass extinction, also known as an **extinction event**, is a decrease in the number of species over a short period of time. While there are many theories as to the causes of mass extinction, it occurs when a relatively large number of species die off or when fewer species evolve than expected. Extinction events are classified as major and minor. It is generally accepted that there have been five **major extinction events** in Earth's history. The five most significant mass extinction events are Ordovician-Silurian, Permian-Triassic, Late Devonian, Triassic-Jurassic, and Cretaceous-Tertiary.

Uniformitarianism, Catastrophism, and Superposition

- **Uniformitarianism**: Also known as gradualism, uniformitarianism is the belief that the forces, processes, and laws that we see today have existed throughout geologic time. It involves the belief that the present is the key to the past, and that relatively slow processes have shaped the geological features of Earth.
- **Catastrophism**: This is the belief that the Earth was shaped by sudden, short-term catastrophic events.
- **Superposition**: In geology, the law of superposition is that underground layers closer to the surface were deposited more recently.

Geologic Time Scale

One year is 365.25 days long. The **International System of Units (SI)** uses the symbol "a" for a standard year or **annum**. The prefixes "M" for **mega** and "G" for **giga** are used to refer to one million and one billion years, respectively. Ma stands for a **megannum** (10^6 years) and Ga stands for a **gigannum** (10^9 years). For example, it can be said that the Earth was formed 4.5 billion years ago, or 4.5 Ga. Use of the abbreviation "mya" for millions of years (ago) is discouraged, but it is still occasionally used. The abbreviation "BP" stands for "before present." The "present" is defined as January 1, 1950, since present changes from year to year. Another abbreviation used is BCE, which stands for "Before the Common Era."

Geologists use the **geologic time scale** when discussing Earth's chronology and the formation of rocks and minerals. Age is calculated in millions of years before the present time. Units of time are often delineated by geologic or paleontologic events. Smaller units of time such as **eras** are distinguished by the abundance and/or extinction of certain plant and animal life. For example, the extinction of the dinosaurs marks the end of the Mesozoic era and the beginning of the Cenozoic, the present, era. We are in the Holocene epoch. The **supereon** encompasses the greatest amount of time. It is composed of eons. Eons are divided into eras, eras into periods, and periods into epochs. Layers of rock also correspond to periods of time in geochronology. Current theory holds that the Earth was formed 4.5 billion years ago.

History of Time Scale

The first known observations of **stratigraphy** were made by **Aristotle**, who lived before the time of Christ. He observed seashells in ancient rock formations and on the beach, and concluded that the fossilized seashells were similar to current seashells. **Avicenna**, a Persian scholar from the 11th century, also made early advances in the development of stratigraphy with the concept of superposition. **Nicolas Steno**, a Danish scientist from the 17th century, expounded upon this with the belief that layers of rock are piled on top of each other. In the 18th century, **Abraham Werner** categorized rocks from four different periods: the Primary, Secondary, Tertiary, and Quaternary periods. This fell out of use when the belief emerged that rock layers containing the same fossils had been deposited at the same time, and were therefore from the same age. British geologists created the names for many of the time divisions in use today. For example, the Devonian period was named after the county of Devon, and the Permian period was named after Perm, Russia.

Relative and Absolute Time

A **numerical**, or "**absolute**," age is a specific number of years, such as 150 million years ago. A "**relative**" age refers to a time range, such as the Mesozoic era. It is used to determine whether one rock formation is older or younger than another formation. Radioactive dating is a form of **absolute dating** and stratigraphy is a form of **relative dating**. Radioactive dating techniques have provided the most information about the absolute age of rocks and other geological features. Together, geochronologists have created a geologic time scale. **Biostratigraphy** uses plant and animal fossils within rock to determine its relative age.

Paleozoic Era

The **Paleozoic era** began about 542 Ma and lasted until 251 Ma. It is further divided into six periods. The Paleozoic era began after the supercontinent Pannotia started to break up and at the end of a global ice age. By the end of the era, the supercontinent Pangaea had formed. The beginning of the Paleozoic era is marked by **Cambrian Explosion**, a time when there were abundant life forms according to the fossil record. The end of the era is marked by one of the major extinction events, the Permian extinction, during which almost 90 percent of the species living at the time became extinct. Many plant and animal forms appeared on the land and in the sea during this era. It is also when large land plants first appeared in the fossil record. There are many invertebrates found in the fossil record of the Paleozoic era, and fish, amphibians, and reptiles also first appeared in the fossil record during this era. There were also large swamps and forests, some of which were formed into coal deposits that exist today.

Mesozoic Era

The **Mesozoic era** is known as the **Age of the Dinosaurs**. It is also the era during which the dinosaurs became extinct. The fossil record also shows the appearance of mammals and birds. Trees that existed included gymnosperms, which have uncovered seeds and are mostly cone bearing, and angiosperms, which have covered seeds and are flowering plants. The angiosperm group is currently the dominant plant group. It was also during this era that the supercontinent **Pangaea** divided into the continental pieces that exist today. During the **Cretaceous period**, sea levels rose until one-third of the Earth's present land mass was underwater, and then receded. This period created huge marine deposits and chalk. The extinction of the dinosaurs occurred about 65 Ma, and was believed to have been triggered by the impact of an asteroid.

Cenozoic Era

The **Cenozoic era** began about 65.5 Ma and continues to the present. It is marked by the **Cretaceous-Tertiary extinction event** (extinction of the dinosaurs as well as many invertebrates and plants). The Cenozoic era is further divided into the Paleogene, Neogene, and Quaternary periods. During the Cenozoic era, Pangaea continued to drift, and the plates eventually moved into their present positions. The **Pleistocene Ice Age**, also known as Quaternary glaciation or the current ice age began about 2.58 Ma and includes the glaciation occurring today. Mammals continued to evolve and other plants and animals came into existence during this era. The fossil record includes the ancestors of the horse, rhinoceros, and camel. It also includes the first dogs and cats and the first humanlike creatures. The first humans appeared less than 200,000 years ago.

Stratigraphy

Stratigraphy is a branch of geology that involves the study of rock layers and layering. **Sedimentary rocks** are the primary focus of stratigraphy. Subfields include **lithostratigraphy**, which is the study of the vertical layering of rock types, and **biostratigraphy**, which is the study of fossil evidence in rock layers. **Magnetostratigraphy** is the study of changes in detrital remnant magnetism (DRM), which is used to measure the polarity of Earth's magnetic field at the time a stratum was deposited. **Chronostratigraphy** focuses on the relative dating of rock strata based on the time of rock formation. **Unconformity** refers to missing layers of rock.

Fossil

Fossils are preservations of plants, animals, their remains, or their traces that date back to about 10,000 years ago. Fossils and where they are found in rock strata makes up the fossil record. Fossils are formed under a very specific set of conditions. The fossil must not be damaged by predators and scavengers after death, and the fossil must not decompose. Usually, this happens when the organism is quickly covered with sediment. This sediment builds up and molecules in the organism's body are replaced by minerals. Fossils come in an array of sizes, from single-celled organisms to large dinosaurs.

Fossils provide a wealth of information about the past, particularly about the flora and fauna that once occupied the Earth, but also about the geologic history of the Earth itself and how Earth and its inhabitants came to be. Some fossilized remains in the **geohistorical record** exemplify ongoing processes in the Earth's environment, such as weathering, glaciation, and volcanism. These have all led to evolutionary changes in plants and animals. Other fossils support the theory that **catastrophic events** caused drastic changes in the Earth and its living creatures. One example of this type of theory is that a meteor struck the Earth and caused dinosaurs to become extinct. Both types of fossils provide scientists with a way to hypothesize whether these types of events will happen again.

Formation of the Earth

Earth's early development began after a **supernova** exploded. This led to the formation of the **Sun** out of hydrogen gas and interstellar dust. These same elements swirled around the newly-formed Sun and formed the **planets**, including Earth. Scientists theorize that about 4.5 billion years ago, Earth was a chunk of rock surrounded by a cloud of gas. It is believed it lacked water and the type of atmosphere that exists today. Heat from radioactive materials in the rock and pressure in the Earth's interior melted the interior. This caused the heavier materials, such as iron, to sink. Lighter silicate-type rocks rose to the

Earth's surface. These rocks formed the Earth's earliest crust. Other chemicals also rose to the Earth's surface, helping to form the water and atmosphere.

Formation of the Atmosphere

It is generally believed that the Earth's **atmosphere** evolved into its present state. Some believe Earth's early atmosphere contained hydrogen, helium, methane, ammonia, and some water vapor. These elements also played a role in planet formation. Earth's early atmosphere was developed before the emergence of living organisms as we know them today. Eventually, the hot hydrogen and helium escaped Earth's gravity and drifted off. Others believe the early atmosphere contained a large amount of carbon dioxide. Either way, there was probably little oxygen at the time.

Another theory is that a second stage of the atmosphere evolved over several hundred million years through a process during which methane, ammonia, and water vapor broke down and reformed into nitrogen, hydrogen, and carbon dioxide. About two billion years ago, higher levels of oxygen were found in the atmosphere, which is indicated by large deposits of iron ore. At the same time, iron ores created in oxygen-poor environments stopped forming. The oxygen in the atmosphere today comes mainly from plants and microorganisms such as algae.

Review Video: Earth's Atmosphere
Visit mometrix.com/academy and enter code: 417614

Layers of the Atmosphere

The **atmosphere** consists of 78% nitrogen, 21% oxygen, and 1% argon. It also includes traces of water vapor, carbon dioxide and other gases, dust particles, and chemicals from Earth. The atmosphere becomes thinner the farther it is from the Earth's surface. It becomes difficult to breathe at about 3 km above sea level. The atmosphere gradually fades into space.

The main layers of the Earth's atmosphere (from lowest to highest) are:

- **Troposphere** (lowest layer): where life exists and most weather occurs; elevation 0–15 km
- **Stratosphere**: has the ozone layer, which absorbs UV radiation from the sun; hottest layer; where most satellites orbit; elevation 15–50 km
- **Mesosphere**: coldest layer; where meteors will burn up; elevation 50–80 km
- **Thermosphere**: where the international space station orbits; elevation 80–700 km
- **Exosphere** (outermost layer): consists mainly of hydrogen and helium; extends to ~10,000 km

Tropospheric Circulation

Most weather takes place in the **troposphere**. Air circulates in the atmosphere by convection and in various types of "cells." Air near the equator is warmed by the Sun and rises. Cool air rushes under it, and the higher, warmer air flows toward Earth's poles. At the poles, it cools and descends to the surface. It is now under the hot air, and flows back to the equator. Air currents coupled with ocean currents move heat around the planet, creating winds, weather, and climate. Winds can change direction with the seasons. For example, in Southeast Asia and India, summer monsoons are caused by air being heated by the Sun. This air rises, draws moisture from the ocean, and causes daily rains. In winter, the air cools, sinks, pushes the moist air away, and creates dry weather.

Meteorology, Weather, and Climate

Meteorology is the study of the atmosphere, particularly as it pertains to forecasting the weather and understanding its processes. **Weather** is the condition of the atmosphere at any given moment. Most weather occurs in the troposphere. Weather includes changing events such as clouds, storms, and temperature, as well as more extreme events such as tornadoes, hurricanes, and blizzards. **Climate** refers to the average weather for a particular area over time, typically at least 30 years. Latitude is an indicator of climate. Changes in climate occur over long time periods.

Review Video: Climate and Weather
Visit mometrix.com/academy and enter code: 455373

Common Weather Phenomenon

Common atmospheric conditions that are frequently measured are temperature, precipitation, wind, and humidity. These weather conditions are often measured at permanently fixed **weather stations** so weather data can be collected and compared over time and by region. Measurements may also be taken by ships, buoys, and underwater instruments. Measurements may also be taken under special circumstances. The measurements taken include temperature, barometric pressure, humidity, wind speed, wind direction, and precipitation. Usually, the following instruments are used: A **thermometer** is used for measuring temperature; a **barometer** is used for measuring barometric/air pressure; a **hygrometer** is used for measuring humidity; an **anemometer** is used for measuring wind speed; a **weather vane** is used for measuring wind direction; and a **rain gauge** is used for measuring precipitation.

Latitude

Latitude is a measurement of the distance from the equator. The distance from the equator indicates how much **solar radiation** a particular area receives. The equator receives more sunlight, while polar areas receive less. The Earth tilts slightly on its **rotational axis**. This tilt determines the seasons and affects weather. There are eight **biomes** or **ecosystems** with particular climates that are associated with latitude. Those in the high latitudes, which get the least sunlight, are tundra and taiga. Those in the mid latitudes are grassland, temperate forest, and chaparral. Those in latitudes closest to the equator are the warmest. The sixth and seventh biomes are desert and tropical rain forest. The eighth biome is the ocean, which is unique because it consists of water and spans the entire globe. Insolation refers to incoming solar radiation. **Diurnal variations** refer to the daily changes in **insolation**. The greatest insolation occurs at noon.

Tilt of the Earth

The **tilt of the Earth** on its axis is 23.5°. This tilt causes the **seasons** and affects the **temperature** because it affects the amount of Sun the area receives. When the Northern or Southern Hemispheres are tilted toward the Sun, the hemisphere tilted toward the sun experiences summer and the other hemisphere experiences winter. This reverses as the Earth revolves around the Sun. Fall and spring occur between the two extremes. The **equator** gets the same amount of sunlight every day of the year, about 12 hours, and doesn't experience seasons. Both poles have days during the winter when they are tilted away from the Sun and receive no daylight. The opposite effect occurs during the summer. There are 24 hours of daylight and no night. The **summer solstice**, the day with the most amount of sunlight, occurs on June 21st in the Northern Hemisphere and on December 21st in the Southern Hemisphere. The **winter solstice**, the day with the least amount of sunlight, occurs on December 21st in the Northern Hemisphere and on June 21st in the Southern Hemisphere.

Review Video: Tilt of Earth and Seasons
Visit mometrix.com/academy and enter code: 602892

Sea and Land Breezes

Sea breezes and land breezes help influence an area's prevailing **winds**, particularly in areas where the wind flow is light. **Sea breezes**, also called onshore breezes, are the result of the different capacities for absorbing heat of the ocean and the land. The sea can be warmed to a greater depth than the land. It warms up more slowly than the land's surface. Land heats air above it as its temperature increases. This heated, warmer air is less dense and rises as a result. The cooler air above the sea and higher sea level pressure create a wind flow in the direction of the land. Coastal areas often receive these cooler breezes. Land cools slower at night than the ocean, and coastal breezes weaken at this time. When the land becomes so cool that it is cooler than the sea surface, the pressure over the ocean is lower than the land. This creates a **land breeze**. This can cause rain and thunderstorms over the ocean.

Causes of Wind and Wind Belts

Winds are the result of air moving by **convection**. Masses of warm air rise, and cold air sweeps into their place. The warm air also moves, cools, and sinks. The term "**prevailing wind**" refers to the wind that usually blows in an area in a single direction. **Dominant winds** are the winds with the highest speeds. Belts or bands that run latitudinally and blow in a specific direction are associated with convection cells. **Hadley cells** are formed directly north and south of the equator. The **Farrell cells** occur at about 30° to 60°. The **jet stream** runs between the Farrell cells and the polar cells. At the higher and lower latitudes, the direction is easterly. At mid latitudes, the direction is westerly. From the North Pole to the south, the surface winds are Polar High Easterlies, Subpolar Low Westerlies, Subtropical High or Horse Latitudes, North-East Trade winds, Equatorial Low or Doldrums, South-East Trades, Subtropical High or Horse Latitudes, Subpolar Low Easterlies, and Polar High.

Local Atmospheric Variations

Terrain affects several local **atmospheric conditions**, including temperature, wind speed, and wind direction. When there are land forms, heating of the ground can be greater than the heating of the surrounding air than it would be at the same altitude above sea level. This creates a thermal low in the region and amplifies any existing thermal lows. It also changes the wind circulation. Terrain such as hills and valleys increase friction between the air and the land, which disturbs the air flow. This physical block deflects the wind, and the resulting air flow is called a barrier jet. Just as the heating of the land and air affects sea and land breezes along the coast, rugged terrain affects the wind circulation between mountains and valleys.

Thunderstorms

A **thunderstorm** is one of the many weather phenomena that can be created during the ongoing process of heat moving through Earth's atmosphere. Thunderstorms form when there is moisture to form rain clouds, unstable air, and lift. Unstable air is usually caused by warm air rising quickly through cold air. Lift can be caused by fronts, sea breezes, and elevated terrain, such as mountains. **Single cell thunderstorms** have one main draft. **Multicell clusters** have clusters of storms. **Multicell lines** have severe thunderstorms along a squall line. **Supercell thunderstorms** are large and severe, and have the capacity to produce destructive tornadoes. **Thunder** is a sonic shock wave caused by the rapid expansion of air around lightning. **Lightning** is the discharge of electricity during a thunderstorm. Lightning can also occur during volcanic eruptions or dust storms.

Cyclones

Cyclones generally refer to large air masses rotating in the same direction as the Earth. They are formed in low pressure areas. Cyclones vary in size. Some are **mesoscale systems**, which vary in size from about 5 km to hundreds of kilometers. Some are **synoptic scale systems**, which are about 1,000 km in size. The size of subtropical cyclones is somewhere in between. Cold-core polar and extratropical cyclones are synoptic scale systems. Warm-core tropical, polar low, and mesocyclones are mesoscale systems. Extratropical cyclones, sometimes called mid-latitude cyclones or wave cyclones, occur in the middle latitudes. They have neither tropical nor polar characteristics. Extratropical cyclones are everyday phenomena which, along with anticyclones, drive the weather over much of the Earth. They can produce cloudiness, mild showers, heavy gales, and thunderstorms. **Anticyclones** occur when there is a descending pocket of air of higher than average pressure. Anticyclones are usually associated with clearing skies and drier, cooler air.

Tornados

During a **tornado**, wind speeds can be upward of 300 miles per hour. Tornados are rotating funnel-like clouds. They have a very high energy density, which means they are very destructive to a small area. They are also short-lived. About 75% of the world's tornadoes occur in the United States, mostly in an area of the Great Plains known as **Tornado Alley**. If there are two or more columns of air, it is referred to as a **multiple vortex tornado**. A **satellite tornado** is a weak tornado that forms near a larger one within the same mesocyclone. A **waterspout** is a tornado over water. The severity of tornadoes is measured using the **Enhanced Fujita Scale**. An EF-0 rating is associated with a 3-second wind gust between 65 and 85 miles per hour, while an EF-5 is associated with wind speeds of greater than 200 mph.

Review Video: Tornadoes
Visit mometrix.com/academy and enter code: 540439

Hurricanes

A **hurricane** is one of the three weather phenomena that can occur as a result of a tropical cyclone. Hurricanes appear well-organized and sometimes have a recognizable eye with strong rotation. Its wind speed is more than 73 mph. Hurricanes are classified using the **Saffir-Simpson Scale**, which ranges from category 1 to category 5. A category 5 hurricane has wind speeds greater than 155 mph. Hurricanes are named alphabetically through the season starting with "A." The letters "Q," "U," and "Z" are not used. There are six lists of names that are used from year to year. The names of devastating hurricanes are retired from the list.

Humidity

Humidity refers to water vapor contained in the air. The amount of moisture contained in air depends upon its **temperature**. The higher the air temperature, the more moisture it can hold. These higher levels of moisture are associated with higher humidity. **Absolute humidity** refers to the total amount of moisture air is capable of holding at a certain temperature. **Relative humidity** is the ratio of water vapor in the air compared to the amount the air is capable of holding at its current temperature. As temperature decreases, absolute humidity stays the same and relative humidity increases. A **hygrometer** is a device used to measure humidity. The **dew point** is the temperature at which water vapor condenses into water at a particular humidity.

Precipitation

After clouds reach the dew point, **precipitation** occurs. Precipitation can take the form of a liquid or a solid. It is known by many names, including rain, snow, ice, dew, and frost. **Liquid** forms of precipitation include rain and drizzle. Rain or drizzle that freezes on contact is known as freezing rain or freezing drizzle. **Solid** or frozen forms of precipitation include snow, ice needles or diamond dust, sleet or ice pellets, hail, and graupel or snow pellets. **Virga** is a form of precipitation that evaporates before reaching the ground. It usually looks like sheets or shafts falling from a cloud. The amount of rainfall is measured with a **rain gauge**. Intensity can be measured according to how fast precipitation is falling or by how severely it limits visibility. Precipitation plays a major role in the **water cycle** since it is responsible for depositing much of the Earth's fresh water.

Review Video: Hydrologic Cycle
Visit mometrix.com/academy and enter code: 426578

Heat Waves

A **heat wave** is a stretch of hotter than normal weather. Some heat waves may involve high humidity and last longer than a week. Heat waves can form if a **warm high-pressure weather system** stalls in an area. The **jet stream** is a flow that moves air through the middle latitudes. If the jet stream shifts, it can bring a pattern of unusually warm weather into a region, creating a heat wave. Heat can be trapped by cities. If there is no rain or clouds to help cool the weather, the heat wave can linger. In humans, heat waves can lead to heat stroke, heat exhaustion, cramps, dehydration, and even death. Plants can dry up and crops can fail. There is also a greater threat of **fires** during a heat wave in dry areas.

Formation of Clouds

Clouds **form** when air cools and warm air is forced to give up some of its **water vapor** because it can no longer hold it. This vapor condenses and forms tiny droplets of water or ice crystals called clouds. Particles, or aerosols, are needed for water vapor to form water droplets. These are called **condensation nuclei**. Clouds are created by surface heating, mountains and terrain, rising air masses, and weather fronts. Clouds precipitate, returning the water they contain to Earth. Clouds can also create **atmospheric optics**. They can scatter light, creating colorful phenomena such as rainbows, colorful sunsets, and the green flash phenomenon.

Review Video: Clouds
Visit mometrix.com/academy and enter code: 803166

Cloud Types

Most clouds can be classified according to the altitude of their base above Earth's surface. **High clouds** occur at altitudes between 5,000 and 13,000 meters. **Middle clouds** occur at altitudes between 2,000 and 7,000 meters. **Low clouds** occur from the Earth's surface to altitudes of 2,000 meters. Types of high clouds include cirrus (Ci), thin wispy mare's tails that consist of ice; cirrocumulus (Cc), small, pillow-like puffs that often appear in rows; and cirrostratus (Cs), thin, sheet-like clouds that often cover the entire sky. Types of middle clouds include altocumulus (Ac), gray-white clouds that consist of liquid water; and altostratus (As), grayish or blue-gray clouds that span the sky. Types of low clouds include stratus (St), gray and fog-like clouds consisting of water droplets that take up the whole sky; stratocumulus (Sc), low-lying, lumpy gray clouds; and nimbostratus (Ns), dark gray clouds with uneven bases that indicate rain or snow. Two types of clouds, cumulus (Cu) and cumulonimbus (Cb), are capable of great vertical growth. They can start at a wide range of altitudes, from the Earth's surface to altitudes of 13,000 meters.

Contrails, or condensation trails, are thin white streaks caused by jets. These are created from water vapor condensing and freezing the jet's exhaust particles. Contrails can be further classified as short-lived, persistent non-spreading, and persistent. **Lenticular** or lee wave clouds are created by an air current over an obstacle, such as a mountain. They appear to be stationary, but are actually forming, dissipating, and reforming in the same place. **Kelvin-Helmholtz** clouds are formed by winds with different speeds or directions. They look like ocean waves. **Mammatus** clouds hang down from the base of a cloud, usually a cumulonimbus cloud. They often occur during the warmer months.

Air Masses

Air masses are large volumes of air in the troposphere of the Earth. They are categorized by their temperature and by the amount of water vapor they contain. Arctic and Antarctic air masses are cold. Polar air masses are cool. Tropical and equatorial air masses are hot. Other types of air masses include maritime and monsoon, both of which are moist and unstable. There are also continental and superior air masses, which are dry. A **weather front** separates two masses of air of different densities. It is the principal cause of meteorological phenomena. Air masses are quickly and easily affected by the land they are above. They can have certain characteristics, and then develop new ones when they get blown over a different area.

Pressure Systems

The concept of atmospheric pressure involves the idea that air exerts a force. An imaginary column of air 1 square inch in size rising through the atmosphere would exert a force of 14.7 pounds per square inch (psi). Both temperature and altitude affect atmospheric pressure. Low and high **pressure systems** tend to want to equalize. Air tends to move from areas of high pressure to areas of low pressure. When air moves into a low pressure system, the air that was there gets pushed up, creating lower temperatures and pressures. Water vapor condenses and forms clouds and possibly rain and snow. A **barometer** is used to measure air pressure.

Review Video: Rotation of Low Pressure Systems
Visit mometrix.com/academy and enter code: 258356

Frontal Systems

A **cold front** is a mass of cold air, usually fast moving and dense, that moves into a warm air front, producing clouds. This often produces a temperature drop and rain, hail (frozen rain), thunder, and lightning. A **warm front** is pushed up by a fast-moving cold front. It is often associated with high wispy clouds, such as cirrus and cirrostratus clouds. A **stationary front** forms when a warm and cold front meet, but neither is strong enough to move the other. Winds blowing parallel to the fronts keep the front stationary. The front may remain in the same place for days until the wind direction changes and both fronts become a single warm or cold front. In other cases, the entire front dissipates. An **occluded front** forms when a cold front pushes into a warm front. The warm air rises and the two masses of cool air join. These types of fronts often occur in areas of low atmospheric pressure.

Short and Long-term Weather Forecasting

Short and long-term **weather forecasting** is important because the day-to-day weather greatly affects humans and human activity. Severe weather and natural events can cause devastating harm to humans, property, and sources of livelihood, such as crops. The **persistence method** of forecasting can be used to create both short and long-term forecasts in areas that change very little or change slowly. It assumes that the weather tomorrow will be similar to the weather today. **Barometric pressure** is measured because a change in air pressure can indicate the arrival of a cold front that could lead to precipitation. **Long-term forecasts** based on climate data are useful to help people prepare for seasonal changes and severe events such as hurricanes.

Weather Fronts and Weather Maps

A **weather front** is the area between two differing masses of air that affects weather. **Frontal movements** are influenced by the jet stream and other high winds. Movements are determined by the type of front. **Cold fronts** move up to twice as fast as **warm fronts**. It is in the turbulent frontal area where weather events take place. This area also creates temperature changes. Weather phenomena include rain, thunderstorms, high winds, tornadoes, cloudiness, clear skies, and hurricanes. Different fronts can be plotted on weather maps using a set of designated symbols. **Surface weather maps** can also include symbols representing clouds, rain, temperature, air pressure, and fair weather.

The Ozone Layer, the Ionosphere, the Homosphere, and the Heterosphere

- The **ozone layer**, although contained within the stratosphere, is determined by ozone (O_3) concentrations. It absorbs the majority of ultraviolet light from the Sun.
- The **ionosphere** encompasses the mesosphere, thermosphere, and parts of the exosphere. The has molecules in this layer are partially ionized by solar radiation. It affects radio wave transmission and auroras.
- The **homosphere** encompasses the troposphere, stratosphere, and mesosphere. Gases in the homosphere are considered well mixed.
- The **heterosphere** encompasses the thermosphere and exosphere. In this layer, the distance that particles can move without colliding is large. As a result, gases are **stratified** according to their molecular weights. Heavier gases such as oxygen and nitrogen occur near the bottom of the heterosphere, while hydrogen, the lightest element, is found at the top.

Hydrosphere

Much of Earth is covered by a layer of water or ice called the **hydrosphere**. Most of the hydrosphere consists of ocean water. The **water cycle** and the many processes involved in it take place in the hydrosphere.

There are several theories regarding how the Earth's hydrosphere was formed. Earth contains more surface water than other planets in the inner solar system. **Outgassing**, the slow release of trapped water vapor from the Earth's interior, is one theory used to explain the existence of water on Earth. This does not really account for the quantity of water on Earth, however. Another hypothesis is that the early Earth was subjected to a period of bombardment by **comets** and **water-rich asteroids**, which resulted in the release of water into the Earth's environment. If this is true, much of the water on the surface of the Earth today originated from the outer parts of the solar system beyond Neptune.

Frontal Systems and Weather Maps

Cold fronts are represented on weather maps as a blue line. Solid blue triangles are used to indicate the direction of movement. **Warm fronts** are represented with a red line. Solid red semi-circles are used to indicate the direction of the front. The cold and warm front symbols are merged and alternated to point in opposite directions to indicate a **stationary front**. An **occluded front** is represented by a purple line with alternating solid purple triangles and semi-circles. A **surface trough** is represented by an orange dashed line. A **squall** or **shear line** is represented by a red line. Two dots and a dash are alternated to form the line. A **dry line** is represented by an orange line with semi-circles in outline form. A **tropical wave** is represented by a straight orange line. An "L" is used to indicate an area of **low atmospheric pressure** and an "H" is used to indicate an area of **high atmospheric pressure**.

Bergeron Classification System

The **Bergeron classification system** uses three sets of letters to identify the following characteristics of air masses: moisture content, thermal characteristics from where they originated, and the stability of the atmosphere. "**Moisture content**" abbreviations are as follows: "c" represents the dry continental air masses and "m" stands for the moist maritime air masses. "**Thermal characteristics**" abbreviations are as follows: "T" indicates the air mass is tropical in origin; "P" indicates the air mass is polar in origin; "A" indicates the air mass is Antarctic in origin; "M" stands for monsoon; "E" indicates the air mass is equatorial in origin; and "S" is used to represent superior air, which is dry air formed by a downward motion. "**Stability of the Atmosphere**" abbreviations are as follows: "k" indicates the mass is colder than the ground below it, while "w" indicates the mass is warmer than the ground. For example, cP is a continental polar air mass, while cPk is a polar air mass blowing over the Gulf Stream, which is warmer than the mass.

Shearline, Dry Line, Squall Line, and Tropical Waves

- **Shearline**: This evolves from a stationary front that has gotten smaller. Wind direction shifts over a short distance.
- **Dry line or dew point line**: This separates two warm air masses of differing moisture content. At lower altitudes, the moist air mass wedges under the drier air. At higher altitudes, the dry air wedges under the moist air. This is a frequent occurrence in the Midwest and Canada, where the dry air of the Southwest and the moister air of the Gulf of Mexico meet. This can lead to extreme weather events, including tornadoes and thunderstorms.
- **Squall line**: Severe thunderstorms can form at the front of or ahead of a cold front. In some cases, severe thunderstorms can also outrun cold fronts. A squall line can produce extreme weather in the form of heavy rain, hail, lightning, strong winds, tornadoes, and waterspouts.
- **Tropical waves or easterly waves**: These are atmospheric troughs or areas of low air pressure that travel westward in the tropics, causing clouds and thunderstorms.

Latitude, Longitude, and the Equator

For the purposes of tracking time and location, the Earth is divided into sections with imaginary lines. Lines that run vertically around the globe through the poles are lines of **longitude**, sometimes called meridians. The **Prime Meridian** is the longitudinal reference point of 0. Longitude is measured in 15-degree increments toward the east or west. Degrees are further divided into 60 minutes, and each minute is divided into 60 seconds. Lines of **latitude** run horizontally around the Earth parallel to the equator, which is the 0-reference point and the widest point of the Earth. Latitude is the distance north or south from the equator, and is also measured in degrees, minutes, and seconds.

Tropic of Cancer, Tropic of Capricorn, Antarctic, and Arctic Circles

- **Tropic of Cancer**: This is located at 23.5 degrees north. The Sun is directly overhead at noon on June 21st in the Tropic of Cancer, which marks the beginning of summer in the Northern Hemisphere.
- **Tropic of Capricorn**: This is located at 23.5 degrees south. The Sun is directly overhead at noon on December 21st in the Tropic of Capricorn, which marks the beginning of winter in the Northern Hemisphere.

- **Arctic Circle**: This is located at 66.5 degrees north, and marks the start of when the Sun is not visible above the horizon. This occurs on December 21st, the same day the Sun is directly over the Tropic of Capricorn.
- **Antarctic Circle**: This is located at 66.5 degrees south, and marks the start of when the Sun is not visible above the horizon. This occurs on June 21st, which marks the beginning of winter in the Southern Hemisphere and is when the Sun is directly over the Tropic of Cancer.

Properties of Water

Water contains an extensive network of **hydrogen bonds**. As a result, water has a high **heat capacity**, meaning that it can absorb a large amount of heat without changing temperature, and a high **heat of vaporization**, meaning that it can absorb a large amount of heat before it transforms from a liquid to a gas state. One result of these properties is that water helps to regulate the Earth's climate by absorbing **thermal radiation**.

The presence of hydrogen bonds is also responsible for **capillary action**, which allows water to rise into a narrow tube against the force of gravity. This is part of the reason that water can be transported into the body of trees.

When water freezes, it becomes less dense and **expands**, allowing ice to float on water. This **insulates** the water below, preventing a lake from freezing from the bottom up. If a lake froze from the bottom up, it might destroy life in the lake, and might not completely thaw during the summer.

Review Video: Properties of Water
Visit mometrix.com/academy and enter code: 279526

Ocean

The **ocean** is a salty body of water that covers 71% of the Earth's surface. Geographically, the ocean is divided into three large oceans: the **Pacific Ocean**, the **Atlantic Ocean**, and the **Indian Ocean**. There are also other divisions, such as gulfs, bays, and various types of seas, including Mediterranean and marginal seas. The ocean's depth is greatest at **Challenger Deep** in the Mariana Trench (10,924 meters below sea level).

Salinity is a measure of the amount of dissolved salts in ocean water. It is defined in terms of conductivity. Salinity is influenced by the geologic formations in the area, with igneous formations leading to lower salinity and sedimentary formations leading to higher salinity. Dryer areas with greater rates of evaporation also have higher salt concentrations. Areas where fresh water mixes with ocean water have lower salt concentrations. Hydrogen and oxygen make up about 96.5% of sea water. The major constituents of the dissolved solids of sea water at an atomic level are chlorine (55.3%), sodium (30.8%), magnesium (3.7%), sulfur (2.6%), calcium (1.2%), and potassium (1.1%). The salinity of ocean water is fairly constant, ranging from 34.60 to 34.80 parts per thousand, which is 200 parts per million. Measuring variation on this small of a scale requires instruments that are accurate to about one part per million.

Ocean Floor

The **ocean floor** includes features similar to those found on land, such as mountains, ridges, plains, and canyons. Other features of the ocean floor are as follows:

- The oceanic **crust** is a thin, dense layer that is about 10 km thick.
- A **seamount** is an undersea volcanic peak that rises to a height of at least 1,000 meters.

- A **guyot** is a seamount with a flat top.
- A **mid-ocean ridge** is a continuous undersea mountain chain.
- **Sills** are low parts of ridges separating ocean basins or other seas.
- **Trenches** are long, narrow troughs.

Gyres and Coriolis Effect

Gyres are surface ocean currents that form large circular patterns. In the Northern Hemisphere, they flow clockwise. In the Southern Hemisphere, they flow counterclockwise. These directions are caused by the **Coriolis effect**. The Coriolis effect occurs due to the fact that the Earth is a rotating object. In the Northern Hemisphere, currents appear to be curving to the right. In the Southern Hemisphere, currents appear to be curving to the left. Gyres tend to flow in the opposite direction near the Earth's poles. In the portion of the Pacific Ocean north of the equator, the major currents are North Pacific, California, North Equatorial, and Kuroshio. In the South Pacific, they are South Equatorial, East Australia, South Pacific, and Peru. In the North Atlantic, they are the North Atlantic Drift, Canary, North Equatorial, and Gulf Stream. In the South Atlantic, they are South Equatorial, Brazil, South Atlantic, and Benguela.

Ocean Currents

Surface currents are caused by winds. **Subsurface currents**, which occur deep beneath the ocean's surface, are caused by land masses and the Earth's rotation. The density of ocean water can also affect currents. Sea water with a higher salinity is denser than sea water with a lower salinity. Water from denser areas flows to areas with water that is less dense. Currents are classified by **temperature**. Colder polar sea water flows south towards warmer water, forming **cold currents**. **Warm water currents** swirl around the basins and equator. In turn, heat lost and gained by the ocean creates winds. Ocean currents play a significant role in transferring this heat toward the poles, which aids in the development of many types of weather phenomena.

Upwelling and Ekman Transport

Upwelling occurs where wind blows parallel to a coast. This causes the ocean surface to move away from the coast. Deep-sea water, which is usually cold and rich in nutrients, rises to takes its place. **Ekman transport** refers to the impact of the Coriolis effect when wind moves water. Wind blowing in one direction tries to move the surface layer of water in a straight line, but the rotation of the Earth causes water to move in a curved direction. The wind continues to blow the surface of the water and the surface water turns slightly. Below the surface, the water turns even more, eventually creating a spiral. This creates water movement at a right angle to the wind direction. The importance of upwelling is that it brings the nutrient-rich dead and rotting sea creatures closer to the ocean's surface. Here, they are consumed by **phytoplankton**, which is in turn eaten by **zooplankton**. Fish eat the zooplankton, and larger creatures and humans eat the fish. **Downwelling** is the opposite of upwelling.

Deep Sea Currents and Ocean Waves

Deep sea currents are often likened to a conveyor belt because they circumnavigate the entire ocean, albeit weakly, and slowly mix deeper and shallower water. In the winter, deep circulation carries cold water from high latitudes to lower latitudes throughout the world. This takes place in areas where most water is at a depth of between 4 and 5 km. This water mass can reach temperatures of 4°C or lower. Surface ocean temperatures average about 17°C, but can vary from 2°C to 36°C. The vast cold mass of sea water is also dense and has a high saline content, which forces it to sink at high latitudes. It spreads out, stratifies, and fills the ocean basins. Deep mixing occurs and then the water upwells. The manner in which deep sea currents move can be described as **abyssal circulation**.

Most waves in the ocean are formed by winds. The stronger the winds are, the larger the waves will be. The highest point of a wave is the **crest**. The lowest point of a wave is the **trough**. The **wavelength** is measured from crest to crest. The wave **height** is measured from the trailing trough to the peak of the crest. The wave **frequency** refers to the number of wave crests passing a designated point each second. A wave **period** is the time it takes for a wave crest to reach the point of the wave crest of the previous wave. The **energy** in the wave runs into the shallow sea floor. This causes the wave to become steeper and then fall over, or break.

Waves that reach the shore are not all the same size. They can be larger or smaller than average. About once an hour, there is usually a wave that is twice the size of others. There are even larger, but rare, **rogue waves**, which often travel alone and in a different direction from other waves. **Swells** are waves that have traveled a great distance. These types of waves are usually large waves with flatter crests. They are very regular in shape and size.

Tides

The sea level slowly rises and falls over the period of a day. These types of waves on the sea surface are known as **tides**. Tides have wavelengths of thousands of kilometers. They differ from other wave types in that they are created by slow and very small changes in gravity due to the motion of the Sun and the Moon relative to Earth.

The **gravitational pull** of the Sun and Moon causes the oceans to rise and fall each day, creating high and low tides. Most areas have two high tides and two low tides per day. Because the Moon is closer to the Earth than the Sun, its gravitational pull is much greater. The water on the side of the Earth that is closest to the Moon and the water on the opposite side experience **high tide**. The two **low tides** occur on the other sides. This changes as the Moon revolves around the Earth. **Tidal range** is the measurement of the height difference between low and high tide. Tidal range also changes with the location of the Sun and Moon throughout the year, creating spring and neap tides. When all these bodies are aligned, the combined gravitational pull is greater and the tidal range is also greater. This is what creates the **spring tide**. The **neap tide** is when the tidal range is at its lowest, which occurs when the Sun and Moon are at right angles.

Review Video: Moon and Sun on Ocean Tides
Visit mometrix.com/academy and enter code: 902956

Seismic Sea Waves

Seismic sea waves or **tsunamis** (sometimes mistakenly called tidal waves) are formed by **seismic activity**. A tsunami is a series of waves with long wavelengths and long periods. Far out at sea, the heights of these waves are typically less than one meter. The wavelength may be 100 km and the wave period may range from five minutes to one hour. However, as seismic sea waves approach the shoreline, the bottom of the wave is slowed down by the shallower sea floor. The top is not slowed as much, and wave height increases to as much as 20 meters. These waves can hit the shore at speeds of up to 30 miles per hour. Tsunamis are caused by earthquakes, submarine landslides, and volcanic eruptions.

Rift Valleys

Rift valleys occur both on land and in the ocean. They are a result of **plate tectonics** and occur when plates are spreading apart. In the ocean, this is part of the crust development cycle in which new crust is created at mid-ocean ridges and old crust is lost at the trenches. The Mid-Atlantic Ridge is an example of this. It occurs at divergent Eurasian and North American plates and in the South Atlantic, African, and

South American plates. The East Pacific Rise is also a mid-oceanic ridge. The most extensive rift valley is located along the crest of the mid-ocean ridge system. It is a result of sea floor spreading.

Shorelines and Coastal Processes

The area where land meets the sea is called the **shoreline**. This marks the average position of the ocean. Longshore currents create **longshore drift** or **transport** (also called beach drift). This is when ocean waves move toward a beach at an angle, which moves water along the coast. Sediment is eroded from some areas and deposited in others. In this way, it is moved along the beach. **Rip currents** are strong, fast currents that occur when part of longshore current moves away from the beach. Hard, man-made structures built perpendicular to the beach tend to trap sand on the up-current side. Erosion occurs on the down-current side. Features formed by the sediment deposited by waves include spits, bay-mouth bars, tombolos, barrier islands, and buildups. **Sand** is composed of weather-resistant, granular materials like quartz and orthoclase. In some locations, it is composed of rock and basalt.

Weathering erodes rock and soil into sand. Other parts of the soil such as clay and silt are deposited in areas of the continental shelf. The larger sand particles get deposited in the form of a **beach**. This includes a **near shore**, which is underwater, a **fore shore**, the area typically considered the beach, and a **back shore**. The **offshore** starts about 5 meters from the shoreline and extends to about 20 meters. The beach also includes wet and dry parts and a fore dune and rear dune. Waves typically move sand from the sea to the beach, and gravity and wave action move it back again. Wind gradually pushes sand particles uphill in a jumping motion called saltation. Sand stays deposited in the form of **dunes** and the dunes appear as if they roll backward. Storms can both erode a beach and provide additional deposition.

Black Smokers

A **black smoker** is a type of hydrothermal vent formed when superheated water from below Earth's crust emerges from the ocean floor. This hot water is also rich in sulfides and other minerals from the Earth's crust. When the hot water comes in contact with the cold ocean water, it creates a black chimney-like structure around the vent. Water temperatures around black smokers have been recorded at 400°C. However, water pressure is too great on the sea floor to allow for boiling. The water is also very acidic (twice that of vinegar). It is estimated that the yearly volume of water passing through black smokers is 1.4×10^{14} kg.

Carbon Cycle, Phytoplankton, and Zooplankton

- The **carbon and nutrient cycles** of the ocean are processes that are due in part to the deep currents, mixing, and upwelling that occur in the ocean. **Carbon dioxide** (CO_2) from the atmosphere is dissolved into the ocean at higher latitudes and distributed to the denser deep water. Where upwelling occurs, CO_2 is brought back to the surface and emitted into the tropical air.
- **Phytoplankton** are typically single-celled organisms that are nourished by the Sun. They are photosynthetic autotrophs, meaning they convert water, carbon dioxide, and solar energy into food. They drift with the currents, produce oxygen as a byproduct, and serve as a food source. Zooplankton feed on phytoplankton.
- **Zooplankton** are heterotrophic organisms, meaning they do not synthesize their own food. Zooplankton can be single-celled creatures or much larger organisms, such as jellyfish, mollusks, and crustaceans.

El Niño-Southern Oscillation (ENSO)

The **El Niño-Southern Oscillation (ENSO)** is a climate pattern of the Pacific Ocean area that lasts 6 to 18 months and causes weather that is different from the expected seasonal patterns and variations. There are two sets of events associated with ENSO: El Niño and La Niña. The usual weather patterns for the Pacific Ocean involve the movement of sea water by winds from the eastern part of the tropical Pacific to the western part of the Pacific Ocean. This pattern causes cold deep water upwells in the eastern Pacific. This creates wet weather and is considered a low-pressure system. Conversely, the eastern Pacific is a dry, high-pressure system. **El Niño** weakens upwelling because equalization in air pressure leads to less wind, which leads to more water staying in the eastern Pacific. **La Niña** increases upwelling because winds grow stronger because of higher air pressures across the Pacific. Both El Niño and La Niña cause extreme weather events such as droughts, heavy rain, and flooding.

North Atlantic Oscillation (NAO).

The **North Atlantic Oscillation** is a climatic occurrence that affects winter weather in the Northern Hemisphere, particularly in the east coast regions of the United States, Europe, and North Africa. Atmospheric pressure over the North Atlantic caused by the Icelandic Low and the high pressure Azores leads to the North Atlantic Oscillation. There is both a "**positive**" and "**negative**" phase of the NAO. The positive phase is when strong winds caused by a large difference in air pressure send wet winter storms from eastern North America to northern Europe. Weaker winds associated with a smaller difference in air pressure cause eastern North America and northern Europe to have fewer winter storms. Instead, the weather is rainy in southern Europe and North Africa.

Beaufort Wind Scale.

The **Beaufort wind scale** assigns a numerical value to wind conditions and the appearance of the sea. **Zero** represents a calm, mirror-like sea with no measurable wind. **Twelve** is the maximum on the Beaufort scale, and represents hurricane force winds with speeds of 35.2 meters per second (m/s). Visibility is greatly reduced, the sea air is filled with foam, and the sea is completely white with driving spray. The scale is as follows: 1 is light wind with a speed of 1.2 m/s; 2 is a light breeze of 2.8 m/s; 3 is a gentle breeze of 4.9 m/s; 4 is a moderate breeze of 7.7 m/s; and 5 is a fresh breeze of 10.5 m/s. At 5, there are moderate waves, many white caps, and some spray. Six is a strong breeze of 13.1 m/s; 7 is a near gale with wind speeds of 15.8 m/s; 8 is gale force winds of 18.8 m/s; 9 is strong gales of 22.1 m/s; 10 is considered a storm with wind speeds of 25.9 m/s; and 11 is a violent storm.

Describe the process of deposition.

Deposition, or **sedimentation**, is the geological process in which previously eroded material is transported or added to a land form or land mass. Erosion and sedimentation are complementary geological processes. **Running water** causes a substantial amount of deposition of transported materials in both fresh water and coastal areas. Examples include gravity transporting material down the slope of a mountain and depositing it at the base of the slope. Another example is when sandstorms deposit particles in other locations. When glaciers melt and retreat, it can result in the deposition of sediments. **Evaporation** is also considered to cause deposition since dissolved materials are left behind when water evaporates. Deposition can include the buildup of **organic materials**. For example, chalk is partially made up of the small calcium carbonate skeletons of marine plankton, which helps create more calcium carbonate from chemical processes.

Weathering

There are two basic types of **weathering**: mechanical and chemical. Weathering is a very prominent process on the Earth's surface. Materials weather at different rates, which are known as differential weathering. Mechanical and chemical weathering is interdependent. For example, **chemical weathering** can loosen the bonds between molecules and allow mechanical weathering to take place. **Mechanical weathering** can expose the surfaces of land masses and allow chemical weathering to take place. Impact, abrasion, frost wedging, root wedging, salt wedging, and uploading are types of mechanical weathering.

Types of chemical weathering are dissolution, hydration, hydrolysis, oxidation, biological, and carbonation. The primary type of chemical weathering is caused by **acid rain**. Carbonic and sulfuric acids can enter rain when they are present in the atmosphere. This lowers the pH value of rain, making it more acidic. Normal rain water has a pH value of 5.5. Acid rain has a pH value of 4 or less.

Erosion

Erosion is the wearing-away of rock materials from the Earth's surface. Erosion can be classified as natural geologic erosion and erosion due to human activity. **Natural geologic erosion** occurs due to weathering and gravity. Factors involved in natural geologic erosion are typically long term forces. **Human activities** such as development, farming, and deforestation occur over shorter periods of time. Soil, which supports plant growth, is the topmost layer of organic material. One type of erosion is **sheet erosion**, which is the gradual and somewhat uniform removal of surface soil. **Rills** are small rivulets that cut into soil. **Gullies** are rills that have become enlarged due to extended water run-off. **Sandblows** are caused by wind blowing away particles. Negative effects of erosion include sedimentation in rivers, which can pollute water and damage ecosystems. Erosion can also result in the removal of topsoil, which destroys crops and prevents plants from growing. This reduces food production and alters ecosystems.

Physical Properties

Physical properties (as opposed to chemical structures) used to identify **minerals** are hardness, luster, color, cleavage, and streak. Senses other than sight, such as touch, taste, and smell, may be used to observe physical properties. **Hardness** is the resistance a mineral has to scratches. The *Mohs Hardness Scale* is used to rate hardness from 1 to 10. **Color** can often not be determined definitively as some minerals can be more than one color. **Luster** is determined by reflected light. Luster can be described as metallic (shiny), sub-metallic (dull), non-metallic (vitreous, like glass), or earthy (like dirt or powder). **Streak** is the true color of the mineral in powdered form. It can be determined by rubbing the specimen across an unglazed porcelain tile. Fracture or **cleavage** is how a mineral reacts to stress, such as being struck with a hammer. Other properties that can be used to identify rocks and minerals include magnetism, a salty taste, or a pungent odor in a streak test.

Rocks and Minerals

Minerals are naturally occurring, inorganic solids with a definite chemical composition and an orderly internal crystal structure. A **polymorph** is two minerals with the same chemical composition, but a different crystal structure. **Rocks** are aggregates of one or more minerals, and may also contain **mineraloids** (minerals lacking a crystalline structure) and organic remains. The three types of rocks are sedimentary, igneous, and metamorphic. Rocks are classified based on their formation and the minerals they contain. Minerals are classified by their chemical composition.

Review Video: Rocks vs. Minerals
Visit mometrix.com/academy and enter code: 947587

Geology, Petrology, and Mineralogy

- **Geology** is the study of the planet Earth as it pertains to the composition, structure, and origin of its rocks.
- **Petrology** is the study of rocks, including their composition, texture, structure, occurrence, mode of formation, and history.
- **Mineralogy** is the study of minerals.

Mineral Classification

Minerals are **classified** by chemical composition and internal crystalline structure. They are organized into **classes**. Native elements such as gold and silver are not classified in this manner. The eight classes are sulfides, oxides\hydroxides, halides, carbonates, sulfates, phosphates, and silicates. These classes are based on the dominant **anion** (negatively charged ion) or anionic group. Minerals are classified in this way for three main reasons. First, minerals with the same anion have unmistakable resemblances. Second, minerals with the same anion are often found in the same geologic environment. For example, calcite and dolomite, which belong to the same group, are often found together. Last, this method is similar to the naming convention used to identify inorganic compounds in chemistry. Minerals can be further separated into groups on the basis of **internal structure**.

Sedimentary Rocks

Sedimentary rocks are formed by the process of **lithification**, which involves compaction, the expulsion of liquids from pores, and the cementation of the pre-existing rock. It is pressure and temperature that are responsible for this process. Sedimentary rocks are often formed in layers in the presence of water, and may contain organic remains, such as fossils. Sedimentary rocks are organized into three groups: detrital, biogenic, and chemical. **Texture** refers to the size, shape, and grains of sedimentary rock. Texture can be used to determine how a particular sedimentary rock was created. **Composition** refers to the types of minerals present in the rock. The **origin** of sedimentary rock refers to the type of water that was involved in its creation. Marine deposits, for example, likely involved ocean environments, while continental deposits likely involved dry land and lakes.

Metamorphic Rocks

Metamorphic rock is that which has been changed by great heat and pressure. This results in a variety of outcomes, including deformation, compaction, destruction of the characteristics of the original rock, bending, folding, formation of new minerals because of chemical reactions, and changes in the size and shape of the mineral grain. For example, the igneous rock ferromagnesian can be changed into schist and gneiss. The sedimentary rock carbonaceous can be changed into marble. The texture of metamorphic rocks can be classified as foliated and unfoliated. **Foliation**, or layering, occurs when rock is compressed along one axis during recrystallization. This can be seen in schist and shale. **Unfoliated** rock does not include this banding. Rocks that are compressed equally from all sides or lack specific minerals will be unfoliated. An example is marble.

Igneous Rocks

Igneous rock is formed from **magma**, which is molten material originating from beneath the Earth's surface. Depending upon where magma cools, the resulting igneous rock can be classified as intrusive, plutonic, hypabyssal, extrusive, or volcanic. Magma that solidifies at a depth is **intrusive**, cools slowly, and has a coarse grain as a result. An example is granite. Magma that solidifies at or near the surface is **extrusive**, cools quickly, and usually has a fine grain. An example is basalt. Magma that actually flows out of the Earth's surface is called **lava**. Some extrusive rock cools so quickly that crystals do not have time to form. These rocks have a glassy appearance. An example is obsidian. **Hypabyssal** rock is igneous rock that is formed at medium depths.

Review Video: Igneous, Sedimentary, and Metamorphic Rocks
Visit mometrix.com/academy and enter code: 689294

Granite and Basalt

Both granite and basalt are plentiful igneous rocks, but granite is intrusive and basalt is extrusive. Intrusive rocks come from **magma** within the Earth's crust and cool slowly. Extrusive rocks are formed from **lava** on the Earth's surface and cool more quickly than intrusive rocks. **Granite** is an igneous rock with a medium to coarse texture that is formed from magma. It can be a variety of colors. It is intrusive, massive, hard, and coarse grained. It forms a major part of continental crust. It can be composed of potassium feldspar, plagioclase feldspar, and quartz, as well as various amounts of muscovite, biotite, and hornblende-type amphiboles. **Basalt** is extrusive and usually colored gray to black. It has a fine grain due to quicker cooling. Basalt is porphyritic, meaning it contains larger crystals in a fine matrix. Basalt is usually composed of amphibole and pyroxene, and sometimes of plagioclase, feldspathoids, and olivine.

Soil Profiles

A **soil profile** depicts the parallel layers of rock and soil in the earth's crust. The layers are:

- **O** (organic matter) – consists of non-decomposed organic material
- **A** (surface soil) – organic substances mixed with minerals
- **B** (subsoil) – clay and organic substances
- **C** (parent rock) – large, unbroken rock layer
- **R** (bedrock) – layer of primarily unbroken rock

Earth's Structure and Layers

The Earth is **ellipsoid**, not perfectly spherical. This means the diameter is different through the poles and at the equator. Through the poles, the Earth is about 12,715 km in diameter. The approximate center of the Earth is at a depth of 6,378 km. The Earth is divided into a crust, mantle, and core. The **core** consists of a solid inner portion. Moving outward, the molten outer core occupies the space from about a depth of 5,150 km to a depth of 2,890 km. The **mantle** consists of a lower and upper layer. The lower layer includes the D' (D prime) and D" (D double-prime) layers. The solid portion of the upper mantle and crust together form the **lithosphere**, or rocky sphere. Below this, but still within the mantle, is the **asthenosphere**, or weak sphere. These layers are distinguishable because the lithosphere is relatively rigid, while the asthenosphere resembles a thick liquid.

The Earth's **core** consists of hot iron and forms of nickel. The **mantle** consists of different materials, including iron, magnesium, and calcium. The **crust** covers the mantle, consists of a thin layer of much lighter rocks, and is further subdivided into continental and oceanic portions. The **continental portion** consists mainly of silicates, such as granite. The **oceanic portion** consists of heavier, volcanic rocks, such as basalt. The upper 10 miles of the lithosphere layer (the crust and part of the mantle) is made up of 95% igneous rock (or its metamorphic equivalent), 4% shale, 0.75% sandstone, and 0.25% limestone. There are over 4,000 known minerals, but only about 20 make up some 95% of all rocks. There are, however, more than 3,000 individual kinds of minerals in the Earth's crust. **Silicates** are the largest group of minerals.

Mountains

Orogeny refers to the formation of mountains, particularly the processes of folding and faulting caused by plate tectonics. **Folding** is when layers of sedimentary rock are pressed together by continental plate movements. Sections of rock that are folded upward are called **anticlines**. Sections of rock that are folded downward are called **synclines**. Examples of folded mountains are the Alps and the Himalayans. **Fault-block mountains** are created when tectonic plate movement produces tension that results in displacement. Mountains in the Southwest United States are examples of fault-blocking mountains. Mountains can also be caused by **volcanic activity** and **erosion**.

Maps

Traditional maps represent land in two dimensions, while **topographic maps** represent elevation through the use of contour lines. **Contour lines** help show changes to elevations above the surface of the Earth and on the ocean floor. They also help show the shape of Earth's surface features. The United States Geological Survey (USGS) produces frequently used quadrangle maps in various scales. A **quadrangle topographic map** is bounded by two lines of latitude and two lines of longitude. A **7.5-minute map** shows an area that spans 7.5 minutes of latitude and 7.5 minutes of longitude. The name of the quadrangle map appears at the top, and usually indicates the name of a prominent feature. Topographic maps that show much less detail are also available. They might show a much larger area, such as a country or state. USGS quad maps also refer to **adjacent quad maps**. Other information contained on quad maps includes the projection and grid used, scale, contour intervals, and magnetic declination, which is the difference between true north and magnetic north.

Plate Tectonics

The **theory of plate tectonics** states that the lithosphere, the solid portion of the mantle and Earth's crust, consists of **major and minor plates**. These plates are on top of and move with the viscous upper mantle, which is heated because of the **convection cycle** that occurs in the interior of the Earth. There are different estimates as to the exact number of major and minor plates. The number of major plates is believed to be between 9 and 15, and it is thought that there may be as many as 40 minor plates. The United States is atop the North American plate. The Pacific Ocean is atop the Pacific plate. The point at which these two plates slide horizontally along the San Andreas fault is an example of a **transform plate boundary**. The other two types of boundaries are **divergent** (plates that are spreading apart and forming new crust) and **convergent** (the process of subduction causes one plate to go under another). The movement of plates is what causes other features of the Earth's crust, such as mountains, volcanoes, and earthquakes.

Heat is transferred through the process of **convection**, which is a cycle. Hot material rises and spreads, cooling as it spreads. The cool material then sinks, where it is heated again. The process of convection can be seen in a pot of boiling water. It is believed this same process is happening deep within the Earth. Greater depths are associated with more pressure and heat. The weight of all the rocks causes the increase in pressure, while the decay of heavy radioactive elements such as uranium produces heat. This creates hot areas of molten material that find their way upward and to the surface in an effort to **equalize**, which means pressure and temperature are reduced. This causes the processes involved in **plate tectonics**.

Review Video: Plate Tectonic Theory
Visit mometrix.com/academy and enter code: 535013

Volcanoes and Plate Tectonics

Volcanoes can occur along any type of tectonic plate boundary. At a **divergent boundary**, as plates move apart, magma rises to the surface, cools, and forms a ridge. An example of this is the mid-Atlantic ridge. **Convergent boundaries**, where one plate slides under another, are often areas with a lot of volcanic activity. The **subduction process** creates magma. When it rises to the surface, volcanoes can be created. Volcanoes can also be created in the middle of a plate over hot spots. **Hot spots** are locations where narrow plumes of magma rise through the mantle in a fixed place over a long period of time. The Hawaiian Islands and Midway are examples. The plate shifts and the island moves. Magma continues to rise through the mantle, however, which produces another island. Volcanoes can be active, dormant, or extinct. **Active volcanoes** are those that are erupting or about to erupt. **Dormant volcanoes** are those that might erupt in the future and still have internal volcanic activity. **Extinct volcanoes** are those that will not erupt.

Seafloor-Spreading

Seafloor spreading is the result of underwater volcanic activity. It is a process in which new oceanic crust is formed through volcanic activity at a mid-ocean ridge and then moves away from the ridge. This process provides a mechanism for continental drift.

Volcanoes

The three types of volcanoes are shield, cinder cone, and composite. A **shield volcano** is created by a long-term, relatively gentle eruption. This type of volcanic mountain is created by each progressive lava flow that occurs over time. A **cinder cone volcano** is created by explosive eruptions. Lava is spewed out of a vent into the air. As it falls to the ground, the lava cools into cinders and ash, which build up around the volcano in a cone shape. A **composite volcano** is a combination of the other two types of volcanoes. In this type, there are layers of lava flows and layers of ash and cinder.

Earthquakes

Most **earthquakes** are caused by tectonic plate movement. They occur along fractures called **faults** or **fault zones**. Friction in the faults prevents smooth movement. Tension builds up over time, and the release of that tension results in earthquakes. Faults are grouped based on the type of slippage that occurs. The types of faults are dip-slip, strike-slip, and oblique-slip. A **dip-slip fault** involves vertical movement along the fault plane. In a normal dip-slip fault, the wall that is above the fault plane moves down. In a reverse dip-slip fault, the wall above the fault plane moves up. A **strike-slip fault** involves horizontal movement along the fault plane. **Oblique-slip faults** involve both vertical and horizontal movement. The **Richter magnitude scale** measures how much seismic energy was released by an earthquake. The **epicenter** is the area on the earth's surface that is directly above the point where an earthquake originates.

Review Video: Earthquakes
Visit mometrix.com/academy and enter code: 252531

Review Video: Measuring Earthquakes
Visit mometrix.com/academy and enter code: 393730

Seismic Deformation

There are two types of deformations created by an earthquake fault rupture: static and dynamic. **Static deformation** permanently displaces the ground. Examples are when a road or railroad track becomes distorted by an earthquake. Plate tectonics stresses the fault by creating tension with slow plate movements. An earthquake releases the tension. Plate tectonics also cause a second type of deformation. This type results in dynamic motions that take the form of **seismic waves**. These sound waves can be **compression waves**, also known as primary or P waves, or **shear waves**, also known as secondary or S waves. P waves travel fastest, with speeds ranging between 1.5 and 8 kilometers per second. Shear waves are slower. P waves shake the ground in the direction they are propagating. S waves shake perpendicularly or transverse to the direction of propagation. **Seismographs** use a simple pendulum to record earthquake movement in a record called a **seismogram**. A seismogram can help seismologists estimate the distance, direction, Richter magnitude, and type of faulting of an earthquake.

Hydrologic Cycle

The **hydrologic**, or **water**, **cycle** refers to water movement on, above, and in the Earth. Water can be in any one of its three states during different phases of the cycle. The three states of water are liquid water, frozen ice, and water vapor. Processes involved in the hydrologic cycle include precipitation, canopy interception, snow melt, runoff, infiltration, subsurface flow, evaporation, sublimation, advection, condensation, and transpiration. **Precipitation** occurs when condensed water vapor falls to Earth. Examples include rain, fog drip, and various forms of snow, hail, and sleet. **Canopy interception** occurs when precipitation lands on plant foliage instead of falling to the ground and evaporating. **Snowmelt** is runoff produced by melting snow. **Infiltration** occurs when water flows from the surface into the ground. **Subsurface flow** refers to water that flows underground. **Evaporation** occurs when water in a liquid state changes to a gas. **Sublimation** occurs when water in a solid state (such as snow or ice) changes to water vapor without going through a liquid phase. Advection is the movement of water through the atmosphere. **Condensation** occurs when water vapor changes to liquid water. **Transpiration** occurs when water vapor is released from plants into the air.

Components and Properties of the Solar System and the Universe

Astronomy

Astronomy is the scientific study of celestial objects and their positions, movements, and structures. **Celestial** does not refer to the Earth in particular, but does include its motions as it moves through space. Other objects include the Sun, the Moon, planets, satellites, asteroids, meteors, comets, stars, galaxies, the universe, and other space phenomena. The term astronomy has its roots in the Greek words "astro" and "nomos," which means "laws of the stars."

Review Video: Astronomy
Visit mometrix.com/academy and enter code: 640556

The Sun

The **Sun** is at the center of the solar system. It is composed of 70% hydrogen (H) and 28% helium (He). The remaining 2% is made up of metals. The Sun is one of 100 billion stars in the **Milky Way galaxy**. Its diameter is 1,390,000 km, its mass is 1.989×10^{30} kg, its surface temperature is 5,800 K, and its core temperature is 15,600,000 K. The Sun represents more than 99.8% of the total mass of the solar system. At the core, the temperature is 15.6 million K, the pressure is 250 billion atmospheres, and the density is more than 150 times that of water. The surface is called the **photosphere**. The **chromosphere** lies above this, and the **corona**, which extends millions of kilometers into space, is next. **Sunspots** are relatively cool regions on the surface with a temperature of 3,800 K. Temperatures in the corona are over 1,000,000 K. Its **magnetosphere**, or heliosphere, extends far beyond Pluto.

Review Video: The Sun
Visit mometrix.com/academy and enter code: 699233

The Moon

The **Moon** is the fifth largest satellite in the solar system. It orbits the Earth about every 27.3 days. The changes of the Earth, Sun, and Moon in relation to each other cause the **phases** of the Moon, which repeat every 29.5 days. The Moon's **gravitational pull** (along with the Sun's) is responsible for the tides on Earth. Its diameter is about 3,474 km and its gravity is about 17% of Earth's. The **lunar maria** (plural of mare) on the Moon's surface is dark thin layers composed of dark basalt. They were formed by ancient volcanoes. There are many impact craters on the Moon. There were numerous impact craters on Earth at one time, but they have been transformed by erosion over time. Very few are still visible.

Equinox, Solstice, Perihelion, and Aphelion

- **Equinox**: This occurs twice each year when the Sun crosses the plane of the Earth's celestial equator. During an equinox, Earth is not tilted away from or toward the Sun. The length of day and night are roughly equal. The two equinoxes are the **March equinox** and the **September equinox**.
- **Solstice**: The **summer solstice**, the day with the most amount of sunlight, occurs on June 21st in the Northern Hemisphere and on December 21st in the Southern Hemisphere. The **winter solstice**, the day with the least amount of sunlight, occurs on December 21st in the Northern Hemisphere and on June 21st in the Southern Hemisphere.

- **Perihelion**: This is the point in an object's orbit when it is closest to the Sun.
- **Aphelion**: This is the point in an object's orbit when it is farthest from the Sun.

Origin of the Universe

The **Big Bang theory**, which is widely accepted among astronomers, was developed to explain the origin of the universe. The Big Bang theory states that all the matter in the universe was once in one place. This matter underwent a huge explosion that spread the matter into space. Galaxies formed from this material and the universe is still expanding. There are other theories regarding the origin of the universe, such as the **Steady-State theory** and the **Intelligent Design theory**.

Structure of the Universe

What can be seen of the universe is believed to be at least 93 billion light years across. To put this into perspective, the Milky Way galaxy is about 100,000 light years across. Our view of matter in the universe is that it forms into clumps. Matter is organized into stars, galaxies, clusters of galaxies, superclusters, and the Great Wall of galaxies. Galaxies consist of stars, some with planetary systems. Some estimates state that the universe is about 13 billion years old. It is not considered dense, and is believed to consist of 73 percent dark energy, 23 percent cold dark matter, and 4 percent regular matter. Cosmology is the study of the universe. Interstellar medium (ISM) is the gas and dust in the interstellar space between a galaxy's stars.

Life Cycle of a Star

There are different life cycle possibilities for **stars** after they initially form and enter into the main sequence stage. Small, relatively cold **red dwarfs** with relatively low masses burn hydrogen slowly, and will remain in the main sequence for hundreds of billions of years. Massive, hot **supergiants** will leave the main sequence after just a few million years. The Sun is a mid-sized star that may be in the **main sequence** for 10 billion years. After the main sequence, the star expands to become a **red giant**. Depending upon the initial mass of the star, it can become a **white dwarf** (from a medium-sized star), and then a small, cooling **black dwarf**. Massive stars become **red supergiants** (and sometimes **blue supergiants**), explode in a supernova, and then become **neutron stars.** The largest stars can become **black holes**.

Review Video: Types of Stars
Visit mometrix.com/academy and enter code: 831934

Birth of a Star

A **nebula** is a cloud of dust and gas that is composed primarily of hydrogen (97%) and helium (3%). Gravity causes parts of the nebula to clump together. This accretion continues adding atoms to the center of an unstable **protostar**. Equilibrium between gravity pulling atoms and gas pressure pushing heat and light away from the center is achieved. A star dies when it is no longer able to maintain equilibrium. A protostar may never become a star if it does not reach a critical core temperature. It may become a **brown dwarf** or a **gas giant** instead. If nuclear fusion of hydrogen into helium begins, a star is born. The "main sequence" of a star's life involves nuclear fusion reactions. During this time, the star contracts over billions of years to compensate for the heat and light energy lost. In the star's core, temperature, density, and pressure increase as the star contracts and the cycle continues.

Black Holes, Quasars, and Blazars

- A **black hole** is a space where the gravitational field is so powerful that everything, including light, is pulled into it. Once objects enter the surface, the event horizon, they cannot escape.
- **Quasar** stands for quasi-stellar radio source, which is an energetic galaxy with an active galactic nucleus. Quasars were first identified by their emissions of large amounts of electromagnetic energy, such as radio waves and visible light. These emissions differed from those associated with other galaxies.
- A **blazar** is a compact quasar associated with galaxies containing supermassive black holes.
- Although its existence has not yet been proven, **dark matter** may account for a large proportion of the mass of the universe. It is undetectable because it does not emit any radiation, but is believed to exist because of gravitational forces exerted on visible objects.

Galaxies

Galaxies consist of stars, stellar remnants, and dark matter. **Dwarf galaxies** contain as few as 10 million stars, while **giant galaxies** contain as many as 1 trillion stars. Galaxies are gravitationally bound, meaning the stars, star systems, other gases, and dust orbit the galaxy's center. The Earth exists in the **Milky Way galaxy** and the nearest galaxy to ours is the **Andromeda galaxy**. Galaxies can be classified by their visual shape into elliptical, spiral, irregular, and starburst galaxies. It is estimated that there are more than 100 billion galaxies in the universe ranging from 1,000 to 100,000 parsecs in diameter. Galaxies can be megaparsecs apart. **Intergalactic space** consists of a gas with an average density of less than one atom per cubic meter. Galaxies are organized into clusters which form superclusters. **Dark matter** may account for up to 90% of the mass of galaxies. Dark matter is still not well understood.

Review Video: Galaxies
Visit mometrix.com/academy and enter code: 226539

Review Video: Milky Way
Visit mometrix.com/academy and enter code: 445889

Sidereal and Solar Days

A **sidereal day** is four minutes shorter than a solar day. A **solar day** is the time it takes the Earth to complete one revolution and face the Sun again. From noon to noon is 24 hours. A sidereal day is measured against a distant "fixed" star. As the Earth completes one rotation, it has also completed part of its revolution around the Sun, so it completes a sidereal rotation in reference to the fixed star before it completes a solar rotation. The Sun travels along the ecliptic in 365.25 days. This can be tracked day after day before dawn. After one year, the stars appear back in their original positions. As a result, different constellations are viewable at different times of the year.

Sidereal years are slightly longer than **tropical years**. The difference is caused by the precession of the equinoxes. A calendar based on the sidereal year will be out of sync with the seasons at a rate of about one day every 71 years.

Astronomical Unit, Light Years, and Parsecs

An **astronomical unit**, also known as **AU**, is a widely used measurement in astronomy. One AU is equal to the distance from the Earth to the Sun, which is 150 million km, or 93 million miles. These distances can also be expressed as 149.60×10^9 m or 92.956×10^6 mi. A **light year (ly)** is the distance that light travels in a vacuum in one year. A light year is equal to about 10 trillion km, or 64,341 AU, and is used to measure large astronomical units. Also used for measuring large distances is the **parsec (pc)**, which is the preferred unit since it is better suited for recording observational data. A parsec is the parallax of one arcsecond, and is about 31 trillion km (about 19 trillion miles), or about 3.26 light years. It is used to calculate distances by triangulation. The AU distance from the Earth to the Sun is used to form the side of a right triangle.

Review Video: Measures of Distance used in Astronomy
Visit mometrix.com/academy and enter code: 961792

Hertzsprung-Russell Diagram

A **Hertzsprung-Russell diagram (H-R diagram or HRD)** is a plot or scattergraph depicting stars' temperatures and comparing them with stars' luminosities or magnitudes. This can help determine the age and evolutionary state of a star. A Hertzsprung-Russell diagram is also known as a **color-magnitude diagram (CMD)**. It helps represent the life cycles of stars. In these plots, temperatures are plotted from highest to lowest, which aids in the comparison of H-R diagrams and observations. Hertzsprung-Russell diagrams can have many variations. Most of the stars in these diagrams lie along the line called **main sequence**, which contains stars that are fusing hydrogen. Other groupings include white dwarfs, subgiants, giants, and supergiants.

Morgan-Keenan Classification System

Stars use the **Morgan-Keenan classification system**, which is based on spectral traits that indicate the ionization of the chromosphere. The following letter designations are used to indicate **temperature**, from hottest to coolest: O, B, A, F, G, K, and M. The phrase "Oh, be a fine girl/guy, kiss me" can be used as a memory aid. Different types of stars also have different corresponding colors. O stars are blue; A stars are white; G stars are yellow; and M stars are red. The numbers 0 to 9 are used to indicate tenths between two star classes. Zero indicates 0/10 and 9 indicates 9/10. **Luminosity output** is an indicator of size, and is expressed with the Roman numerals I, II, III, IV, and V. Supergiants are included in class I, giants are included in class III, and main sequence stars are included in class V. Using the Sun as an example, the spectral type G2V could be expressed as "a yellow two-tenths towards an orange main sequence star."

Solar Systems

The **solar system** is a planetary system of objects that exist in an ecliptic plane. Objects orbit around and are bound by gravity to a star called the **Sun**. Objects that orbit around the Sun include: planets, dwarf planets, moons, asteroids, meteoroids, cosmic dust, and comets. The definition of planets has changed. At one time, there were nine planets in the solar system. There are now eight. Planetary objects in the solar system include four inner, **terrestrial planets**: Mercury, Venus, Earth, and Mars. They are relatively small, dense, rocky, lack rings, and have few or no moons. The four outer, or **Jovian, planets** are Jupiter, Saturn, Uranus, and Neptune, which are large and have low densities, rings, and moons. They are also known as **gas giants**. Between the inner and outer planets is the **asteroid belt**. Beyond Neptune is the **Kuiper belt**. Within these belts are five **dwarf planets**: Ceres, Pluto, Haumea, Makemake, and Eris.

The theory of how the solar system was created is that it started with the collapse of a cloud of interstellar gas and dust, which formed the **solar nebula**. This collapse is believed to have occurred because the cloud was disturbed. As it collapsed, it heated up and compressed at the center, forming a flatter protoplanetary disk with a **protostar** at the center. **Planets** formed as a result of accretion from the disk. Gas cooled and condensed into tiny particles of rock, metal, and ice. These particles collided and formed into larger particles, and then into objects the size of small asteroids. Eventually, some became large enough to have significant gravity.

Review Video: Solar System
Visit mometrix.com/academy and enter code: 273231

Sizes of the Earth, Sun, and Moon

The **Earth** is about 12,765 km (7,934 miles) in diameter. The **Moon** is about 3,476 km (2,160 mi) in diameter. The distance between the Earth and the Moon is about 384,401 km (238,910 mi). The diameter of the Sun is approximately 1,390,000 km (866,000 mi). The distance from the Earth to the Sun is 149,598,000 km, also known as 1 **Astronomical Unit (AU)**. The star that is nearest to the solar system is **Proxima Centauri**. It is about 270,000 AU away.

Solar Energy

The Sun's energy is produced by **nuclear fusion reactions**. Each second, about 700,000,000 tons of hydrogen are converted (or fused) to about 695,000,000 tons of helium and 5,000,000 tons of energy in the form of gamma rays. In nuclear fusion, four hydrogen nuclei are fused into one helium nucleus, resulting in the release of energy. In the Sun, the energy proceeds towards the surface and is absorbed and re-emitted at lower and lower temperatures. Energy is mostly in the form of visible light when it reaches the surface. It is estimated that the Sun has used up about half of the hydrogen at its core since its birth. It is expected to radiate in this fashion for another 5 billion years. Eventually, it will deplete its hydrogen fuel, grow brighter, expand to about 260 times its diameter, and become a red giant. The outer layers will ablate and become a dense white dwarf the size of the Earth.

Four Innermost Planets

- **Mercury**: Mercury is the closest to the Sun and is also the smallest planet. It orbits the Sun every 88 days, has no satellites or atmosphere, has a Moon-like surface with craters, appears bright, and is dense and rocky with a large iron core.
- **Venus**: Venus is the second planet from the Sun. It orbits the Sun every 225 days, is very bright, and is similar to Earth in size, gravity, and bulk composition. It has a dense atmosphere composed of carbon dioxide and some sulfur. It is covered with reflective clouds made of sulfuric acid and exhibits signs of volcanism. Lightning and thunder have been recorded on Venus's surface.
- **Earth**: Earth is the third planet from the Sun. It orbits the Sun every 365 days. Approximately 71% of its surface is salt-water oceans. The Earth is rocky, has an atmosphere composed mainly of oxygen and nitrogen, has one moon, and supports millions of species. It contains the only known life in the solar system.
- **Mars**: Mars it the fourth planet from the Sun. It appears reddish due to iron oxide on the surface, has a thin atmosphere, has a rotational period similar to Earth's, and has seasonal cycles. Surface features of Mars include volcanoes, valleys, deserts, and polar ice caps. Mars has impact craters and the tallest mountain, largest canyon, and perhaps the largest impact crater yet discovered.

Review Video: The Inner Planets of Our Solar System
Visit mometrix.com/academy and enter code: 103427

Asteroid Belt, Kuiper Belt, and Oort Cloud

The **asteroid belt** is between Mars and Jupiter. The many objects contained within are composed of rock and metal similar to those found on the terrestrial planets.

The **Kuiper Belt** is beyond Neptune's orbit, but the influence of the gas giants may cause objects from the Kuiper Belt to cross Neptune's orbit. Objects in the Kuiper Belt are still being discovered. They are thought to be composed of the frozen forms of water, ammonia, and methane, and may be the source of short-period comets. It is estimated that there are 35,000 Kuiper Belt objects greater than 100 km in diameter and perhaps 100 million objects about 20 km in diameter.

There is also a hypothetical **Oort Cloud** that may exist far beyond the Kuiper Belt and act as a source for long-period comets.

Review Video: Asteroid Belt, Kuiper Belt, and Oort Cloud
Visit mometrix.com/academy and enter code: 208584

Four Outermost Planets

- **Jupiter**: Jupiter is the fifth planet from the Sun and the largest planet in the solar system. It consists mainly of hydrogen, and 25% of its mass is made up of helium. It has a fast rotation and has clouds in the tropopause composed of ammonia crystals that are arranged into bands sub-divided into lighter-hued zones and darker belts causing storms and turbulence. Jupiter has wind speeds of 100 m/s, a planetary ring, 63 moons, and a **Great Red Spot**, which is an anticyclonic storm.
- **Saturn**: Saturn is the sixth planet from the Sun and the second largest planet in the solar system. It is composed of hydrogen, some helium, and trace elements. Saturn has a small core of rock and ice, a thick layer of metallic hydrogen, a gaseous outer layer, wind speeds of up to 1,800 km/h, a system of rings, and 61 moons.
- **Uranus**: Uranus is the seventh planet from the Sun. Its atmosphere is composed mainly of hydrogen and helium and also contains water, ammonia, methane, and traces of hydrocarbons. With a minimum temperature of 49 K, Uranus has the coldest atmosphere. Uranus has a ring system, a magnetosphere, and 13 moons.
- **Neptune**: Neptune is the eighth planet from the Sun and is the planet with the third largest mass. It has 12 moons, an atmosphere similar to Uranus, a **Great Dark Spot**, and the strongest sustained winds of any planet (wind speeds can be as high as 2,100 km/h). Neptune is cold (about 55 K) and has a fragmented ring system.

Review Video: The Outer Planets of Our Solar System
Visit mometrix.com/academy and enter code: 683995

Phases of the Moon

It takes about one month for the Moon to go through all its phases. **Waxing** refers to the two weeks during which the Moon goes from a new moon to a full moon. About two weeks is spent **waning**, going from a full moon to a new moon. The lit part of the Moon always faces the Sun. The **phases of waxing** are: new moon, during which the Moon is not illuminated and rises and sets with the Sun; crescent moon, during which a tiny sliver is lit; first quarter, during which half the Moon is lit and the phase of the Moon is due south on the meridian; gibbous, during which more than half of the Moon is lit and has a shape similar to a football; right side, during which the Moon is lit; and full moon, during which the Moon is fully illuminated, rises at sunset, and sets at sunrise. After a full moon, the Moon is waning. The **phases of waning** are: gibbous, during which the left side is lit and the Moon rises after sunset and sets after sunrise; third quarter, during which the Moon is half lit and rises at midnight and sets at noon; crescent, during which a tiny sliver is lit; and new moon, during which the Moon is not illuminated and rises and sets with the Sun.

Earth-Moon-Sun System

The **Earth-Moon-Sun system** is responsible for **eclipses**. From Earth, the Sun and the Moon appear to be about the same size. An **eclipse of the Sun** occurs during a new Moon, when the side of the Moon facing the Earth is not illuminated. The Moon passes in front of the Sun and blocks its view from Earth. Eclipses do not occur every month because the orbit of the Moon is at about a 5° angle to the plane of Earth's orbit. An **eclipse of the Moon** happens during the full Moon phase. The Moon passes through the shadow of the Earth and blocks sunlight from reaching it, which temporarily causes darkness. During a lunar eclipse, there are two parts to the shadow. The **umbra** is the dark, inner region. The sun is completely blocked in this area. The **penumbra** is a partially lighted area around the umbra. Earth's shadow is four times longer than the Moon's shadow.

Review Video: Lunar Eclipse
Visit mometrix.com/academy and enter code: 908819

Meteoroids

A **meteoroid** is the name for a rock from space before it enters the Earth's atmosphere. Most meteoroids burn up in the atmosphere before reaching altitudes of 80 km. A **meteor** is the streak of light from a meteoroid in the Earth's atmosphere, and is also known as a shooting star. Meteor showers are associated with comets, happen when the Earth passes through the debris of a comet, and are associated with a higher than normal number of meteors. **Meteorites** are rocks that reach the Earth's surface from space. **Fireballs** are very bright meteors with trails that can last as long as 30 minutes. A **bolide** is a fireball that burns up when it enters Earth's atmosphere. There are many types of meteorites, and they are known to be composed of various materials. Iron meteorites consist of iron and nickel with a criss-cross, or Widmanstatten, internal metallic crystalline structure. Stony iron meteorites are composed of iron, nickel, and silicate materials. Stony meteorites consist mainly of silicate and also contain iron and nickel.

Review Video: Meteoroids, Meteors, and Meteorites
Visit mometrix.com/academy and enter code: 454866

Comets

A **comet** consists of frozen gases and rocky, metallic materials. Comets are usually small and typically have long tails. A comet's tail is made of ionized gases. It points away from the Sun and follows the comet as it approaches the Sun. The tail precedes the head as the comet moves away from the Sun. It is believed that as many as 100 billion comets exist. About 12 new ones are discovered each year. Their orbits are elliptical, not round. Some scientists theorize that short-period comets originate from the **Kuiper Belt** and long-period comets originate from the **Oort Cloud**, which is thought to be 100,000 AU away. Comets orbit the Sun in time periods varying from a few years to hundreds of thousands of years. A well-known comet, **Halley's Comet**, has an orbit of 76 years. It is 80 percent water, and consists of frozen water, carbon dioxide (dry ice), ammonia, and methane.

Natural Satellites

There are about 335 **moons**, or **satellites**, that orbit the planets and objects in the solar system. Many of these satellites have been recently discovered, a few are theoretical, some are asteroid moons (moons orbiting asteroids), some are moonlets (small moons), and some are moons of dwarf planets and objects that have not been definitively categorized, such as trans-Neptunian objects. Mercury and Venus do not have any moons. There are several moons larger than the dwarf planet Pluto and two larger than Mercury. Some consider the Earth and Moon a pair of double planets rather than a planet and a satellite. Some satellites may have started out as asteroids. They were eventually captured by a planet's gravity and became moons.

Types of Orbit

A **geosynchronous orbit** around the Earth has an orbital period matching the Earth's sidereal rotation period. **Sidereal rotation** is based on the position of a fixed star, not the Sun, so a sidereal day is slightly shorter than a 24-hour solar day. A satellite in a geosynchronous orbit appears in the same place in the sky at the same time each day. Technically, any object with an orbit time period equal to the Earth's rotational period is geosynchronous. A **geostationary orbit** is a geosynchronous orbit that is circular and at zero inclination, which means the object is located directly above the equator. Geostationary orbits are useful for communications satellites because they are fixed in the same spot relative to the Earth. A **semisynchronous orbit** has an orbital period of half a sidereal day.

Piloted Space Missions

The Soviet space program successfully completed the first space flight by orbiting **Yuri Gagarin** in 1961 on Vostok 1. His orbit lasted 1 hour, 48 minutes. Later in 1961, the U.S. completed its first piloted space flight by launching **Alan Shepard** into space in the Mercury-Redstone 3. This space mission was suborbital. The first woman in space was **Valentina Tereshkova**, who orbited the Earth 48 times aboard Vostok 6 in 1963. The first space flight with more than one person and also the first that didn't involve space suits took place on the Voskhod in 1964. The first person on the Moon was American **Neil Armstrong**. In 1969, he traveled to the Moon on Apollo 11, which was the 11th manned space flight completed in the Apollo program, which was conducted from 1968 to 1972. In 2003, **Yang Liwei** became the first person from China to go into space. He traveled onboard the Shenzhou 5. The **Space Shuttle Orbiter** has included piloted space shuttles from 1981 until the present. The program was suspended after two space shuttle disasters: **Challenger** in 1986 and **Columbia** in 2003.

Noteworthy Satellites

The first satellite to orbit the Earth was the Soviet Union's **Sputnik 1** in 1957. Its two radio transmitters emitted beeps that were received by radios around the world. Analysis of the radio signals was used to gather information about the electron density of the ionosphere. Soviet success escalated the American space program. In 1958, the U.S. put **Explorer 1** into orbit. The **Osumi** was the first Japanese satellite, which was put into orbit in 1970. The **Vanguard 1** is the satellite that has orbited the Earth the longest. It was put into orbit in 1958 and was still in orbit in October 2016. The **Mir Space Station** orbited Earth for 11 years, and was assembled in space starting in 1986. It was almost continuously occupied until 1999. The **International Space Station** began being assembled in orbit in 1998. At 43,000 cubic feet, it is the largest manned object sent into space. It circles the Earth every 90 minutes.

Limitations of Space Exploration

There are many limitations of space exploration. The main limitation is **knowledge**. Space exploration is currently time-consuming, dangerous, and costly. Manned and unmanned missions, even within the solar system, take years of planning and years to complete. The associated **financial costs** are great. **Technological advances** are needed before interstellar and intergalactic missions can be carried out. By some estimates, it would take more than 70 years to travel to Proxima Centauri (the nearest star) using the fastest rocket technology available. It would take much longer using less advanced technologies. Space travel is **dangerous** for many reasons. Rocket fuel is highly explosive. Non-Earth environments are uninhabitable for humans. Finally, astronauts are exposed to larger than usual amounts of radiation.

Unpiloted Space Missions

The first artificial object to reach another space object was **Luna 2**. It crashed on the Moon in 1959. The first automatic landing was by **Luna 9**. It landed on the Moon in 1966. **Mariner 2**'s flyby of Venus in 1962 was the first successful interplanetary flyby. **Venera 7** landing on and transmitting data from Venus was the first interplanetary surface landing, which took place in 1970. The first soft landing on Mars was in 1971. Unpiloted spacecraft have also made successful soft landings on the asteroids Eros and Itokawa, as well as Titan, a moon of Saturn. The first flyby of Jupiter was in 1973 by **Pioneer 10**. Pioneer 10 was also the first craft of its kind to leave the solar system. The first flyby of Mercury was in 1974 by **Mariner**. The first flyby of Saturn was in 1979 by **Pioneer 11**. The first flyby of Uranus was in 1986 by **Voyager 2**, which also flew by Neptune in 1989.

Evidence of Water

Much of the search for life on other planets has centered on the search for **water**. This is because water is a vital resource for life on Earth and could potentially support life on other planets.

Scientists have long speculated that water once covered a large portion of the planet **Mars**. The Curiosity Rover recently found evidence of liquid water in the soil of Mars.

Scientists also believe that there may be liquid water beneath the crusts of three of **Jupiter's moons** (Europa, Ganymede, and Callisto) and two of Saturn's moons (Enceladus and Titan). Titan is also thought to have lakes of liquid hydrocarbon.

TExES Practice Test

1. Which of the following describes the process skill of concluding?

   a. Explaining or interpreting observations
   b. Making a determination based on the results of a controlled experiment
   c. Reading an instrument during an experiment
   d. Listing similarities and differences between two objects

2. A chemistry experiment is performed to determine the effect of a nonvolatile solute on the boiling point of water. Three trials are performed in which 10 mg, 20 mg and 30 mg of salt are added to 500 ml of distilled water. Each solution is heated on a hot plate, and the elevated boiling points are recorded. Which of the following correctly identifies the independent and dependent variables?

   a. The independent variable is the amount of salt, and the dependent variable is the temperature at which the water boils.
   b. The independent variable is the amount of water, and the dependent variable is the temperature at which the water boils.
   c. The independent variable is the temperature at which the water boils, and the dependent variable is the amount of salt.
   d. The independent variable is the amount of salt, and the dependent variable is the amount of water.

3. Which of the following is NOT true concerning forming and testing hypotheses?

   a. A controlled experiment should have only one independent variable.
   b. A controlled experiment may have several constants.
   c. A good hypothesis should take all of the available background material on the topic into consideration.
   d. A good hypothesis will not be disproved by testing.

4. Which of the following is the correct expression of 0.0034050 in scientific notation?

   a. 34.050×10^{-3}
   b. 3.4050×10^{-2}
   c. 3.4050×10^{-3}
   d. 3.4050×10^{3}

5. Which of the following numbers has 4 significant figures?

   a. 3020.5
   b. 0.003020
   c. 3.2005
   d. 0.0325

6. What is the correct expression of $91{,}000 \times 87{,}000$ using scientific notation and significant figures?

   a. 7.91×10^{9}
   b. 7.9×10^{9}
   c. 79.2×10^{8}
   d. 79×10^{8}

7. Students experimentally determine that the specific heat of copper is 0.410 $\frac{J}{g \cdot °C}$. If the known value of the specific heat of copper is 0.385 $\frac{J}{g \cdot °C}$, what is the percent error?

a. 6.10%
b. 16.4%
c. 6.49%
d. 15.4%

8. Two balances in a classroom laboratory are used to determine the mass of an object. The actual mass of the object is 15.374 grams. Which of the following statements is true concerning the accuracy and precision of these two balances?

Measurement	Triple Beam Balance	Digital Balance
1	15.38 grams	15.375 grams
2	15.39 grams	15.376 grams
3	15.37 grams	15.376 grams
4	15.38 grams	15.375 grams

a. The triple beam balance is both more accurate and more precise.
b. The triple beam balance is more accurate, but the digital balance is more precise.
c. The digital balance is more accurate, but the triple beam balance is more precise.
d. The digital balance is both more accurate and more precise.

9. Which of the following subskills best fits the process skill of observing?

a. Using the five senses to collect evidence and write descriptions
b. Grouping objects based on similarities, differences, and interrelationships
c. Explaining or interpreting collected evidence
d. Reporting to others what has been found by experimentation

10. Which of the following sets of quantities are equivalent?

a. 2,310 mg and 2.310 g
b. 2.310 g and 231.0 mg
c. 2.310 kg and 231.0 g
d. 2.310 kg and 231,000 mg

11. Which of the following best describes the relationship of this set of data?

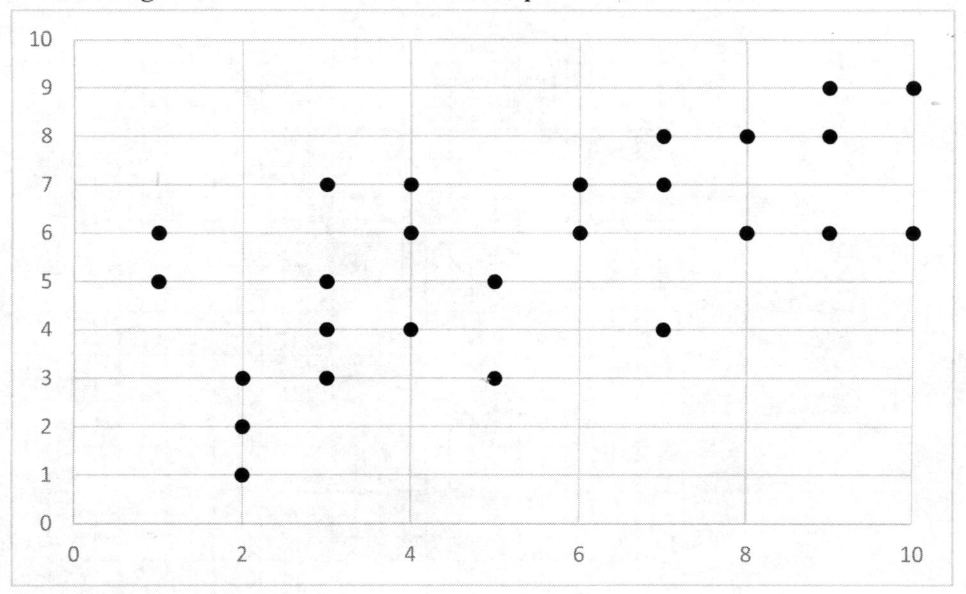

a. High positive correlation
b. Low positive correlation
c. Low negative correlation
d. No correlation

12. Which of the following is NOT true concerning correlation?
a. Correlation can show the relationship between variables.
b. Correlation can show cause and effect.
c. Correlation can show linear relationships.
d. Correlation can show nonlinear relationships.

13. Which of the following is NOT a recommended storage practice for laboratory chemicals?
a. Chemicals should be stored at the appropriate temperature and humidity.
b. Chemicals should be dated when received and when opened.
c. Chemicals may be routinely stored on bench tops.
d. Chemicals should be stored on shelves with raised outer edges.

14. Which of the following is the best prediction for solubility at 150 degrees Celsius?

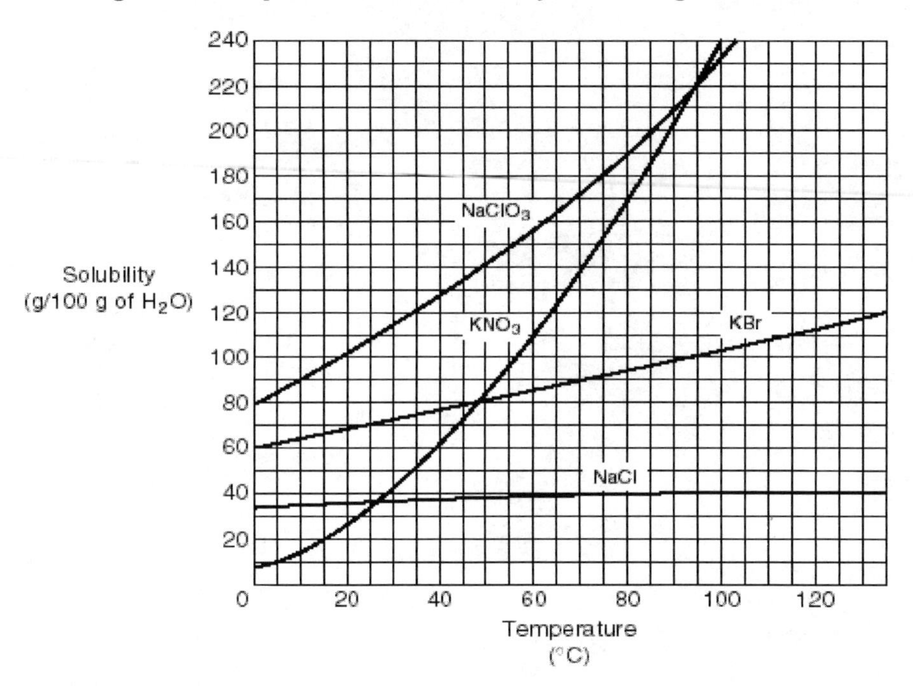

a. 260 g $NaClO_3$ per 100 g H_2O
b. 250 g KNO_3 per 100 g H_2O
c. 130 g KBr per 100 g H_2O
d. 80 g NaCl per 100 g H_2O

15. Which of the following conclusions can be drawn from the data presented in the graph below?

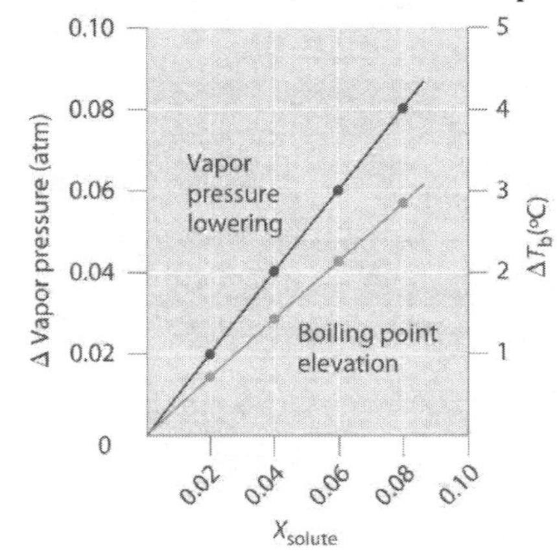

a. Increasing the solute increases the vapor pressure and decreases the boiling point of this solution.
b. Increasing the solute increases the vapor pressure and increases the boiling point of this solution.
c. Increasing the solute decreases the vapor pressure and decreases the boiling point of this solution.
d. Increasing the solute decreases the vapor pressure and increases the boiling point of this solution.

16. What are pure substances that consist of more than one type of atom?

a. Elements
b. Compounds
c. Molecules
d. Mixtures

17. Which of the following statements concerning the states of matter is NOT true?

a. Plasmas are high temperature collections of ions and free electrons.
b. Solids are the least compressible due to the more rigid positions of the particles.
c. Gases have no definitc volume and expand to fill their containers
d. Liquids have no definite shape and no definite volume.

18. The symbol for a calcium ion is Ca^{2+}. Which of the following statements is true concerning this ion?

a. This cation has fewer electrons than protons.
b. This anion has fewer electrons than protons.
c. This cation has more electrons than protons.
d. This anion has more electrons than protons.

19. Which of the following subatomic particles has the smallest mass?

a. Protons
b. Electrons
c. Quarks
d. Neutrons

20. A uranium isotope is represented by the symbol $^{238}_{92}U$. How many neutrons does an atom of this isotope contain?

a. 92
b. 330
c. 238
d. 146

21. Which if the following represents an alpha particle?

a. $^{0}_{-1}e$
b. $^{2}_{1}H^{+}$
c. $^{4}_{2}He^{2+}$
d. $^{0}_{+1}e$

22. Which of the following is an example of a chemical change?

a. Salt dissolving in water
b. Water evaporating
c. Silver tarnishing
d. Dry ice sublimating

23. Which temperature scales have exactly 100 degrees between the freezing point and the boiling point of water?

a. Celsius only
b. Celsius and Kelvin
c. Celsius and Fahrenheit
d. Celsius, Fahrenheit, and Kelvin

24. Which is an example of convection as a method of heat transfer?

a. A person warming his hands by placing them on an electric blanket
b. A person warming his hands by placing them near the sides of a light bulb
c. A person warming his hands by washing with hot water
d. A person warming his hands by rubbing them together

25. The energy flow through an ecosystem is represented by an energy pyramid. In the energy pyramid for a terrestrial ecosystem, the producers utilize 6,000 kilocalories per square meter per year. What approximate amount of energy is transferred to the third trophic level of this ecosystem?

a. 0.6 kilocalories per square meter per year
b. 6 kilocalories per square meter per year
c. 60 kilocalories per square meter per year
d. 600 kilocalories per square meter per year

26. Which of the following general statements concerning ideal gases is true?

a. Volume is inversely proportional to kinetic energy.
b. Volume is inversely proportional to number of moles.
c. Volume is inversely proportional to temperature.
d. Volume is inversely proportional to pressure.

27. According to the kinetic theory of matter, which of the following statements is true?

a. The average kinetic energy is inversely proportional to the square of the average velocity of the particles.
b. The average kinetic energy is inversely proportional to the average velocity of the particles.
c. The average kinetic energy is directly proportional to the square of the average velocity of the particles.
d. The average kinetic energy is directly proportional to the average velocity of the particles.

28. In general, where in the periodic table of elements are the elements with the largest atomic radii located?

a. Upper-right corner
b. Upper-left corner
c. Bottom-left corner
d. Bottom-right corner

29. What is the name of the compound $CuCl_2$?

a. Copper (I) chloride
b. Copper (II) chloride
c. Copper (I) chlorine
d. Copper (II) chlorine

30. Which of the following molecules exhibits ionic bonding?

a. NaCl
b. CO_2
c. $C_6H_{12}O_6$
d. H_2O

31. Given the chemical reaction $4Al(s) + 3O_2(g) \rightarrow 2Al_2O_3(s)$, how many moles of $O_2(g)$ are needed to produce 100.0 moles of $2Al_2O_3(s)$?

a. 100.0
b. 150.0
c. 200.0
d. 250.0

32. Which of the following is Avogadro's number?

a. 2.063×10^{23}
b. 6.023×10^{22}
c. 6.022×10^{23}
d. 2.063×10^{22}

33. What type of reaction is $Cu(s) + 2AgNO_3(aq) \rightarrow 2Ag(s) + Cu(NO_3)_2(aq)$?

a. Single replacement
b. Double replacement
c. Synthesis
d. Decomposition

34. Which of the following is NOT true regarding exothermic and endothermic processes or reactions?

a. Exothermic reactions release heat energy.
b. The melting of ice is an endothermic process.
c. The burning of butane is an exothermic process.
d. The change in enthalpy is positive for an exothermic reaction.

35. Which of the following substances has a pH closest to 1?

a. Bleach
b. Water
c. Ammonia
d. Vinegar

36. Which of the following describes the correct procedure to prepare 100.0 ml of 3.00 M HCl solution from an 18.0 M HCl stock solution?

a. Dilute 16.7 ml of 18.0 M HCl to a total volume of 100.0 ml.
b. Dilute 18.0 ml of 18.0 M HCl to a total volume of 100.0 ml.
c. Dilute 54.0 ml of 18.0 M HCl to a total volume of 100.0 ml.
d. Dilute 14.3 ml of 18.0 M HCl to a total volume of 100.0 ml.

37. Which of the following is NOT generally true regarding solubility?

a. Increasing temperature increases the solubility of a solid in a liquid.
b. Increasing temperature increases the solubility of a gas in a liquid.
c. Increasing the pressure has little effect on the solubility of a solid in a liquid.
d. Increasing partial pressure of a gas decreases the solubility of a gas in a liquid.

38. Which of the following would most likely dissolve in a nonpolar solvent?

a. $AgNO_3$
b. NH_3
c. CCl_4
d. KI

39. Which of the following characteristics is consistent with an acid?

a. Turns litmus paper blue
b. Accepts a proton
c. Reacts with zinc to produce hydrogen gas
d. Produces OH^- ions in aqueous solutions

40. Which of the following is a solute?

a. Salt in a mixture of salt and pepper
b. Air in mixture of ash and air
c. Water in a mixture of salt and water
d. Sugar in a mixture of sugar and water

41. Which of the following is a scalar quantity?

a. Acceleration
b. Velocity
c. Speed
d. Force

42. Which of Newton's laws explains why seatbelts are needed?

a. Second Law of Motion
b. Law of Universal Gravitation
c. First Law of Motion
d. Third Law of Motion

43. According to Newton's Law of Universal Gravitation, what happens to the force of attraction between two objects if the distance between them is doubled?

a. The force is reduced to one half of the original amount.
b. The force is reduced to one fourth of the original amount.
c. The force is quadrupled.
d. The force is doubled.

44. Which of the following is the best description of pressure?

a. Mass per unit volume
b. Force per unit area
c. Force per unit volume
d. Mass per unit area

45. What is the volume of a 378 gram block of quartz that has a density of 2.65 g/cm^3?

a. 1012 cm^3
b. 143 cm^3
c. 375 cm^3
d. 721 cm^3

46. Which of the following statements is NOT true about the period of a simple pendulum?

a. As the mass of a pendulum increases, the period increases.
b. For small amplitudes, the period of a pendulum is approximately independent of amplitude.
c. A pendulum swings more slowly at higher elevation.
d. To double the period of a pendulum, the length must be quadrupled.

47. A worker applies a force of 500.0 N to a pulley for a distance of 1.5 m to move a crate that weighs 1000.0 N a distance of 0.5 m. What is the ideal mechanical advantage of this pulley?

a. 4
b. 2
c. 3
d. 5

48. According to Coulomb's Law of Electric Force, which of the following statements is true?

a. The force between two charged objects is directly related to the square of the distance between them.
b. The force between two charged objects is inversely related to the square of the distance between them.
c. The force between two charged objects is inversely related to the distance between them.
d. The force between two charged objects is inversely related to the square root of the distance between them.

49. What is the current through a resistor of 20.0 ohms if the voltage is 6.0 volts?

a. 0.30 amperes
b. 120 amperes
c. 3.3 amperes
d. 0.20 amperes

50. An electromagnet has a lifting force of 5 N. If the current through the coil is doubled, what is the lifting force?

a. 2 N
b. 5 N
c. 10 N
d. 20 N

51. Which color of light has the highest frequency?

a. Blue
b. Red
c. Green
d. Violet

52. On what does the energy of a photon depend?

a. Speed
b. Mass
c. Frequency
d. Amplitude

53. Under which conditions will light undergo total internal reflection?

a. When the angle of incidence is equal to the critical angle
b. When the angle of incidence is greater than the critical angle
c. When the angle of incidence is less than the critical angle
d. When the angle of incidence is zero

54. Which of the following correctly describes the image of a double concave lens?

a. Reduced, upright, virtual image
b. Enlarged, upright, virtual image
c. Reduced, inverted, virtual image
d. Reduced, upright, real image

55. Which of the following can be described as the way the human ear perceives the amplitude of a sound wave?

a. Loudness
b. Pitch
c. Intensity
d. Frequency

56. Which substance is most likely to be a solid at STP?

a. Kr
b. Na
c. NH_3
d. Xe

57.Which of the following tend to increase the melting point of a solid?

1. Increasing molecular weight
2. Decreasing polarity
3. Increasing surface area

a. I and II
b. II
c. III
d. I and III

58. A gas at constant volume is cooled. Which statement about the gas must be true?

a. The kinetic energy of the gas molecules has decreased.
b. The gas has condensed to a liquid.
c. The weight of the gas has decreased.
d. The density of the gas has increased.

59. One mole of oxygen gas and two moles of hydrogen are combined in a sealed container at STP. Which of the following statements is true?

a. The mass of hydrogen gas is greater than the mass of oxygen.
b. The volume of hydrogen is greater than the volume of oxygen.
c. The hydrogen and oxygen will react to produce 2 mol of water.
d. The partial pressure of hydrogen is greater than the partial pressure of oxygen.

60. Graham's law is best used to determine what relationship between two different materials?

a. pressure and volume
b. volume and temperature
c. mass and diffusion rate
d. Diffusion rate and temperature

61. Which of the following statements is true about the physical properties of liquids and gases?

I. Liquids and gases are both compressible
II. Liquids flow, but gases do not
III. Liquids flow, and gases are incompressible
IV. Liquids flow and gases are compressible
V. Gases flow and liquids are incompressible

a. I and III
b. II and IV
c. III and V
d. IV and V

62. Which of the following statements **generally** describes the trend of electronegativity considering the Periodic Table of the Elements?

a. Electronegativity increases going from left to right and from top to bottom
b. Electronegativity increases going from right to left and from bottom to top
c. Electronegativity increases going from left to right and from bottom to top
d. Electronegativity increases going from right to left and from top to bottom

63. A solid is heated until it melts. Which of the following is true about the solid melting?

a. ΔH is positive, and ΔS is positive
b. ΔH is negative and ΔS is positive
c. ΔH is positive and ΔS is negative
d. ΔH is negative and ΔS is negative

64. A liquid is held at its freezing point and slowly allowed to solidify. Which of the following statements about this event are true?

a. During freezing, the temperature of the material decreases
b. While freezing, heat is given off by the material
c. During freezing, heat is absorbed by the material
d. During freezing, the temperature of the material increases

65. Which of the following radioactive emissions results in an increase in atomic number?

a. Alpha
b. Beta
c. Gamma
d. Neutron

66. A material has a half life of 2 years. If you started with 1 kg of the material, how much of it would still be the original material after 8 years?

a. 1 kg
b. 0.5 kg
c. 0.06 kg
d. 0.12 kg

67. The hydrogen bonds in a water molecule make water a good

a. Solvent for lipids
b. Participant in replacement reactions
c. Surface for small particles and living organisms to move across
d. Solvent for polysaccharides such as cellulose

68. The breakdown of a disaccharide releases energy which is stored as ATP. This is an example of a(n)
   a. Combination reaction
   b. Replacement reaction
   c. Endothermic reaction
   d. Exothermic reaction

69. Which of the following metabolic compounds is composed of only carbon, oxygen, and hydrogen?
   a. Phospholipids
   b. Glycogen
   c. Peptides
   d. RNA

70. When an animal takes in more energy that it uses over an extended time, the extra chemical energy is stored as:
   a. Fat
   b. Starch
   c. Protein
   d. Enzymes

71. Which of the following molecules is thought to have acted as the first enzyme in early life on earth?
   a. Protein
   b. RNA
   c. DNA
   d. Triglycerides

72. Which of the following organelles is/are formed when the plasma membrane surrounds a particle outside of the cell?
   a. Golgi bodies
   b. Rough endoplasmic reticulum
   c. Secretory vesicles
   d. Endocytic vesicles

73. Which of the following plant organelles contain(s) pigment that give leaves their color?
   a. Centrioles
   b. Cell walls
   c. Chloroplasts
   d. Central vacuole

74. Prokaryotic and eukaryotic cells are similar in having which of the following?
   a. Membrane-bound organelles
   b. Protein-studded DNA
   c. Presence of a nucleus
   d. Integral membrane proteins in the plasma membrane

75. Which of the following cell types has a peptidoglycan cell wall?
   a. Algae
   b. Bacteria
   c. Fungi
   d. Land plants

76. Enzymes catalyze biochemical reactions by

a. Lowering the potential energy of the products
b. Separating inhibitors from products
c. Forming a complex with the products
d. Lowering the activation energy of the reaction

77. Which of the following is not a characteristic of enzymes?

a. They change shape when they bind their substrates
b. They can catalyze reactions in both forward and reverse directions
c. Their activity is sensitive to changes in temperature
d. They are always active on more than one kind of substrate

78. In a strenuously exercising muscle, NADH begins to accumulate in high concentration. Which of the following metabolic process will be activated to reduce the concentration of NADH?

a. Glycolysis
b. The Krebs cycle
c. Lactic acid fermentation
d. Oxidative phosphorylation

79. Which of the following statements regarding chemiosmosis in mitochondria is not correct?

a. ATP synthase is powered by protons flowing through membrane channels
b. Energy from ATP is used to transport protons to the intermembrane space
c. Energy from the electron transport chain is used to transport protons to the intermembrane space
d. An electrical gradient and a pH gradient both exist across the inner membrane

80. In photosynthesis, high-energy electrons move through electron transport chains to produce ATP and NADPH. Which of the following provides the energy to create high energy electrons?

a. NADH
b. $NADP^+$
c. Water
d. Light

81. Which of the following kinds of plants is most likely to perform CAM photosynthesis?

a. Mosses
b. Grasses
c. Deciduous trees
d. Cacti

82. The combination of DNA with histones is called

a. A centromere
b. Chromatin
c. A chromatid
d. Nucleoli

83. In plants and animals, genetic variation is introduced during

a. Crossing over in mitosis
b. Chromosome segregation in mitosis
c. Cytokinesis of meiosis
d. Anaphase I of meiosis

84. DNA replication occurs during which of the following phases?

a. Prophase I
b. Prophase II
c. Interphase I
d. Interphase II

85. The synaptonemal complex is present in which of the following phases of the cell cycle?

a. Metaphase of mitosis
b. Metaphase of meiosis I
c. Telophase of meiosis I
d. Metaphase of meiosis II

86. A length of DNA coding for a particular protein is called a(n)

a. Allele
b. Genome
c. Gene
d. Transcript

87. In DNA replication, which of the following enzymes is required for separating the DNA molecule into two strands?

a. DNA polymerase
b. Single strand binding protein
c. DNA gyrase
d. Helicase

88. Which of the following chemical moieties forms the backbone of DNA?

a. Nitrogenous bases
b. Glycerol
c. Amino groups
d. Pentose and phosphate

89. Which of the following is required for the activity of DNA polymerase?

a. Okazaki fragments
b. RNA primer
c. Single-strand binding protein
d. Leading strand

90. Which of the following is the substrate for DNA ligase?

a. Okazaki fragments
b. RNA primer
c. Single-strand binding protein
d. Leading strand

91. Which of the following is true of the enzyme telomerase?

a. It is active on the leading strand during DNA synthesis
b. It requires a chromosomal DNA template
c. It acts in the $3' \rightarrow 5'$ direction
d. It adds a repetitive DNA sequence to the end of chromosomes

92. Which enzyme in DNA replication is a potential source of new mutations?

a. DNA ligase
b. Primase
c. DNA gyrase
d. DNA polymerase

93. Which of the following mutations is most likely to have a dramatic effect on the sequence of a protein?

a. A point mutation
b. A missense mutation
c. A deletion
d. A silent mutation

94. Which of the following best describes igneous rock?

a. Includes intrusive and extrusive rock categories
b. Includes foliated and non-foliated rock categories
c. Includes chemical and mechanical rock categories
d. Includes organic and inorganic rock categories

95. To which class of minerals do opal, corundum, magnetite, and quartz belong?

a. Halides
b. Silicates
c. Native elements
d. Oxides

96. Which of the following soil or rock types has a high porosity and a low permeability?

a. Sand
b. Granite
c. Gravel
d. Clay

97. In relation to the water cycle, which of the following statements concerning transpiration is NOT true?

a. As relative humidity increases, the rate of transpiration increases.
b. As winds increase, the rate of transpiration increases.
c. As temperatures increase, the rate of transpiration increases.
d. As soil moisture decreases, the rate of transpiration decreases.

98. Which of the following statements concerning earthquakes is NOT true?

a. The epicenter is located on the earth's surface directly above the focus.
b. Large earthquakes near or beneath a large body of water can generate deadly tsunamis.
c. The epicenter may be located by combining seismograms from two widely separate locations.
d. P waves, which travel faster than S waves, tend to have lower amplitude than S waves, causing little damage.

99. Which of the following statements regarding the principle of uniformitarianism is true?

a. Uniformitarianism is an argument for catastrophism.
b. Uniformitarianism is a key building block for Darwin's theory of evolution.
c. Uniformitarianism states that the past is the key to the present.
d. Uniformitarianism states that the fittest organisms will survive to reproduce.

100. According to the geologic time scale, which of the following statements is NOT true?

a. The rise of human civilization occurred between six thousand and twelve thousand years ago.
b. The Cambrian Explosion occurred after the Jurassic Period.
c. Amphibians appeared before reptiles, mammals, and birds.
d. Spontaneous generation of the first cells occurred approximately 4,000,000,000 years ago.

101. Which of the following is NOT a correct representation of the average salinity of seawater?

a. 35 parts per thousand
b. 3.5 parts per hundred
c. 3.5%
d. 35%

102. Which of the following is NOT a factor as to why lakes don't freeze solid in winter?

a. Water has its lowest volume at zero degrees Celsius.
b. As water freezes, the ice floats due to its lower density than the surrounding water.
c. Due to hydrogen bonding, water forms six-sided crystals that have a larger volume than six water molecules.
d. The water exposed to the cold air freezes first forming a good insulator between the air and the water beneath it.

103. Which of the following layers of the earth make up the lithosphere?

a. The crust only
b. The crust and the rigid upper portion of the upper mantle
c. The crust and the upper mantle
d. The crust, upper mantle, and lower mantle

104. Which of the following is a type of physical weathering?

a. Oxidation
b. Hydrolysis
c. Exfoliation
d. Carbonation

105. Which of the following states the correct atmospheric percentages of the major gases?

a. Nitrogen 78% and oxygen 21%
b. Oxygen 78% and carbon dioxide 21 %
c. Oxygen 78% and nitrogen 21%
d. Carbon dioxide 78% and oxygen 21%

106. Which of the following statements regarding the layers of the atmosphere is NOT true?

a. In the troposphere, temperature decreases as altitude increases.
b. In the mesosphere, temperature decreases as altitude increases.
c. In the stratosphere, temperature decreases as altitude increases.
d. In the thermosphere, temperature increases as altitude increases.

107. Which of the following correctly describes cloud formation?

a. Clouds form when evaporation and condensation are in dynamic equilibrium.
b. Clouds form when there are no condensation nuclei in the air.
c. Clouds form when the atmospheric temperature reaches the dew point.
d. Clouds form when the relative humidity is 0%.

108. Which of the following descriptions concerning air masses is true?

a. Maritime tropical air masses bring warm, dry weather.
b. Continental polar air masses bring warm, moist weather.
c. Continental tropical air masses bring cold, dry weather.
d. Maritime polar air masses bring cold, moist weather.

109. According to Kepler's Laws of Planetary Motion, which of the following statements is true?

a. The planets orbit the sun in circular paths.
b. While orbiting the sun, planets sweep out equal areas in equal amounts of time.
c. Planets located further from the sun have shorter periods than planets located nearer to the sun.
d. While orbiting the sun, the closer the planet is to the sun, the slower it travels.

110. Which of the following statements about the moon is NOT true?

a. Only one side of the moon is seen from earth.
b. The moon only rotates once in one orbit around the earth.
c. The moon is slowly moving closer to the earth.
d. The gravitational acceleration on the surface of the moon is approximately one sixth of the gravitational acceleration on the surface of the earth.

111. Between which two planets is the asteroid belt located?

a. Saturn and Uranus
b. Jupiter and Saturn
c. Earth and Mars
d. Mars and Jupiter

112. Which of the following apparent color of stars indicates the coolest temperature?

a. Orange red
b. Yellow orange
c. Yellow white
d. Blue white

113. Which of the following statements correctly describes a similarity or difference between rocks and minerals?

a. Minerals may contain traces of organic compounds, while rocks do not.
b. Rocks are classified by their formation and the minerals they contain, while minerals are classified by their chemical composition and physical properties.
c. Both rocks and minerals can be polymorphs.
d. Both rocks and minerals may contain mineraloids.

114. Which of the following is the best description of mineraloids?

a. Mineraloids are organic compounds found in rocks.
b. Mineraloids are inorganic solids containing two or more minerals with different crystalline structures.
c. Mineraloids are inorganic solids containing one or more minerals with the same crystalline structure.
d. Mineraloids are minerals that lack a crystalline structure.

115. All of the following are branches of petrology EXCEPT:

a. Metamorphic petrology.
b. Igneous petrology.
c. Mineralogical petrology.
d. Sedimentary petrology.

116. Which of the following is NOT one of the five major physical properties of minerals?

a. Chemical composition
b. Hardness
c. Luster
d. Streak

117. Which of these minerals would have the lowest score on the Mohs scale?

a. Gypsum
b. Fluorite
c. Talc
d. Diamond

118. A mineral's true color is observed by:

a. Conducting a streak test on white paper.
b. Conducting a streak test on unglazed porcelain tile.
c. Inspecting the mineral's outer surface.
d. Shining a light on the mineral to inspect its luster.

119. According to the Dana classification system, gold, silver, and copper belong to which class?

a. Organic
b. Elemental
c. Oxide
d. Sulfide

120. According to the Dana classification system, minerals that contain the anion SO_4^{2-} are part of which chemical class?

a. Sulfate
b. Sulfite
c. Halide
d. Phosphate

121. Which of the following is the most immediate effect of acid rain?

a. Loss of fish due to toxicity of water
b. Disease- and pest-ridden forest trees
c. Unwanted algae growth where a river enters the ocean
d. Deterioration of buildings and monuments

122. Which of the following options is a serious direct impact of climate change?

a. Soil erosion
b. Deforestation
c. Water pollution
d. Increase in average sea level

123. Which of the following is NOT an environmental impact of an irrigation scheme that draws water from a river?

a. Reduction in the downstream river discharge
b. Raising of the level of the water table
c. Decreased evaporation in the area
d. Increased drainage flow

124. Which of the following is a negative impact of reservoirs or dams?

a. Flood control
b. Decreased dissolved oxygen
c. Hydroelectricity
d. Irrigation

125. Which of the following is a negative effect of groundwater or aquifer depletion?

a. Possible saltwater contamination of the water supply
b. Decreased cost as water must be pumped further
c. Increased surface water supplies
d. Raising of the water table

126. Which of the following is NOT a result of ozone layer depletion?

a. Higher UV levels reaching the earth
b. More skin cancer, sunburn, and premature aging of skin
c. Damage to marine life such as plankton
d. Increased crop yields of wheat, corn, and soybeans

127. How does the loss of biodiversity impact the environment and society?

a. Increase of access to raw materials
b. Increase of access to clean water
c. Decrease of food supply
d. Decrease of vulnerability to natural disasters

128. Which of the following activities has impacted society with improved weather forecasting, development of a global positioning system, and the development of lightweight materials?

a. Conservation and recycling
b. Space exploration
c. Biotechnology
d. Land reclamation

129. Which of the following has the potential for negative impacts including soil contamination, surface water contamination, pollution, and leachate?

a. Landfills
b. Incinerators
c. Recycling centers
d. Irrigation systems

130. Which of the following is a source of renewable energy?

a. Nuclear power
b. Natural gas
c. Geothermal power
d. Crude oil

131. Which of the following is a source of nonrenewable energy?

a. Solar power
b. Wind power
c. Wood
d. Coal

132. Which type of plant does not produce fruits?

a. Monocots
b. Angiosperms
c. Gymnosperms
d. Nonvascular plants

133. Which of the following natural resource is NOT used in the manufacturing of glass?

a. Bauxite
b. Sand
c. Soda ash
d. Limestone

134. Which of the following is a benefit of wind energy?

a. Wind turbines are space efficient.
b. Wind is fluctuating as a source of energy.
c. Wind turbines are expensive to manufacture and install.
d. Wind turbines are a threat to wildlife.

135. Which of the following is a drawback of solar energy?

a. Solar energy is environmentally friendly
b. Solar energy is intermittent
c. Solar energy is low maintenance
d. Solar energy is silent

Answers and Explanations

1. B: Making a determination based on the results of a controlled experiment is a description of concluding. Inferring can be described as explaining or interpreting observations. Reading an instrument during an experiment is one type of quantitative observation. Comparing includes noting similarities and differences.

2. A: In a scientific experiment, the dependent variable is the condition that is being tested and measured. The independent variable is the condition that is being changed or controlled. In this example, the amount of salt is varied, and the boiling point of water is measured. Therefore, the independent variable is the amount of salt, and the dependent variable is the temperature at which the water boils.

3. D: A good hypothesis must be testable. This means it may be proved or disproved by testing using a controlled experiment. A controlled experiment may have several constants but only one independent variable.

4. C: The number 0.0034050 is written as 3.4050×10^{-3} in scientific notation. The correct form for scientific notation is $M \times 10^{n}$ in which M is a number between 1 and 10, and n is an integer. Numbers greater than or equal to 10 have a positive exponent, and numbers less than 1 have a negative exponent.

5. B: When working with numbers with decimals, the number of significant figures is determined by starting at the first nonzero digit on the left and counting to the last digit on the right. The number 0.003020 has 4 significant figures. The number 3020.5 has 5 significant figures. The number 3.2005 has 5 significant figures. The number 0.0325 has 3 significant figures.

6. B: Before taking significant figures into consideration, the product of 91,000 × 87,000 is 7,917,000,000. In scientific notation, the product is 7.917×10^{9}. Since each factor has two significant figures, the product should have two significant figures. The correct answer is 7.9×10^{9}.

7. C: Percent error is calculated by the following equation.

$$Percent\ error = \frac{Experimental\ value - Theoretical\ value}{Theoretical\ value} \times 100\%$$

$$Percent\ error = \frac{0.410 - 0.385}{0.385} \times 100\% = 6.49\%$$

The percent error for the students' specific heat of copper of 6.49%.

8. D: Accuracy is determined by finding the range of differences between the measured values and the actual value. The smaller the differences, the greater the accuracy. The range of differences for the triple beam balance is between 0.004 - 0.016. The range of differences for the digital balance is 0.001 - 0.002. Therefore, the digital balance is more accurate. Precision is determined by finding the difference between the highest and lowest readings for each balance. The smaller the difference, the greater the precision. This range for the triple beam balance is 0.02. This range for the digital balance is 0.001. Therefore, the digital balance is also more precise.

9. A: Observation includes collecting evidence, using the five senses, and writing descriptions. Classifying includes grouping items based on similarities, differences, and interrelationships. Inferring includes explaining or interpreting collected evidence. Communication is reporting to others what has been found by experimentation.

10. A: Since 1 g is equal to 1,000 mg, 2,310 mg is equivalent to 2.310 g. Since 1 kg is equal to 1,000 g, 2.310 kg is equivalent to 2,310 g, and 2.310 kg is equivalent to 2,310,000 mg.

11. B: Since the points in this scatterplot "tend" to be rising, this is a positive correlation. However, since the points are not clustered to resemble a straight line, this is a low positive correlation.

12. B: Correlations may be positive or negative and linear or nonlinear. However, correlation does not determine cause and effect. Correlation does not necessarily mean causation.

13. C: Chemicals should not be stored routinely on bench tops. Each chemical should be stored in a location for that specific type of chemical. When in use chemicals maybe be temporarily kept on bench tops, but only in the quantities that are required for that particular situation. Chemicals should be returned to an appropriate location after use.

14. C: Predictions of the solubility of each chemical at 150 degrees Celsius can be made by extending the lines or curves. Since the data for KBr is relatively linear, it is reasonable to assume that the solubility may increase to about 130 g per 100 g H_2O. If the curves for $NaClO_3$ and KNO_3 continue along the same lines, then these predictions are too low. The prediction for NaCl is too high.

15. D: This graph shows the effect of increasing the amount of solute in a solution on both vapor pressure lowering and boiling point elevation. The change in vapor pressure is a decrease due to the label of *vapor pressure lowering*. As the amount of solute increases, the amount the vapor pressure is lowered continually increases. Increasing the solute decreases the vapor pressure. Increasing the solute also increases the amount the boiling point is elevated. Increasing the solute increases the boiling point of the solution.

16. B: Elements and compounds are both pure substances. Elements consist of only one type of atom. Compounds consist of more than one type of atom. Molecules may make up either elements or compounds. Mixtures are two or more substances that are physically combined but not chemically united.

17. D: Liquids have no definite shape, but they do have a definite volume. While the particles of liquids move more freely than those in solids, they do maintain a definite volume.

18. A: Cations are positively charged ions. Anions are negatively charged ions. Therefore, the ion Ca^{2+} is a cation. Cations are positively charged because they have lost one or more electrons. This cation has lost two electrons and has fewer electrons than protons.

19. B: Electrons, protons, and neutrons are subatomic particles. Electrons have the smallest mass. Protons and neutrons, which are nearly equal in mass, are several orders of magnitude more massive than electrons. Quarks are believed to be the components of protons and neutrons; while a quark has less mass than a complete proton or neutron, it still has more mass than an electron.

20. D: Since the atomic number of this isotope is 92, the atom contains 92 protons. Since the mass number is 238, the atom contains 238 protons and neutrons. Since the difference between 238 and 92 is 146, the atom contains 146 neutrons.

21. C: Alpha particles are identical to helium nuclei and may be represented as He^{2+}, ${}^{4}_{2}He$, or ${}^{4}_{2}He^{2+}$. They may also be represented by the Greek letter alpha as α, α^{2+} or ${}^{4}_{2}\alpha^{2+}$. Beta particles are high speed electrons or positrons and are designated by the Greek letter beta as β^- and β^+ or ${}_{-1}^{0}e$ and ${}_{+1}^{0}e$.

22. C: A chemical change involves a chemical reaction. New substances are produced. When silver tarnishes, a thin layer of corrosion is formed indicating a chemical change. A physical change does not produce new substances. Phase changes such as evaporation and sublimation are physical changes. Salt dissolving in water is also a physical change, because the ions just separate, and no new substances are formed.

23. B: On the Celsius scale, water freezes at 0 °C and boils at 100 °C. On the Kelvin scale, water freezes at 273.15 K and boils at 373.15 K. Both the Celsius and Kelvin scales have exactly 100 degrees between the freezing and boiling points of water. Since water freezes at 32 °F and boils at 212 °F on the Fahrenheit scale, the Fahrenheit scale has 180 degrees between the freezing and boiling points of water.

24. C: Methods of heat transfer include conduction, convection, and radiation. With convection, heat is transferred by moving currents in fluids such as air or water. When a person washes his hands with hot water, heat is transmitted to his hands by means of convection. With conduction, heat is transferred by direct contact such as when someone touches an electric blanket. In radiation, heat is transferred by electromagnetic waves such as when someone places his hands near the sides of a light bulb. When a person warms his hands by rubbing them together, heat is generated by friction.

25. C: Producers always form the base of an energy pyramid as the first trophic level. Each successive level receives about 10% of the energy from the previous level. In this energy pyramid, the second trophic level receives 10% of 6000 or 600 kilocalories per square meter per year. The third trophic level receives 10% of 600 or 60 kilocalories per square meter per year.

26. D: According to Boyle's Law, the volume of a gas is inversely proportional to pressure. As pressure increases, volume decreases. According to Avogadro's Law, the volume of a gas is proportional to the number of moles. As the number of moles increases, volume increases. According to Charles's Law, the volume of a gas is proportional to the temperature in Kelvins. As the temperature increases, volume increases. Since temperature is a measure of the kinetic energy of a gas, volume is proportional to the kinetic energy.

27. C: According to the kinetic theory of matter, the kinetic energy of a particle is found by $KE = \frac{1}{2}mv^2$ in which *KE* is the kinetic energy in Joules, *m* is the mass of the particle in kilograms, and *v* is the velocity of the particle in meters per second squared. This formula shows that the average kinetic energy is directly proportional to the square of the average velocity of the particles.

28. C: In general, atomic radius increases moving down a group due to the increasing number of electron shells. In general, atomic radius decreases moving from left to right across a period due to the increasing number of protons in the energy level. Therefore, atoms of elements in the bottom left corner of the periodic table tend to have the largest atomic radii.

29. B: The compound $CuCl_2$ is an ionic compound consisting of Cu^{2+} ions and Cl^- ions. Ionic compounds are named from the cation and anion names. The name of this compound is copper (II) chloride. The Roman number II inside the parentheses indicates which copper ion is present.

30. A: Sodium chloride exhibits ionic bonding due to the attraction between Na^+ ions and Cl^- ions. Typically, elements on the opposite sides of the periodic table (a metal and a nonmetal) form ionic bonds. Carbon dioxide, water, and glucose exhibit covalent bonding. Typically, elements on the same side of the periodic (two or more nonmetals) form covalent bonds.

31. B: The coefficients of the balanced chemical equation can be used to form a mole ratio to be used in dimensional analysis. Since 3 moles of $O_2(g)$ produce 2 moles of $2Al_2O_3(s)$, the needed mole ratio is $\left(\frac{3 \text{ moles } O_2}{2 \text{ moles } Al_2O_3}\right)$. Using dimensional analysis, (100.0 moles Al_2O_3) $\left(\frac{3 \text{ moles } O_2}{2 \text{ moles } Al_2O_3}\right)$ yields 150.0 moles of $O_2(g)$.

32. C: Avogadro's number is the number of particles in one mole of a substance. Avogadro's number is 6.022×10^{23}. One mole of any substance contains 6.022×10^{23} particles of that substance.

33. A: This is a single replacement reaction in which copper replaces silver. The copper combines with the nitrate ions, and the silver precipitates out. Single replacement reactions have the general form of $A + BC \rightarrow AC + B$. Double replacement reactions have the general form of $AB + CD \rightarrow AD + CB$. Synthesis reactions have the general form of $A + B \rightarrow AB$. Decomposition reactions have the general form of $AB \rightarrow A + B$.

34. D: Exothermic reactions release heat energy while endothermic reactions absorb heat energy. Since the burning of butane releases heat energy, the reaction is exothermic. Since the melting of ice absorbs energy, the process is endothermic. Since an exothermic reaction releases heat energy, the change in enthalpy is negative.

35. D: Vinegar is a 5% solution of acetic acid. The pH scale ranges from 0 to 14. Substances with pH's near zero are strong acids, and substances with pH's near 14 are strong bases. Substances with pH's of 7 are neutral. Bleach is a strong base, and ammonia is a relatively weak base. Water is neutral. Since vinegar is the only acid listed, the pH of vinegar is the closest to a pH of 1.

36. A: The needed volume of the stock solution is found by $V_{Stock}M_{Stock} = V_{Dilute}M_{Dilute}$ in which V_{Stock} is the unknown variable, M_{Stock} is the molarity of the stock solution, V_{Dilute} is the volume of the diluted solution, and M_{Dilute} is the molarity of the diluted solution. Then, $V_{Stock} = \frac{V_{Dilute}M_{Dilute}}{M_{Stock}}$. For this problem, $V_{Stock} = \frac{(100.0 \text{ ml})(3.00 \text{ M})}{18.0 \text{ M}}$ is approximately 16.7 ml. To prepare 100.0 ml of 3.00 M HCl solution from an 18.0 M HCl stock solution, dilute 16.7 ml of 18.0 M HCl to 100.0 ml.

37. B: Solubility is the amount of solute present in saturated solution. For a gas solute in a liquid solvent, increasing the temperature increases the kinetic energy of the gas molecules, which decreases the solubility of the gas in the liquid. Increasing the pressure of the gas increases the number of particles escaping from the surface and decreases the solubility. For a liquid solute in a liquid solvent, increasing the temperature increases the kinetic energy, which increases the number of collisions and increases the solubility. Increasing the pressure of a solute in a liquid has little or no effect on solubility.

38. C: A general rule of thumb for solubility is "like dissolves like". Polar solutes tend to dissolve in polar solvents such as water. Nonpolar solutes tend to dissolve in nonpolar solvents. Since CCl_4 has a tetrahedral shape with the polar covalent bonds arranged symmetrically around the carbon atom, CCl_4 is a nonpolar molecule which should dissolve in a nonpolar solvent. Since $AgNO_3$, NH_3, and KI are polar molecules, they probably won't dissolve in a nonpolar solvent.

39. C: Acids react with metals like zinc to produce hydrogen gas. Acids turn litmus red, not blue. Acids donate protons, not accept them. Acids produce H^+ ions in aqueous solution, not OH^- ions.

40. D: In a homogeneous solution, the substance that is dissolved is the solute. A mixture of sugar and water is a homogenous solution in which the sugar is the solute, and the water is the solvent. A mixture of salt and water is a homogeneous solution in which the salt is the solute, and the water is the solvent. A mixture of ash in air is a description of smoke which is a colloid. A mixture of salt and pepper is a heterogeneous mixture.

41. C: Vectors are quantities with both magnitude and direction. Scalars are quantities with magnitude but not direction. Since a velocity, an acceleration, and a force have magnitude and direction, they are all vectors. Since speed only has magnitude, speed is a scalar.

42. C: Newton's first law of motion states that an object in motion tends to remain in motion at a constant velocity unless acted upon by an external force. This tendency to resist changes in motion is known as inertia. Newton's First Law of Motion is often referred to as the Law of Inertia.

43. B: According to the Law of Universal Gravitation, the force of attraction between two objects is inversely proportional to the square of the distance between the two objects. If the distance increases, the force decreases. If the distance is doubled, the force is reduced to one fourth of the original amount.

44. B: Pressure can be defined as force per unit area. This is evident from common pressure units such as lb/in^2 and N/m^2. Mass per unit volume is a description of density.

45. B: Density is mass per unit volume. Then volume can be calculated by dividing mass by density. For this block of quartz, $V = \frac{378 \text{ g}}{2.65 \text{ g/cm}^3}$, which equals 143 cm^3.

46. A: The period of a simple pendulum depends on the length and the rate of acceleration due to gravity. The period is independent of mass and amplitude (to a good approximation) for amplitudes less than about 15 degrees. The period of a pendulum is unaffected by increasing the mass.

47. C: The ideal mechanical advantage of a simple machine is determined by the ratio of input distance to output distance. Since the input distance is 1.5 m and the output distance is 0.5 m, the ideal mechanical advantage for this pulley is 3.

48. B: Coulomb's Law of Electric Force is represented by $F = k\frac{q_1 q_2}{d^2}$ in which F is the force of attraction, k is a constant related to the medium between the charges, q_1 and q_2 are the strengths of the charges, and d is the distance between the charges. Since the square of the distance is in the denominator, the force is inversely related to the square of the distance between the charges.

49. A: According to Ohm's Law, $V = IR$ in which V represents voltage in volts; I represents the current or amperage in amperes; and R represents resistance in ohms. Then current is found by $I = \frac{V}{R}$. For this situation, $I = \frac{6.0 \text{ Volts}}{20.0 \text{ Ohms}} = 0.30$ amperes.

50. D: The strength of an electromagnet is directly related to the square of the current flowing through the coil. If the current is doubled, the lifting force is quadrupled. Since the original lifting force is 5 N, when the current is doubled, the lifting force is 20 N.

51. D: The colors of the visible spectrum from the lowest to highest frequency are red, orange, yellow, green, blue, and violet. Therefore, violet has the highest frequency.

52. C: The energy of a photon is determined by $E = hf$ in which E represents the energy of a photon, h is Planck's constant, and f represents the frequency of the photon. Therefore, the energy of a photon depends on the frequency of the photon.

53. B: When the angle of incidence is zero, the angle of refraction is also zero. As the angle of incidence increases, the angle of refraction increases. When the angle of incidence reaches the critical angle, the angle of refraction is 90 degrees. When the angle of incidence is greater than the critical angle, the light undergoes total internal reflection. No light is refracted.

54. A: A double concave lens is a diverging lens in which the light rays are spread apart. Therefore, the image formed by a double concave lens is always reduced, upright and virtual regardless of the distance of the object from the lens.

55. A: The strength of a sound wave is the intensity, which is related to the amplitude. The effect of intensity on the way humans perceive sound is loudness. Pitch, which is the "highness" or "lowness" of a sound, is determined by the frequency of the sound.

56. B: Na (sodium) is a solid at standard temperature and pressure, which is 0°C (273 K) and 100 kPa (0.986 atm), according to IUPAC. The stronger the intermolecular forces, the greater the likelihood of the material being a solid. Kr and Xe are noble gases and have negligible intermolecular attraction. NH_3 has some hydrogen bonding but is still a gas at STP. Sodium is an alkali metal whose atoms are bonded by metallic bonding and is therefore a solid at STP.

57. D: Generally, the larger and heavier the molecule, the higher the melting point. Decreasing polarity will lower intermolecular attractions and lower the melting point. Long, linear molecules have a larger surface area, and therefore more opportunity to interact with other molecules, which increases the melting point.

58. A: The kinetic energy of the gas molecules is directly proportional to the temperature. If the temperature decreases, so does the molecular motion. A decrease in temperature will not necessarily mean a gas condenses to a liquid. Neither the mass nor the density is impacted, as no material was added or removed, and the volume remained the same.

59. D: Since there are twice as many molecules of hydrogen present vs. oxygen, the partial pressure of hydrogen will be greater. The mass of hydrogen will not be greater than the mass of oxygen present even though there are more moles of hydrogen, due to oxygen having a higher molecular weight. Each gas will occupy the same volume. Hydrogen and oxygen gas can coexist in the container without reacting to produce water. There is no indication given that a chemical reaction has occurred.

60. C: Graham's law of diffusion allows one to calculate the relative diffusion rate between two different gases based on their masses.

61. D: Both liquids and gases are fluids and therefore flow, but only gases are compressible. The molecules that make up a gas are very far apart, allowing the gas to be compressed into a smaller volume.

62. C: The most electronegative atoms are found near the top right of the periodic table. Fluorine has a high electronegativity, while Cesium, located near the bottom left of the table, has a low electronegativity.

63. A: Heat is absorbed by the solid during melting, therefore ΔH is positive. Going from a solid to a liquid greatly increases the freedom of the particles, therefore increasing the entropy, so ΔS is also positive.

64. B: Freezing is an exothermic event; therefore heat must be given off. The temperature of the material remains unchanged at the freezing point during the process.

65. B: Negative beta emission represents the spontaneous decay of a neutron into a proton with the release of an electron. Therefore the resulting nucleus will have one more proton than it did before the reaction, and protons represent the atomic number of an atom. Alpha decay results in the emission of a helium nucleus. The resulting nucleus of an alpha decay would lose two protons and two neutrons, causing a decrease in both the atomic number and the mass number. Gamma decay does not affect the numbers of protons or neutrons in the nucleus. It is an emission of a photon, or packet of energy.

66. C: Since each half life is 2 years, eight years would be 4 half lives. So the mass of material is halved 4 times. Therefore if we start with 1 kg, at two years we would have 0.5 kg, at four years we would have 0.25 kg, after 6 years we would have 0.12 kg, and after 8 years we would have 0.06 kg.

67. C: The hydrogen bonds between water molecules cause water molecules to attract each other (negative pole to positive pole. and "stick" together. This gives water a high surface tension, which allows small living organisms, such as water striders, to move across its surface. Since water is a polar molecule, it readily dissolves other polar and ionic molecules such as carbohydrates and amino acids. Polarity alone is not sufficient to make something soluble in water, however; for example, cellulose is polar but its molecular weight is so large that it is not soluble in water.

68. D: An exothermic reaction releases energy, whereas an endothermic reaction requires energy. The breakdown of a chemical compound is an example of a decomposition reaction (AB → A + B.. A combination reaction (A + B →AB. is the reverse of a decomposition reaction, and a replacement (displacement) reaction is one where compound breaks apart and forms a new compound plus a free reactant (AB + C →AC + B or AB + CD → AD + CB.

69. B: Glycogen is a polysaccharide, a molecule composed of many bonded glucose molecules. Glucose is a carbohydrate, and all carbohydrates are composed of only carbon, oxygen, and hydrogen. Most other metabolic compounds contain other atoms, particularly nitrogen, phosphorous, and sulfur.

70. A: Long term energy storage in animals takes the form of fat. Animals also store energy as glycogen, and plants store energy as starch. , but these substances are for shorter-term use. Fats are a good storage form for chemical energy because fatty acids bond to glycerol in a condensation reaction to form fats (triglycerides). This reaction, which releases water, allows for the compacting of high-energy fatty acids in a concentrated form.

71. B: Some RNA molecules in extant organisms have enzymatic activity; for example the formation of peptide bonds on ribosomes is catalyzed by an RNA molecule. This and other information has led scientists to believe that the most likely molecules to first demonstrate enzymatic activity were RNA molecules.

72. D: Endocytosis is a process by which cells absorb larger molecules or even tiny organisms, such as bacteria, than would be able to pass through the plasma membrane. Endocytic vesicles containing molecules from the extracellular environment often undergo further processing once they enter the cell.

73. C: Chloroplasts contain the light-absorbing compound chlorophyll, which is essential in photosynthesis. This gives leaves their green color. Chloroplasts also contain yellow and red carotenoid pigments, which give leaves red and yellow colors in the fall as chloroplasts lose their chlorophyll.

74. D: Both prokaryotes and eukaryotes interact with the extracellular environment and use membrane-bound or membrane-associated proteins to achieve this. They both use diffusion and active transport to move materials in and out of their cells. Prokaryotes have very few proteins associated with their DNA, whereas eukaryotes' DNA is richly studded with proteins. Both types of living things can have flagella, although with different structural characteristics in the two groups. The most important differences between prokaryotes and eukaryotes are the lack of a nucleus and membrane-bound organelles in prokaryotes.

75. B: Bacteria and cyanobacteria have cell walls constructed from peptidoglycans – a polysaccharide and protein molecule. Other types of organisms with cell walls, for instance, plants and fungi, have cell walls composed of different polysaccharides. Plant cell walls are composed of cellulose, and fungal cell walls are composed of chitin.

76. D: Enzymes act as catalysts for biochemical reactions. A catalyst is not consumed in a reaction, but, rather, lowers the activation energy for that reaction. The potential energy of the substrate and the product remain the same, but the activation energy—the energy needed to make the reaction progress—can be lowered with the help of an enzyme.

77. D: Enzymes are substrate-specific. Most enzymes catalyze only one biochemical reaction. Their active sites are specific for a certain type of substrate and do not bind to other substrates and catalyze other reactions.

78. C: Lactic acid fermentation converts pyruvate into lactate using high-energy electrons from NADH. This process allows ATP production to continue in anaerobic conditions by providing NAD^+ so that ATP can be made in glycolysis.

79. B: Proteins in the inner membrane of the mitochondrion accept high-energy electrons from NAD and $FADH_2$, and in turn transport protons from the matrix to the intermembrane space. The high proton concentration in the intermembrane space creates a gradient which is harnessed by ATP synthase to produce ATP.

80. D: Electrons trapped by the chlorophyll P680 molecule in photosystem II are energized by light. They are then transferred to electron acceptors in an electron transport chain.

81. D: CAM photosynthesis occurs in plants that grow where water loss must be minimized, such as cacti. These plants open their stomata and fix CO_2 at night. During the day, stomata are closed, reducing water loss. Thus, photosynthesis can proceed without water loss.

82. B: DNA wrapped around histone proteins is called chromatin. In a eukaryotic cell, DNA is always associated with protein; it is not "naked" as with prokaryotic cells.

83. D: In anaphase I, homologous chromosome pairs segregate randomly into daughter cells. This means that each daughter cell contains a unique combination of chromosomes that is different from the mother cell and different from its cognate daughter cell.

84. C: Although there are two cell divisions in meiosis, DNA replication occurs only once. It occurs in interphase I, before M phase begins.

85. B: The synaptonemal complex is the point of contact between homologous chromatids. It is formed when nonsister chromatids exchange genetic material through crossing over. Once prophase of meiosis I has completed, crossovers have resolved and the synaptonemal complex no longer exists. Rather, sister chromatids are held together at their centromeres prior to separation in anaphase II.

86. C: Genes code for proteins, and genes are discrete lengths of DNA on chromosomes. An allele is a variant of a gene (different DNA sequence.. In diploid organisms, there may be two versions of each gene.

87. D: The enzyme helicase unwinds DNA. It depends on several other proteins to make the unwinding run smoothly, however. Single-strand binding protein holds the single stranded DNA in place, and topoisomerase helps relieve tension at the replication fork.

88. D: DNA is composed of nucleotides joined together in long chains. Nucleotides are composed of a pentose sugar, a phosphate group, and a nitrogenous base. The bases form the "rungs" of the ladder at the core of the DNA helix and the pentose-phosphates are on its outside, or backbone.

89. B: DNA replication begins with a short segment of RNA (not DNA.. DNA polymerase cannot begin adding nucleotides without an existing piece of DNA (a primer).

90. A: DNA synthesis on the lagging strand forms short segments called Okazaki fragments. Because DNA polymerase can only add nucleotides in the $5' \rightarrow 3'$ direction, lagging strand synthesis is discontinuous. The final product is formed when DNA ligase joins Okazaki fragments together.

91. D: Each time a cell divides; a few base pairs of DNA at the end of each chromosome are lost. Telomerase is an enzyme that uses a built-in template to add a short sequence of DNA over and over at the end of chromosomes—a sort of protective "cap". This prevents the loss of genetic material with each round of DNA replication.

92. D: DNA polymerase does not match base pairs with 100% fidelity. Some level of mismatching is present for all DNA polymerases, and this is a source of mutation in nature. Cells have mechanisms of correcting base pair mismatches, but they do not fix all of them.

93. C: Insertions and deletions cause frameshift mutations. These mutations cause all subsequent nucleotides to be displaced by one position, and thereby cause all the amino acids to be different than they would have been if the mutation had not occurred.

94. A.: Igneous rock forms from solidified magma. If the magma solidifies while underground, it's called intrusive rock. If the magma reaches the surface as lava and then solidifies, it's called extrusive rock. Metamorphic rock includes foliated and non-foliated rock categories. Sedimentary rock includes chemical, mechanical, organic, and inorganic rock categories.

95. D: Opal, corundum, magnetite and quartz are oxides. Opal and quartz are silicon dioxides. Corundum is aluminum oxide, and magnetite is iron oxide. Halides contain a halogen. Silicates contain silicon and oxygen. Native elements such as copper and silver exist as uncombined elements.

96. D: Porosity is a measure of how much water the soil can retain. Permeability is a measure of how easily water can travel through that soil. Clay has a high porosity because it holds a lot of water. Clay has a low permeability. Since it is fine-grained, water flows very slowly through it. Sand and gravel have high porosities and high permeabilities. Granite has a low porosity and a low permeability.

97. A: As the relative humidity in the area surrounding a plant increases, the rate of transpiration decreases. It is more difficult for water to evaporate into the more saturated air. As the relative humidity decreases, the rate of transpiration increases.

98. C: In order to pinpoint the exact location of the epicenter, seismograms are needed from three widely separate locations. A circle is drawn around each location with a radius equal to the distance of the earthquake. Since two circles can cross in two locations, a third circle is needed to pinpoint which intersection is the location of the epicenter. The intersection of the three circles is the location of the epicenter.

99. B: Darwin studied Lyell's work *Principles of Geology* while sailing around South America and the Galapagos islands. He was able to apply this concept of *the present is the key to the past* to the evolutionary history of life on earth. Uniformitarianism is completely opposed to the idea of catastrophism. Natural selection states that the fittest organisms will survive to reproduce.

100. B: The Cambrian Explosion occurred during the Cambrian Period in the Paleozoic Era approximately 541,000,000 years ago. The Jurassic Period known for the first giant dinosaurs occurred during the Mesozoic Era approximately 201,000,000 years ago.

101. D: The average salinity of seawater is 3.5 %. This can also be written as 35 parts per thousand or 3.5 parts per hundred.

102. A: Water actually has its lowest volume at four degrees Celsius. Water stops contracting at four degrees Celsius. Water expands as it cools from four degrees Celsius to zero degrees Celsius.

103. B: The lithosphere is the solid outer section of the earth. This includes the crust and the upper portion of the upper mantle. The asthenosphere, which lies in the upper mantle, is below the lithosphere.

104. C: Exfoliation is a type of physical or mechanical weathering that occurs when rocks peel off in sheets or layers. No chemical change occurs. Oxidation, hydrolysis, and carbonation are all types of chemical weathering.

105. A: The two most abundant atmospheric gases are nitrogen (78%) and oxygen (21%). Argon (0.93%), and neon (0.0018%) are also present in much smaller amounts. Carbon dioxide is present in varying amounts typically ranging from 0.02 to 0.04%.

106. C: In the stratosphere, temperature increases as altitude increases. The stratosphere contains the ozone layer which absorbs ultraviolet radiation and then reemits this energy as heat.

107. C: Clouds form when water in the air condenses onto condensation nuclei in the air. Atmospheric water vapor will condense when the atmospheric temperature reaches the dew point.

108. D: Air masses are named for the areas over which they form. Since maritime polar air masses form over oceans in frigid regions, they bring cold, moist weather. Since maritime tropical air masses form over oceans in warmer regions, they bring warm, moist weather. Since continental polar air masses form over northern Canada or Alaska, they bring cold, dry weather. Since continental tropical air masses form over deserts, they bring warm, dry weather.

109. B: According to the 1st Law of Planetary Motion, planets move in elliptical orbits, not circular. According to the 2nd Law of Planetary Motion, a radius vector connecting a planet to the sun sweeps out equal areas in equal amounts of time. According to the 3rd Law of Planetary Motions, the square of the period of a planet is directly proportional to the cube of the mean distance.

110. C: The moon is slowly moving further away from the earth. The moon is moving a little less than 4 cm a year away from the earth. Since the moon only rotates once in every orbit around the earth, the same side is always seen from earth. The acceleration of gravity on the surface of the moon is approximately one sixth of the gravitational acceleration on the surface of the earth... although the moon has less than 1/80 the mass of the Earth, it also has a smaller radius, and the acceleration of gravity on the surface depends on both.

111. D: The main asteroid belt which contains millions of asteroids is between Mars and Jupiter.

112. A: Orange red stars have temperatures less than 3,700 K. Yellow orange stars range between 3,700 and 5,200 K. Yellow white stars range between 5,200 K and 6,000 K. Blue white stars range between 10,000 and 30,000 K.

113. B: It is true that rocks are classified by their formation and the minerals they contain, while minerals are classified by their chemical composition and physical properties. Answer A is incorrect because rocks may contain traces of organic compounds. Answers C and D are incorrect because only minerals can be polymorphs and only rocks contain mineraloids.

114. D: Mineraloids are best defined as minerals that lack a crystalline structure, and they are typically found in rocks. Inorganic solids containing two or more minerals with different crystalline structures are known as polymorphs.

115. C: Mineralogical petrology is not a branch of petrology. Petrologists study the various categories of rocks, including metamorphic, igneous, and sedimentary. Some petrologists, called experimental petrologists, also study changes in the geochemistry of materials that are exposed to extreme temperatures and pressures. Minerals are studied by mineralogists, not petrologists.

116. A: Chemical composition is not one of the physical properties used to classify minerals. The five major physical properties used to classify minerals are luster, hardness, cleavage, streak, and form. There is a separate classification system based on the chemical composition of minerals.

117. C: On Mohs scale of mineral hardness, talc has the lowest possible score (a one). Diamond is a ten, which is the highest possible score, and gypsum and fluorite have a score of two and four, respectively. Minerals can always scratch minerals that have a Mohs score lower than their own.

118. B: A mineral's true color is observed by conducting a streak test on unglazed porcelain tile. Paper is not appropriate for a streak test because it does not have the correct physical properties. External observation (inspecting the mineral's outer surface) is not sufficient to establish true color since streak tests sometimes reveal a color that is different from the substance's external hue. Finally, the luster test is not used to determine color.

119. B: According to the Dana classification system, gold, silver, and copper belong to the elemental class. Members of the oxide class include chromite and magnetite, and hydrocarbons and acetates are members of the organic class. Sulfide minerals include pyrite and galena.

120. A: According to the Dana system, minerals that contain the anion SO_4^{2-} are part of the sulfate class. Sulfate minerals are typically formed in environments where highly saline water evaporates. Gypsum is an example of a mineral that belongs to the sulfate class.

121. A: Fish may die suddenly after heavy rains due to the lower pH leading to high levels of substances such as aluminum in the water. Over time acid rain may slowly remove nutrients from the forest soil weakening defenses of trees making them more vulnerable to diseases and pests. Excess nitrogen may lead to overgrowth of algae in areas where rivers enter the ocean. Acid rain may slowly deteriorate buildings and monuments made from stone containing calcium carbonate.

122. D: Of these options, the only real direct impact of climate change is the rising sea level. This is due to the melting glaciers and ice sheets. Also, the oceans expand slightly as they get warmer.

123. C: An irrigation scheme that draws water from a river and redistributes the water in the local area leads to an increase in evaporation, not a decrease. This is largely due to the increase of the surface area of contact of the water and the atmosphere.

124. B: Water moves more slowly downstream of a dam. This results in less aeration and diffusion and lowers the dissolved oxygen content in the water.

125. A: Groundwater overuse and depletion has several negative effects including saltwater contamination of the water supply, increased cost as water must be pumped further, decreased surface water supplies, and lowering of the water table.

126. D: Ozone layer depletion results in higher UV levels reaching the earth. These higher levels of UV rays may result in more skin cancers, sunburn, and premature aging of skin, damage to marine life such as plankton, and decreased crop yields of wheat, corn, and soybeans.

127. C: The loss of biodiversity destabilizes ecosystems and impacts society by decreasing the food supply, decreasing the access to raw materials and clean water, and increasing the vulnerability to natural disasters.

128. B: Space exploration has provided many benefits for humanity. Aside from the inspiration for many to undertake further studies in science, many practical benefits have resulted such as improved weather forecasting, development of a global positioning system, and the development of lightweight materials.

129. A: While landfills are necessary, potential problems include soil contamination, surface water contamination, pollution, and leachate.

130. C: Sources of renewable energy include geothermal power, solar energy, and wind power. Sources of nonrenewable energy include nuclear power, natural gas, and fossil fuels like coal, natural gas, and crude oil.

131. D: Coal is a fossil fuel. Fossil fuels like coal, crude oil, and natural gas are nonrenewable.

132: D: Nonvascular plants do not produce fruits like angiosperms and gymnosperms do. They generally reproduce sexually, but produce spores instead of seeds.

133. A: Glass is manufactured from sand, soda ash, and limestone. Aluminum is manufactured from bauxite ore.

134. A: Pros of wind energy include space efficiency, no pollution, and low operational costs. Cons of wind energy include wind fluctuation, threats to wildlife, and the expense to manufacture and install.

135. B: Pros of solar energy include the facts that it is renewable, abundant, environmentally friendly, low maintenance, and silent. Cons of solar energy include that it is expensive and intermittent and requires space.

Thank You

We at Mometrix would like to extend our heartfelt thanks to you, our friend and patron, for allowing us to play a part in your journey. It is a privilege to serve people from all walks of life who are unified in their commitment to building the best future they can for themselves.

The preparation you devote to these important testing milestones may be the most valuable educational opportunity you have for making a real difference in your life. We encourage you to put your heart into it—that feeling of succeeding, overcoming, and yes, conquering will be well worth the hours you've invested.

We want to hear your story, your struggles and your successes, and if you see any opportunities for us to improve our materials so we can help others even more effectively in the future, please share that with us as well. **The team at Mometrix would be absolutely thrilled to hear from you!** So please, send us an email (support@mometrix.com) and let's stay in touch.

If you'd like some additional help, check out these other resources we offer for your exam:

http://MometrixFlashcards.com/TExES

Additional Bonus Material

Due to our efforts to try to keep this book to a manageable length, we've created a link that will give you access to all of your additional bonus material.

Please visit http://www.mometrix.com/bonus948/texessci7-12 to access the information.